Citizens for a National Maat Public Policy

Ata Uchenna Omom

Citizens for a National Maat Public Policy

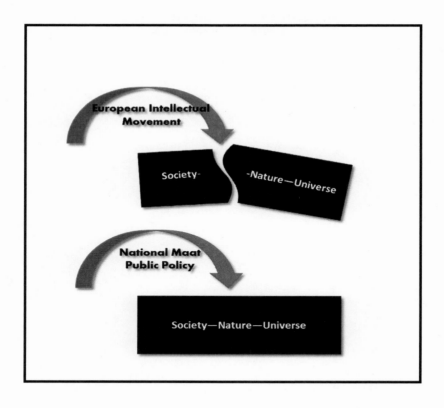

ISBN: 978-0-692-04990-7

Copyediting:
S. L. Waterhouse

Cover and page design and layout:
mitchell&sennaar communications, inc.

Outline

CHAPTER 1: Definition   **p. 1**
CHAPTER 2: Introduction   **p. 3**
CHAPTER 3: Prècis   **p. 7**
CHAPTER 4: Background   **p. 9**
CHAPTER 5: The Problem   **p. 17**
     5.1 Limits of Reason
     5.2 The Age of Enlightenment
CHAPTER 6: Introduction to the National Maat Public Policy   **p. 37**
     6.1 A Summation of Inventions
     6.2 What is Maat?
CHAPTER 7: Introduction to Spiritual Anatomy   **p. 55**
CHAPTER 8: A Perspective on Policy Implementation   **p. 61**
     8.1 Reversing the Industrial Capitalistic
        Cultural Assimilation
          8.1.1 Racial Diversity
          8.1.2 Prerequisite for Moral
            Decision-Making
          8.1.3 U.S. Cabinet
          8.1.4 Cultural Relativism
          8.1.5 Economic Development
     8.2 The Law and Emotions
CHAPTER 9: Morality versus Money   **p. 93**
CHAPTER 10: The Porcupine Climbs Trees   **p. 109**
     Since it is a Monkey
CHAPTER 11: With a Lie You Can Go Very Far,   **p. 115**
     But You Can Never Go Back!
     11.1 A Need for National Moral Leadership
     11.2 Institutional Racism
     11.3 The American Empire
     11.4 Self-Efficacy

CHAPTER 12: Summary   **p. 129**
        12.1 Lying
        12.2 Defense Mechanism
        12.3 Where is Western Knowledge Taking Us?
        12.4 Industrialism is an anti-Ecological
             Defense Mechanism (AEDM)
        12.5 Morality, Melanin, Biosphere, Universe
        12.6 Beyond the World of Materialism:
             Re-Embracing the'Spirit World'
CHAPTER 13: Conclusion   **p. 173**
        References   **p. 181**
        Endnotes   **p. 219**
        About the Author   **p. 225**

Acknowledgements

This writer acknowledges and is thankful for the ancestral spiritual support and *everlasting love* of my mother (Mary Ruth McNeill-Rainey), my father (Carl Rentie, Sr.), and sister (Maggie Bell Rentie-Thompson). To my brothers Carl Jr., Leonard (Len), and Cortez, Hotep! To Tamara, Krishnia, Andrea, Inger, David (Frankie) and Weldon, "Forward Ever, Backward Never."

Chapter 1
Definition

1. <u>Cultural Relativism</u> is the understanding of the norms and values of another culture from the perspective of the members of that culture.

2. <u>Maat</u> is a universal spiritual principle that is represented by whatever is right, true, real, genuine, upright, righteous, and just (Budge 184-185).

3. <u>National Maat Public Policy</u> is a government administrative and management decision-making strategy that gives forthright consideration to the spirits of children, women, men, nature, and universe in addressing government and human affairs.

4. <u>Positivism</u> is a philosophy that states that information derived from the *sensory experience* (smell, sight, hearing, taste, touch) that is interpreted by reason, logic and/or mathematics with no regard for spiritual experience is authoritative knowledge. ("Positivism"; Macionis and Gerber).

5. <u>Reason</u> is a "belief that is able to render an otherwise irrational action rational" (Campbell 9th ed., 626). See the word "*motive.*"

6. <u>Reason-based society</u> is a society that values reason over spirituality in government and human affairs and classifies spirit as non-knowledge.

7. <u>Spirit</u> is "the non-physical parts of a person: the mental, moral and emotional characteristics that make up the core of someone's identity" (VandenBos).

8. <u>Spirit-based society</u> is a society that values spirit in government and human affairs and mandates consideration of spirit in government decision-making and human affairs.

9. <u>42 Declarations of Innocence</u> are an Ancient Egyptian code of ethics and common law.

~ ~ ~

Chapter 2
Introduction

T he reader is asked to read all definitions before reading further. The definitions will help the reader to better understand this proposal. This proposal will be appreciated more if it is read from the beginning to the end without skipping around. It is also helpful to pause and reflect on each chapter before going on to read the next chapter. This proposal is not related to any particular organization in any way. Any shortcomings in this proposal are a reflection of the author's efforts. This work does not go into detail for every point made, instead appropriately focuses on the book's purpose. The writer does give consideration to other potential point-of-views (i.e., counter-arguments) realizing that people have their own perspectives due to varying cultural perspectives, life experiences, and education. So an effort was made, as much as possible without straying too far from the goal of this proposal, to give some documentation to show that there is creditable evidence to support particular assertions being made in this very important, yet delicate, matter.

Please note the terms "ethics" and "morals" are used interchangeably. Likewise, the phrases "indigenous people" and "traditional people" are used interchangeably. Keep in mind that "ecology" is the interactions amongst living things in their environment. "Biosphere" is the land surface, water on and in the Earth, air and atmosphere of the planet, Earth. This work offers evidence that strongly confirms that our decision-making strategies are antagonistic to the spirits of mankind, nature and the universe. Because of this, the topic of *decision-making strategies in government and human affairs* must be in the forefront of national debate.

This proposal is not written in a typical linear fashion. Instead, it is written in a holistic fashion with consideration to interrelated topics. This means that the problem to be addressed in this work is discussed from several different perspectives. Because of this repetition will be apparent throughout, occurring in varying contexts. The repetition functions as a chant. You will also observe that the tone of this work will shift back and forth from a secular (non-spiritual) tone to a spiritual tone. There are some testy areas in pursuing this goal.

Because Americans and racial groups are subcategories of the human species, many points made about Americans and racial groups have significance to our species and vice versa. There is some criticism of science, religion, money, and technology. For example, my complaint about technology is we need technology that promotes life and a balanced ecology. When this author is criticizing science, science is viewed as being OUT OF HARMONY with the "order in nature and society, as established by the act of creation" (Karenga 8). When science is praised it is being viewed as being IN HARMONY with the "order in nature and society, as established by the act of creation." Most of the criticism made in this proposal is counter-balanced with a solution.

To solve our real world problems, we must go right to the underlying cause, lay it upon the tabletop for inspection, and solve (or cure) it in a holistic way so that it does not create further problems or diseases. This work seeks to be solution-oriented. It is unfortunate that many of us believe that if we keep doing the *same* uneventful and foolish things over and over and over again, day after day, and year after year, things will get better. The reader will see that this is wishful thinking!

This proposal will show that things will not get better until we engage problem-solving from a macro (holistic) context rather than the usual micro (atomistic) context. For example, the police force cannot be effective in fighting crime if the institutions of society (i.e., religion, education, politics/law, family, health, and economics) are engaging in decision-making strategies that actually create the problems that cause crime. We will see that this is indeed the case.

The reader will also find out why our society and the world has become increasingly more vulgar, cold-blooded and violent. We will also learn why we tend to not pay heartfelt attention to our emotions and emotions of others. We will learn that moral development has never been a highly-prized social value in the United States of America, conventionally. The standard of comparison is the 42 Declarations of Innocence. If we don't address this problem, we will never solve our persistent social, economic, and environmental problems. Additionally, we will learn why the urban elites and bourgeois should have a minimal leadership role in planning and administrating intervention in addressing climate change.

Many say we've got to prepare the next generation. However, how can we adequately prepare the next generation when most of us are not prepared? We must prepare ourselves as evidence of change-in-motion.

The research herein suggest that the urban elite and bourgeois may be reluctant to be that evidence of change-in-motion.

In short, this proposal offers a holistic decision-making strategy for addressing a wide-range of human problems in the American society. The proposal highlights the importance of "truth and history" in decision-making and provides scholarly evidence that informs us that both truth and history keep our thoughts in touch with reality.

Some have suggested that America is too racist to establish the proposed, National Maat Public Policy. Maat means truth. Question: How do you know when you have NEVER tried??? Some have said this Maat topic needs to be made simple. Well, OK. "You can solve problems better with truth than with falsehood." *There, simple*! This writer has also been told, "Honey, we live in different times, the practice of maat was in ancient times." This is true. The practice of maat was effective in ancient times for over *three millennia*. So it is highly significant to a nation that is in a socio-economic and environmental crisis and has been in existence for *less than two hundred and fifty years*!!

While advocating for a National Maat Public Policy on the streets over the years, I can recall hearing some talk about I am trying to get young people to stir up unrest that could lead to someone being arrested and jailed and damaging people's reputations. I have never been secret about what I am trying to do: to the point where someone needs to speculate about what I am trying to. Over the years the same main message that I circulated to people on the streets also went to: city police commissioners, patrolling police officers (multiracial), a U.S. Homeland Security administrator, a former U.S. president, Members of U.S. Congress, Maryland State legislators, city mayor, city councilpersons, some HBCU's university professors (received a NIH short-term research training grant), civil rights organization, sororities and fraternities, etc. In summary, I have been trying to stir up a socially-sanctioned maat movement.

All living things have basic needs. All animals need air, water, food, and shelter. This means EVERY human being has the responsibility to protect the air, water, plants, and the life-giving and nurturing qualities of Mother Nature. If only we, America, took leadership in preoccupying ourselves with this.

Whether you are black, brown, red, yellow, or white, the writer wishes you a pleasant experience and hopes that you find value in this work. After reading this proposal, if you value Maat, you are a citizen for a *National Maat Public Policy*. This is an ecological restoration proposal.

Chapter 3
Prècis

The purpose of this work is to show the importance of a National Maat Public Policy. A National Maat Public Policy is a government administrative and management decision-making strategy that gives forthright consideration to the spirits of children, women, men, nature, and universe in addressing government and human affairs.

The problem to be addressed in this proposal is: Citizens of America live in a reason-based society (see definition). Because humans have a genetic disposition to be spiritual beings, citizens of America must have the constitutional right to live in a spirit-based society—as spiritual beings! This is a basic human necessity that we have been overlooking.

The significance of this work is that it identifies a serious problem that has been built into the social, economic, health, political/legal, educational and religious infrastructures of this nation. The identification of this problem was useful in helping the writer to analyze "the root" cause of many of this nation's problems and to formulate a practical solution to the problems. Additionally, this work is significant in that it lays out a perspective that can stimulate a much needed "positive" national conversation on race relations.

While not readily apparent, when you start to read Chapter 4, the advocacy for the National Maat Public Policy begins with a very short history on the first humans, initial racial differentiation in Europe, and the prime cultural value of humanity's respected and longest lasting civilization. This is complemented with a brief intro to the personality of traditional/indigenous people.

Next, Chapter 5 discusses the "limits of reason" and the "Age of Enlightenment." These two topics help to clarify the point that we live in a reason-based society. The data in this chapter was useful in helping this analyst to devise a feasible solution to the stated problem.

Chapter 6 presents a very brief analysis of the cumulative negative impact of innovations from 1790 to 2014. Then *Maat* (ma'at) is introduced. In explaining Maat, there is a focus on highlighting the fact that Maat (the universal spiritual principle) is "not" a religion! This is a very important point to keep in mind.

In Chapters 7-11, the author labors creatively to show the reader the appropriateness of a National Maat Public Policy by showing the shortcomings of the white world's intellectual movement, which is called "The Enlightenment."

In Chapter 12, there is a recapitulation and discussion of the main points that have been presented throughout the proposal. Chapter 13 is the conclusion.

Chapter 4
Background

America is racially and culturally diverse. According to the 2010 Census, the national population by race for that year was: whites, alone, 72.4 percent; African Americans, alone,12.6 percent; American Indian and Alaska Native, alone, 0.9 percent; Asians, alone, 4.8 percent; Native Hawaiians and other Pacific Islanders, 0.2 percent; some other race, 6.2 percent; and two or more races, 2.9 percent.

The above diversity is representative of descendants from six continents: Africa, Asia, Australia/Oceania, Europe, North America, and South America. Knowledge of one's history shapes one's views of the present and future. Each racial group has a unique history, which is important to its wellbeing and survival. Without knowledge of our past history, we are limited in understanding how to approach and solve problems in the present and future.

For example, a farmer cannot take the nutrients out of the soil and expect his or her crops to grow plentiful and nutritious. The farmer's past experience should have informed him or her that this would be costly and counterproductive. So, if the farmer values his or her past experience with soil and nutrients, the farmer will *not* deplete the nutrients from the soil. If the soil is deficient in nutrients, the farmer knows to replace the nutrients so the crops can grow to be wholesome and nourishing. Past experience (history) improves our ability to make morally sound decisions. The logic expressed in this paragraph is reflective of the logic to be expressed throughout this work.

As stated earlier, there will be a very short look at the (1.) history of the first Homo sapiens sapiens [modern man and woman], (2.) their migration out of Africa, (3.) initial racial differentiation in Europe, and (4.) prime cultural value of humanity's respected and longest lasting civilization. The history in this chapter belongs to all races, and we should seek to learn from it as history improves our ability to make moral decisions.

Now, we will start with the fact that our species (Homo sapiens sapiens) originated 200,000 years ago in Africa (Gugliotta 56-64). In the book *Civilization or Barbarism: An Authentic Anthropology*, the author states, "the birthplace of humanity is East Africa's Great Lakes region in the area of the Omo Valley" (Diop, "Civilization" 11). Cheikh Anta Diop, Ph.D., of Senegal, Africa was the most influential scholar in the world on the origin of humanity and the origin of human civilization in the twentieth century. It will become more apparent, to those who do not know, that black Africans were the sole representatives of the human race—for an estimated period of 180,000 years— before any other race appeared on Earth!! "The first blacks who went out to populate (and transmit their DNA sequence to) the rest of the world exited Africa through the Strait of Gibraltar, the Isthmus of Suez, and maybe through Sicily and Southern Italy."

Scientific evidence has been found to support this claim. "Tools found at Jwalapuram, a 74,000-year-old site in southern India, match those used in Africa from the same period" (Gugliotta). According to David Imhotep, Ph.D., author of the groundbreaking book *The First Americans Were Africans: Documented Evidence*, "There is evidence of Africans in South America 56,000 years ago and in North America (in the area of South Carolina) 51,700 years ago" (Imhotep 62-63). "Fossil and archaeological records…show that modern humans reached Australia *mil* Papua New Guinea—then part of the same landmass— at least 45,000 years ago and maybe much earlier" (Gugliotta). First humans to enter Europe around 40,000 years ago were black (Imhotep 27, 50), and "…Negroid expansion extended from Western Europe to Lake Baykal in Siberia, by way of the Crimea and the Don Basin" (Diop, "Civilization" 51). Aurignacian culture[i] is a "highly developed Upper Paleolithic Age culture, named after a cave at Aurignac (France) where artifacts were found… Cro-Magnon (white) man, Combe-Capelle man, and Grimaldi (black) man all contributed to Aurignacian culture" (Diop, "Origin" 297). This culture is associated with early Africans and was discovered around Lake Baykal (Imhotep 43). This lake is located in southeastern Russia just north of Mongolia, near North China. "Grimaldi Negroids (Black Africans) have left their numerous traces all over Europe and Asia from the Iberian Peninsula to Lake Baykal in Siberia" (Diop, "Civilization" 15). Russian Professor Mikhail Gerasimov identified Negroid type skulls in this area that are related to the Middle Mousterian period, Diop adds. The first humans—who were black—arrived in China in 17,000 BC (53).

The <u>Aurignacian industry</u> is the tool-making industry and artistic tradition brought to the world from Africa (Editors); it represents "the first complete tradition in the history of art, moving from awkward attempts to a well-developed, mature style" (Editors). "If we accept the assumption of a migration from Africa, it is not surprising to find Aurignacian tools in France, Italy, and Spain" (Diop, "Origin" 67). The following represents the Aurignacian industry: "improved (punch-struck) blade and bladelet (small blade-shaped weapon/tool) technology; new end-scraper and burin forms (stone tools for engraving); increased 'imposed form' in tool manufacture…complex, highly shaped bone, antler and ivory tools; appearance of personal ornaments (perforated teeth, marine shells, shaped stone, and ivory beads); appearance of complex and varied art forms (engravings, sculptures, cave paintings); appearance of symbolic 'notation' systems; new musical instruments (bird-bone flutes); long distance distribution and exchange networks (for marine shells, high quality stone, etc.); improved missile technology (objects forcibly propelled); rapid change in technological patterns; increased population density (increased ability to live in large groups); more highly structured occupation sites; increased 'specialization' in some animal exploitation patterns" (Mellars 13). It is helpful to notice, "On the basis of…new evidence, it is now possible to show beyond any reasonable doubt that many of the most distinctive archeological hallmarks of the classic Middle-Upper Paleolithic transition in Europe can be documented at least 30,000 to 40,000 years earlier in certain parts of Africa than anywhere within Europe itself" (16).

After black Africans represented the human race for 180,000 years, the "first white appeared only around 20,000 years ago… He (white race) is probably the result of a mutation from the Grimaldi Negroid (black African) due to an existence of 20,000 years in the excessively cold climate of Europe at the end of the last glaciation" (Diop, "Civilization" 15-16). "The mutation from Negroid to Cro-Magnon (white) did not happen overnight. There was a long transition period of more than 15,000 years, corresponding to the appearance of numerous intermediate types between Negroid and the Europoid, without any occurrence of interbreeding" (49). What is mutation?

A gene mutation is a permanent alteration in the DNA sequence that makes up a gene, such that the sequence differs from what is found in most people. Hereditary mutations are inherited from a parent and are present throughout a person's life in virtually every cell in the body. These mutations are also called germline mutations because they are present in the parent's egg or sperm cells, which are also called germ cells. When an egg and a sperm cell unite, the resulting fertilized egg cell receives DNA from both parents. If this DNA has a mutation, the child that grows from the fertilized egg will have the mutation in each of his or her cells. ("What is a Gene Mutation…?")

"The Chancelade Man, who would be the prototype of the Yellow Race, appeared in the Reindeer period about 15,000 years ago in the Magdalenian Age. Is he a mongrel born in a cold climate, from both stocks of the Grimaldi [blacks] in Europe and the new Cro-Magnon [whites]?" (Diop, 16). "The brachycephalic races—Yellow, Semites— appeared only around the Mesolithic Age (10,000 to 5,000 BC), probably following great migratory current and interbreeding." Diop emphasizes that "racial differentiation took place in Europe, probably in southern France and Spain, at the end of the last Würm glaciation, between 40,000 and 20,000 years ago" (13).

The American Association of Physical Anthropology reports that "biological differences between human beings reflect both *hereditary factors* and the influences of natural and social *environments*. In most cases, these differences are due to the interaction of both" ("Biological Aspects of Race"). According to Thomas Bouchard, a psychologist and geneticist, "Current thinking holds that each individual picks and chooses from a range of stimuli and events largely on the basis of his or her genotype and creates a unique set of experiences—that is, people help to create their own environments… It also reminds us of our links to the biological world (all living things) and our evolutionary history" (1701).

Psychologist Cara L. Smith, et al. (85) state that individuals who have "openness-to-experience" and are "sensation-seeking" combined are significantly likely to have beliefs in paranormal. According to physician Richard Gerber in his book *Vibrational Medicine*, the "ability to see the universe from different perspectives may be a reflection of the different vantage points of perception..." (159). Temperament is the "basic foundation of personality" (VandenBos 928). Temperament is the "constitutional disposition to react to one's environment in a certain way" (Campbell 9th ed., 976).

The above points are made to emphasis the underlying factors that shape our personality. Now let us briefly look at the origin of Ancient Egypt and the people's personality. Many historians are of the opinion that the Ancient Egyptian culture lasted from 3100 BC to AD 640 while giving the world agriculture, astronomy, architecture, medicine, math, science, writing, etc., before "culturally" collapsing due to repetitive invasions from Hyksos [mixed Semitic and Asian descents], Persians [an ancient nomadic Iranian population], Greeks, Romans, Vandals [barbarian Germanic people], and Arabs (Hilliard). Some scholars, such as Dr. Imhotep, believe Nubian civilizations and Ancient Egypt can be dated much earlier. Imhotep states,

> Ta-Seti (oldest civilization) in Nubia, part of the Great Kushite Empire, predated Egypt and is credited with moving north from Nubia into Egypt *creating* the Egyptian civilization. Then again, at the end of Egyptian civilization, the Nubians *saved* an aging Egyptian nation postponing its doom for almost 100 more years. But that was not the beginning of this civilization. Many of the pieces of Ta-seti's and Egypt's civilizations are seen in Nabta Playa which is given a starting date of between *17,700* and *43,000* years ago. The 17,700 year date is the most conservative of the two given by the astrophysicist Dr. Thomas Brophy. (133)

In humanity's longest-lasting civilization (Ancient Egypt), the personality was called *ka* (Gadalla 108). "*Ka* is our holographic connector—connecting us across many dimensions into an embodied form on earth" (Prakasha 174). *"Ka* provides the infrastructure for the body, emotions, and mind to exist" (175). In Western psychology, spirit is defined as the non-physical parts of a person (moral, emotional, mental characteristics) that make up the core of one's identity (VandenBos).

Professor and Chair of the Department of African American Studies at Temple University, Dr. Molefi Asante, who is *"among the most published contemporary scholars"* makes us aware that *"Ka,* as the *double* of the personality of a man or woman, could be any place... In fact the *ka* could actually separate itself from or unite itself with the body. It could also move freely from place to place and return to its body. When a person died the living had to make sure that the *ka* was taken care of so that the dead person could have eternal life" (Asante 48). The pyramid texts from the Nile Valley region are possibly the oldest known spiritual texts in the world (Wilkinson 6). Please note how the partial quote below from the "Pyramid Text of Unas" [King Unas] describes an aspect of the *ka*:

> That which is sent by thy ka cometh to thee (you), that which is sent by thy father cometh to thee, that which is sent by Ra (sun god) cometh to thee, and it arriveth in the train thy Ra. Thou are pure, thy bones are the gods and the goddesses of heaven, thou existest at the side of God, thou art unfastened, thou comest forth toward thy soul. (trans. by Budge 24)

In your assessment of the above quote keep in mind that a "goddess" is a supernatural force or energy with feminine attributes who regulates certain aspects of the universe, spirit world, nature, and/or society. Plus "god" is a supernatural force or energy with masculine attributes who regulates certain aspects of the universe, spirit world, nature, and/or society. Living in harmony with the goddesses and gods has been a cultural preoccupation for traditional/indigenous people.

Even a contemporary Tibetan mystic adds, "To the enlightened man...whose consciousness embraces the universe, to him the universe becomes his body, while his physical body becomes a manifestation of the Universal mind, his inner vision an expression of higher reality, and his speech an expression of eternal truth and mantric powers" (Capra 305). Geneticist Dean Hamer, Ph.D., who has studied the role of genes in human behavior note: "Spirituality comes from within. The kernel must be there from the start. It must be part of their genes" (Hamer 49).

Emotions are an aspect of spirit. Just how important are emotions? "Developmental psychology views emotions as behavioral adaptations that have occurred during evolutionary development" (Campbell 9th ed., 330). In the field of psychiatry emotions "are genetically programmed responses that have been maintained because they have increased the chances of the organism's survival. Emotions...reflect the organism's value."

With that said, the reader may want to note that Maat (ma'at) is a universal spiritual principle that was highly "valued" in Ancient Egypt for over 3,000 years! Even after major invasions, Maat remained the common law of Ancient Egypt until it culturally collapsed due to repetitive invasions. Egyptologist Shafer et al. explains,

> The fundamental principle of Egyptian culture was expressed in the term Maat: truth, justice, cosmic order, well-ordered state, handed down from the gods, and perfect and intact. Maat codified the cultural status quo, the Egyptian way of life and way of doing things projected back into timelessness before time. Maat was the concept that gave meaning to life...Maat was custom, or tradition, or traditional value, or even culture itself... Maat regulated behavior; it was common law...it was the only way. Abstractly, that which stood outside Maat was unreality or falsehood; in practical terms, anyone, Egyptians or other, who operated beyond its bounds was regarded as a criminal or savage. (128)

The prime social value of humanity's longest lasting civilization in the world is clear! Please notice that Maat is "not" a religion! California State University Professor and Chair of Africana Studies Dr. Maulana Karenga, who is the author of *Maat, the Moral Ideal in Ancient Egypt:*

A Study in Classical African Ethics, states: "Maat is right order in nature and society, as established by the act of creation" (8). According to the 2009 UN's State of the World's Indigenous People report…

> Spirituality is the relationship human beings create with the spirit world in order to manage forces that seem overpowering. Indigenous spirituality is intimately linked to the environment in which the people live. For indigenous peoples, the land is the core of all spirituality and this relationship to the spirit of the earth is central to all the issues that are important to indigenous peoples today. **…Spirituality can be seen as an internal connection to the universe, which includes a sense of meaning or purpose in life, a cosmology or way of explaining one's personal universe and personal moral code.** …What is important here is that spirituality is the relationship to the universe. …Put another way, spirituality defines the relationships of indigenous (traditional) peoples with their environment as custodians of the land; it helps construct social relationships, gives meaning, purpose and hope to life. It is not separated but is an integral, infused part of the whole in the indigenous (traditional) worldview. (State 59-62)

Today in the midst of the world's growing social, economic, and environmental catastrophes, humanity is fortunate to still have a history of humanity's respected and longest-lasting civilization in the world and "more than 370 million traditional (indigenous) people spread across 70 countries worldwide" ("Who Are Indigenous People?") in Africa, Americas, Oceania, Asia, and Europe, whose mission is to reclaim, develop, protect, practice, teach, and live their spiritual traditions ("United Nations Declaration of Indigenous People Rights"). We need their guidance and wisdom today.

~ ~ ~

Chapter 5
The Problem

C hapter 5 is divided into two parts: (1.) Limits of Reason and (2.) the Age of Enlightenment. How did America become a reason-based society? The answer is through the European intellectual movement. This movement is called the Enlightenment. It started in the 1600's. The Age of Enlightenment is also called the "Age of Reason" and "Age of Rationalism."

> *Problem Statement: Citizens of America live in a reason-based society. A reason-based society is a society that values reason over spirituality in government and human affairs and classifies spirit as non-knowledge. Because humans have a genetic disposition toward spirituality, citizens of America must have the "constitutional right" to live in a spirit-based society—as spiritual beings.*

5.1 Limits of Reason

Is it really true that reason is the best strategy for learning the truth? The following experts will provide a final answer for the ages.

"Our own times have inherited a dilemma: Is reason a natural component or datum of our species or is it a painfully arrived at objective that does violence to some of our natural tendencies?" (Palmarini 4). According to *Campbell's Psychiatry Dictionary* 9th ed., reason is a mere "belief that is able to render an otherwise irrational action rational." (see "motive" 626).

In the book *Reason in Human Affairs*, the author points out: "One kind of optimism, or supposed optimism, argues that if we think hard enough or rational enough, we can solve all our problems. The Eighteenth century, the Age of Reasoning, was supposed to have been imbued (saturated) with this kind of optimism. The hopes we hold out for reason in our world today are much more modest" (Simon 3).

In the paper entitled "Why Do Humans Reason? Arguments for an Argumentative Theory," cognitive scientists Hugo Merciera and Dan Sperbera write, "Reasoning is generally seen as a means to improve knowledge and make better decisions. However, much evidence shows that reasoning often leads to epistemic (cognitive) distortions and poor decisions. This suggests that the function of reasoning should be rethought."

In the book *Inevitable Illusions: How Mistakes of Reason Rules Our Mind*, the author writes "…even when we are engaging in high-level administration in courts, in the hospital, or in the family, we are prey to certain cognitive illusions. And we are deluded in complete innocence, in good faith, not even realizing that we are so misled" (Palmarini x).

One standout problem seems to be: "In spite of the norms of logic and the principles of scientific investigation, human beings tend to shun any evidence that disconfirms their beliefs of the world; that is, they are unlikely to negate (cancel) their own hypotheses. Because such shortcomings in reasoning may interfere with accurate personal and social judgments… counselors would serve their clients well by helping them recognize such tendencies" (Bassoff 368-371), according to the article entitled "Neglecting the Negative: Shortcomings of Reasoning."

Neurologist Donald Calne, former director of the Neurodegenerative Disorder Center at the University of British Columbia from 1981 to 2001, asked and answered the following question in his book *Within Reason: Rationality and Human Behavior*:

> Why have so many turned against reason? There are several explanations, but among the foremost must be failure of the quixotic (unrealistic) hopes vested in it. Reason was misrepresented as an all-powerful divine force, with its own supreme mission. In fact, it has no aim and no inherent goodness. <u>Reason is simply and solely a tool, without any legitimate claims to moral content. It is a biological product fashioned…to help us survive in an inhospitable and unpredictable physical environment</u>. (11-12)

As we have seen, reason is not suited for being the 'best' method for learning truth. It helps to notice that the right and left cerebral hemispheres are naturally connected (34). Left hemisphere is more proficient at abstract reasoning, according to Jeffery Shuren M.D., J.D., and neuroscientist Jordan Grafman, Ph.D. (918). Abstract means theoretical, not having concrete existence, ideal, and unreal. <u>The left hemisphere applies rules of formal logic independent of content of the material</u> (917). <u>In contrast, the right hemisphere may use past experiences, factual (real) or emotional, and thus would be more proficient when reasoning involves familiar scenarios</u> (918). "Each hemisphere overextends its perspective on phenomenon to the other side, and therefore both contribute to an extent that depends on the characteristics of the phenomenon at hand" (Deglin and Kinsbourne 285).

People generally reason by analogy (an imaginative comparison) in retrieving past experiences, including the emotions experienced, when confronted with a familiar situation (Deglin and Kinsbourne). <u>If the retrieval of past experiences, including the emotions experienced, does not occur when confronted with a familiar situation, abstract reasoning occurs consistent with sanctioned rules of logic. Therefore, the person is inclined to respond calmly and appear unaffected by any absurdity of or involving the experience or event</u> (Shuren and Grafman 917).

It has been indicated that cognitive scientists are of the opinion that people typically retrieve past experiences, including the emotions attached or surrounding the experience, when reasoning about a familiar situation in order to ensure that thoughts correspond to reality. In this case, it would seem that consideration must be given to not only sensory experience (smell, taste, sound, touch, and sight) but also to emotional, mental, moral, and psychic experiences, which are interrelated, linked!

For example, the American Psychological Association's *APA Dictionary of Psychology* indicates that feelings "are inevitably evaluated as pleasant or unpleasant, but they can have more specific intra-psychic qualities" (VandenBos). So, the "psychic" is "denoting phenomena associated with the mind...a class of phenomena, such as telepathy and clairvoyance, which appears to defy scientific explanation." Hence, to cut off feelings and/or intra-psychic qualities (i.e., telepathy, clairvoyance) is to undermine the pursuit of the whole truth. Therefore, reason cannot possibly be the best tool for running a government.

In closing, Eugene Sadler-Smith (351) who is a professor of organizational behavior points out that a wide number of biologists and psychologists view our species with an evolved moral sense that is initiated by nature toward moral behavior. "<u>The genetic and neural bases of morality exist independently of institutional frameworks and social structures.</u>" The above means the "human brain is designed in such a way as to predispose Homo sapiens to respond to ethical dilemmas intuitively..." (369). While the brain is a very sophisticated organ, the mind is very delicate and tender.

This is to say that "present work (has) revealed that moral judgments of a person can be altered by one seemingly irrelevant and often unavoidable type of information: the group to which that person belongs. Moral agents' group membership was found repeatedly to alter moral judgments" (Ambady 2148). Taken to its extreme, the instrumentality of the institution may separate the individual from his or her intuitive evolved moral nature before morals have a chance to display itself (Smith "Virtue" 369). This point brings us to the second part of the problem: the white world's intellectual movement—the Enlightenment!

5.2 **The Age of Enlightenment**

First, it helps to understand the forces of Nature. We will start with the difference between the meaning of "weather" and "climate." Weather is the condition of the atmosphere over a SHORT period of time. Climate is the average course of weather conditions over a period of many years, decades, centuries, or millennia! Knowing this helps us to better gasp the deep consequences of the origin of the white race which was initiated by an act of Nature (extreme cold and harse climate conditions). The first humans (black Africans), who migrated into Europe, got trapped by unsuspecting brutal cold glacial climate for an estimated 20 millennia! The occurrence caused these Africans to acquire hereditary mutations (i.e., white skin, personality changes). What is most significant here, for our discussion, is NOT the white skin! It is the personality change. Here lies our race relations dilemma.

What we are about to learn, in a rather general way, is how the European world has undermined traditional knowledge. While today's whites had no part in the initial planning and implementation of the white race's Enlightenment, white descendants continue to enjoy the benefits of their European ancestors' horrifying scheme. On the surface, their continued promotion and participation in this scheme appears to be related to the influences of white supremacy, institutional racism (group behavior), and/or low morals.

In the research entitled "Diversities of Knowledge Communities, Their Worldviews and Sciences: On the Challenges of their Co-Evolution," the authors Bertus Haverkort and Coen Reijntjes write, "Human knowledge covers all aspects of human life...in all their dimensions, social, natural and spiritual, and at all levels... Only part of our knowledge is conscious, directly accessible and expressible in language. The other part is subconscious and intuitive, linked to our deepest source of knowledge and centre of life" (12). It is this subconscious and intuitive knowledge that has been misunderstood and under appreciated by the white world.

Before a full discussion on the white world's intellectual movement begins, there will be a brief introduction of Greek philosopher Aristotle and the "Age of Discovery" in order to provide a modest continuum of history. This will help us better see how the Enlightenment fits in the continuum of human history, from the period of cultural decline in Ancient Egypt up to the present time.

* * *

Egypt did not collapse until AD 640. "Aristotle (384 BC to 322 BC) enjoyed tremendous prestige during his time. To some leading Christian, Jewish, and Arab scholars of the Middle Ages...his writings seemed to contain the sum total of human knowledge. Saint Thomas Aquinas, one of the most influential philosophers of the Middle Ages, considered Aristotle "the philosopher" (World Book, vol. 1, 2015: 664). "Even after the intellectual revolutions of the Renaissance, the Reformation, and the Enlightenment, Aristotelian concepts remained embedded in Western thinking" (Kenny).

While this is indeed true, historian Diop puts Aristotle's accomplishments into historical perspective when he points out that the "Ancient Egyptians knew conceptual thought in the most rigorous sense two thousand years before Aristotle (was born)... Aristotle borrowed Egyptian sciences all the while keeping completely quiet about it" (327, 341).

George G.M. James, Ph.D.,[ii] who was a professor of logic and Greek and professor of language and philosophy, writes in his book, *Stolen Legacy: Greek Philosophy is Stolen Egyptian Philosophy*, the following:

> After nearly five thousand years of prohibition against the Greeks, they were permitted to enter Egypt for the purpose of their education. First, through the Persian invasion and secondly through the invasion of Alexander the Great. From sixth century BC therefore to the death of Aristotle (322 BC) the Greeks made the best of their chance to learn all they could about Egyptian culture; most students received instructions directly from the Egyptian Priests, but after the invasion by Alexander the Great, the Royal temples and libraries were plundered and pillaged, and Aristotle's school converted the library at Alexandria into a research centre. There is no wonder then, that the production of the unusually large number of books ascribed to Aristotle has proved a physical impossibility, for any single man within a life time. The history of **Aristotle's life has done him far more harm than good, since it carefully avoids any statement relating to his visit to Egypt**. (7-8)

What is really important for our purpose is that Aristotle believed that "all human beings are not only on Earth but also in the universe, the universe is common to everything" (Kenny), and "all living things—not only human beings—have souls" (Shields). "According to Aristotle, deduction is the strongest form of logical reasoning" (Alexander 265). Aristotle also "stressed the role of experience in the formation of knowledge" (Gottlieb 33). In precolonial times, the above views were common in societies. For instance, the Hitchiti's [a Native American tribe of the Muscogee Creek Confederacy] belief system was based on the concept of order; all things living and non-living possessed spirits, some more powerful than others (Malinowski and Sheets 442).

* * *

Keep in mind that the discussion on Aristotle and the Age of Discovery provides background data for our examination of the Age of Enlightenment. It is vital to know that the Age of Discovery was made possible because of the critical role Africans (Black Moors) played in bringing Europe out of the *chaotic* and *violent* Dark Ages. In his book *Golden Age of the Moor*, Ivan Sertima, Ph.D., who is a historian gives one of many possible examples: "**Nearly all the major universities in Europe**" were built by Black Moors (Sertima 10). He continues,

> "Why did Europe fall into such darkness after all it had received from Greeks who had taken so much from... the Egyptian sciences? G.G.M. James in *Stolen Legacy*, answers this question. James had pointed out that the edicts (order) of Theodosius in the 4th century closed down the temples of Egyptian mysteries as well as the philosophical schools of Greece. The emperor Justinian in AD 529 followed in the same path of Theodosius. Thus an intellectual darkness descended over Christian Europe and the entire Greco-Roman world. It lasted for centuries." (11)

Because of the African Moors' civilizing influence on Europe from AD 711 to AD 1492 (781 years) Europeans were able to start their rise out of the dark ages. The Age of Discovery was possible beginning around AD 1500's to late AD 1800's. In truth, it was a period of European **exploration, discovery, extermination** and **exploitation** of traditional people worldwide, proving the violent behavior had not subdued. "**Renowned historian Cheikh Anta Diop, explains how during the**

Middle Ages (5th-15th centuries), the great empires of the world were Black empires, and the educational and cultural centers of the world were predominately African. Moreover, during that period, it was the Europeans who were the lawless barbarians" (Chengu 5). As the Europeans ascended from the Dark Ages the following occurred. The papal bulls of Dum Diversas, Romanus Pontifex, and Inter Caetera are legal authorizations given by the 15th Century Pope Nicholas and Pope Alexander VI that granted European Christian nations the right to claim lands and subdue and enslave the non-Christian world in the name of Jesus Christ. In 1452 Pope Nicholas V wrote the bull of Dum Diversas, and in 1455 he wrote the bull of Romanus Pontifex. In 1493 Pope Alexander VI wrote the bull of Inter Caetera.

During the Age of Discovery, the weak underdeveloped European economies became increasingly upbeat, stronger, and wealthier from the stolen natural resources (i.e., silver and gold) and human exploitation (i.e., slavery) of traditional people. At the same time traditional people's economies became weaker and poorer. In summary, the above papal bulls established the precedent for the long history of exploration, colonialism, transatlantic slavery, and today's imperialism (International; Castanha; "Inter Caetera"; "Romanus"; "Catholic Church").

* * *

Now we turn our full attention to the Age of Enlightenment, which started in the 1600's. Understanding the Enlightenment will help us to understand today's present industrial-capitalistic society. The Enlightenment was/is a white race intellectual movement. This means there were many scholars, philosophers, scientists, common people (men, women and children) who contributed to the movement in the beginning. The European world's Enlightenment was not an initiative to truly enlighten. The reader will see that the European Enlightenment was actually an initiative to "DE-ENLIGHTEN" the non-white world. It was not about giving or promoting greater knowledge and understanding. There is no nice way to say it: the Enlightenment was/

is *the biggest lie in the history of our species*! This statement will be supported with scholarly references throughout this work.

Sir Francis Bacon's (1561-1626) contributions were a supplement to and interdependent with the Age of Discovery. Bacon is said to be the father of the scientific method (World Book, vol. 22015: 18). "Bacon is considered one of the leading figures in the scientific revolution for his advocacy of empiricism (that all knowledge is derived from the five senses) in the study of nature" (Alexander 298). He is considered the father of empiricism.

In opposition to Aristotle, Bacon "saw induction as an alternative to deduction" (265). It is true, however, that not all of Bacon's contemporaries agreed with him. In spite of that, because of Bacon, today "so much of people's reasoning is actually inductive reasoning (Feeney and Heit 1)...it corresponds to everyday reasoning." Our everyday reasoning tends to be theoretical or speculative.

Bacon also believed "that 'spirit is not virtue (moral), energy, entelechy (real, actual), or some foolishness of that kind, but a body thin and invisible, yet having place, dimension and realness. Thus, for Bacon spirit was not something immaterial such as a soul" (Zagorin 114). "Bacon's idea of spirit...is that matter or body is all that exists in nature" (113-114), and his view "was not unlike that held at the end of the century by Sir Isaac Newton."

Nevertheless, Bacon was an influential and respected philosopher, statesman, lawyer, and intellectual reformer. Bacon believed that scientific truth could best be derived from observation and reason:

> The title of Francis Bacon's 1620 book *Novum Organum* ('New Methods') said it all. Organum was the label philosophers used for Aristotle's six books on logic; Bacon set out to replace them. 'The honour and reverence due to the ancients remain untouched and undiminished,' Bacon insisted; his goal, he said, was to 'appear merely as a guide to point out the road.' Yet once we started down the road, Bacon noted, we would find there was 'but one course left...to commence a total reconstruction of

<u>science, arts, and all human knowledge, raised upon the proper foundation</u>. (Morris 468)

"But what would provide such foundation? 'Simple,' said Bacon: observation" (469). Remember that when reasoning about an observation, it typically involves retrieval of past experience or past history for imaginative comparison with the observation. In the book *From Dawn to Decadence 1500 to the Present*, the author Jacques Barzun helps us to appraise Bacon's attitude toward past experience or history in writing the following:

> The ancients, he (Bacon) pointed out, can no longer be invoked as authority because we know more than they did. We are the ancient and wise; they (the ancients) were the young and ignorant. Besides, authority is worthless. The notion that something is true because a wise man said it is a bad principle. Is the thing true in fact? Test by observation. (203-204)

If one conveniently leaves out truths the observation is justly questionable! However for the father of the scientific method "truth, he (Bacon) said...is 'rightly called the daughter of time, not of authority,' and he therefore condemned 'those enchantments of antiquity and authority'" (Zagorin 226). According to James Hannam, who has a doctorate in the history and philosophy of science, it was with Bacon's influential declaration that "science reason demanded linkage between observation and theory (speculation), and this gave a new order to the world" (Hannam 9)! It was this event that *legitimizes the deletion* of historic truths of antiquity from the equation for calculating truth. "Indigenous and independent systems were destroyed. Colonial and slave structures as well as apartheid and general white supremacy structures, were created, including boarding school as to separate children from parents and communities and cultures, and especially mission schools to destroy the (traditional people's) worldviews and to stigmize colonized and enslaved people as savages, primitives, and pagans. The recent "culture war" over the school curriculum is a continuation in a newer form of ideological structures (to separate)...

children and communities from their tradition" (Hilliard "The State," 6). Below offers the reader insight into why Sir Bacon was so influential:

> Before the edifice of modern science could be built, it required the strong foundations that were laid for it in the Middle Ages. The cornerstone was a widespread acceptance of reason as a valid tool for discovering the truth about the world. <u>Clearly, this could not happen without the approval of the Church, which at the time was the guardian of almost all intellectual endeavors... this means that the development of reasoning and its relationship with faith are both important parts of our story</u>. (Hannam xix)

The attempt to clarify and synchronize this intellectual movement was based on a simple recommendation. German philosopher Immanuel Kant (1724-1804) bluntly explained, "<u>Dare to know! Have the courage to use your own understanding</u>" (qtd. by Morris 471-472). "The first precept was never to accept a thing as true until (you) knew it as such without a single doubt" (Daniels and Hyslop 210). The reader must note that this "autonomous (self-determining), rational, continuous and universal criticism was institutionalized as never before and the modern intellect is the outcome" (Roberts and Westad 694).

The Enlightenment's mission was to celebrate "reason as the best method for learning truth" (World Book, vol. 6 2015: 326a) in order for the white race to take leadership in the world (World Book, vol. 1, 1998: 138; Cooke 722). The application of reason would now be the power by which man would understand the universe and improve his own condition (Encyclopedia Britannica, vol. 4, 2002: 504). Traditional spiritual knowledge began to fade! During the "European intellectual movement of the 17th and 18th centuries, ideas concerning God, reason, nature and man were synthesized into a (*new*) worldview that gained wide assent (approval) and that instigated revolutionary developments in art, philosophy and politics."

It was believed that "if European scientists were right and observation and logic were really the best tools for understanding God's will, then it stood to reason that they would be the best tools for running governments, too" (Morris). Remember logic is an established way one is expected to think or interpret something.

The new modern intellect proved to be problematic as "enlightenment was as much a bundle of attitudes as a collection of ideas, and here lies another difficulty in coming to terms with it. Many streams (of ideas and attitudes) flowed into it, but by no means did they all follow the same course. The roots of enlightenment are confused; development always resembled a continuing debate" (Roberts and Westad 691). During "this period scientists in England and the colonies (in North America), in universities, scientific societies, and in small shops experimented, finding ways of applying logic, mathematics and scientific findings" (Faragher 445).

"Eighteenth century colleges were the primary sites for processing growing and discordant (opposing) bodies of information about human beings, an occupation that marshaled the expertise of theologians and scientists. Scholars struggled—and at times competed—to craft coherent explanations for the diversity of the world's people" (Wilder 190).

Like Sir Bacon and many other Enlightenment thinkers, philosopher Immanuel Kant contributed to the "Enlightenment" by giving "the strongest, if not the only, sufficiently articulated theoretical philosophical justification of the superior/inferior classification of 'races of man' of any European writer up to his time" (Boxill and Hill 452)! "Kant believed that the racial classification he offered was a necessary truth, based on reason alone" (453).

This De-Enlightenment involved every social institution (i.e., politics/law, education, religion, family, economic, health) of European societies, American colonies (later the United States), and eventually most of the world! On the onset, the common man, woman, and child equally participated in the shaping of new ideas and innovations, but with time the influential scholars, scientists and wealthy took on leadership roles. "Education was important to Enlightenment's quest... even at the cost of challenging tradition" (Black 177).

Cultural historian Thomas Berry, author of the book *The Great Works: Our Way into the Future*, reports that some of the universities that were forerunners in this intellectual movement are University of Paris [France]; University of Oxford [England], University of Prague [Czech Republic], University of Vienna [Austria], and University of Bologna [Italy]. "These and other European universities provided the context in which scientific learning could develop and be communicated to our own times" (187).

Some American universities, including "King's College New York (now Columbia University), …the College of Philadelphia (now Penn)…Yale College and the College of William & Mary…even Puritan colleges such as the College of New Jersey (now Princeton) and Harvard, reformed their curricula to include natural philosophy (science), modern astronomy, and math" ("American Enlightenment"). Further discussion on "modern astronomy" will come up again.

"What the Enlightenment invented was the ideal of generalized critical intellect" (Roberts and Westad 694). This merely involved a preoccupation with assertive persuasive inductive argumentation and criticism. This skill was necessary for the process of legitimizing newly forming Enlightenment knowledge over traditional knowledge. The new Enlightenment knowledge could appear in the form of dazzling and convincing rhetoric or intimidating theoretical-philosophical perspectives—or outright *in your face* lies.

With everything considered, Hannam (347) summarizes the four key factors that helped the European intellectual movement to succeed: (*1*) "learning institutions," which were protected by the Catholic Church and state; (*2*) "technology"; (*3*) "metaphysics," which is concerned with explaining the fundamental nature of being; and (*4*) "theoretical" which is concerned with theory (rather than experience and practice). According to *Merriam Webster's Collegiate Dictionary*, theoretical (a.) is "relating to or having the character of theory: abstract, (b.) confined to theory or speculation often in contrast to practical application, (c.) existing only in theory" (1222). In regard to our discussion, theoretical is concerned with presenting a concise systematic way of how you should use words and how you should not use words to ensure "<u>assumptions</u>" <u>steer clear of historical truths</u>.

Hannam also points out that "the power of many European theories was derived from the way they combined mathematics with natural philosophy" (350). "Isaac Newton's *Principia Mathematica* had appeared in 1687, using the new tool of calculus that (he)... developed to express his model of the heavens mathematically. ...Numbers (then) became the measure of reality" (Morris 470). In other words, "number" became the measure of *real life*!

There is a personal side to Isaac Newton that might interest the reader. Isaac was one of the most influential scientists of his time. "In the spring of 1720, Sir Isaac Newton owned shares in the South Sea Company, the hottest stock in England. (The company was involved in slave trade.) Sensing that the market was getting out of hand, the great physicist muttered that he 'could calculate the motions of the heavenly bodies but not the madness of the people.' Newton dumped his South Sea (company) shares, pocketing a 100% profit totaling £7,000. But just months later, swept up in the wild enthusiasm of the market, Newton jumped back in at a much higher price—and lost £20,000. For the rest of his life, he forbade anyone to speak the words 'South Sea' in his presence" (Holony).

Returning to Newton's professional work, neurologist Calne (9-10) quotes Newton himself, writing: "In the words of Isaac Newton, 'Science consists in discovering the frame and operations of nature and reducing them, as far as may be, to general rules and laws, establishing these rules by observation and experiments, and thence deducing the causes and effects of things.'"

"The urge to advance knowledge (based on observation, theory and math)...explains why great effort was made to organize and circulate the results of the scientific research of the time. Many scholars gathered, organized, and published this knowledge. In fact, the Age of Reasoning could be called the Age of the Encyclopédie" (Cobban 139). The circle of new philosophies was increasing, and the "publishers of books, magazines and newspapers were supplying an enlarged market" (Ferguson 77). According to the book *The Eighteenth Century: Europe in the Age of Enlightenment*, "The importance of the Encyclopédie in the Enlightenment is twofold. In the first place, it was a vehicle for the most advanced ideals of the 18th Century. The attack on revealed religion (also known as spirituality) is prominent in its pages" (Cobban 275). "In enlightened thought there seemed to be small room for the divine" (Robert and Westad 692). As a matter of fact, the "most sustained intellectual achievement of the century [was the] 'Encyclopédie'" (268). In short, the intellectual movement functioned like a promotional marketing strategy. "Marketing is the activity, set of institutions, and processes for creating, communicating, delivering, and exchanging offerings that have value for customers, clients, partners, and society at large," according to the American Marketing Association.[iii]

The philosophy of science called "positivism" was conceived to establish a criterion for what would be the defining boundaries of knowledge. Knowledge would be phenomena derived from the five senses, reason, and mathematical proof. Accordingly, anything outside of these criteria—such as the spirit—was to be scientifically unverifiable (Calne; Morris 468-470; Hannam 9). An alternative way of saying it: positivism is the philosophy of science in which information derived from sensory experience [sight, taste, hearing, smell, touch] is interpreted through rational, logical, and/or mathematical treatments; this forms the comprehensive sphere of "Western authoritative knowledge" ("Positivism"; Macionis and Gerber).

Encyclopédie is the trophy of the age of Enlightenment ("Encyclopedie" *ref.*). The Encyclopédie was the first publication of its kind and "famous above all for representing the thought of the Enlightenment." Its purpose: "to change the way people think" and to "...disseminate all this information to the public and future generations" ("Encyclopedie"). For example, enlightenment philosopher "Locke's work influenced the framers of our Constitution and continues to influence contemporary courts" (Gordon 1540). For instance, "the framers of the U.S. Constitution placed great importance on the rights to life, civil liberty, and property (see the 5th Amendment) and this became the credo of the new age" (Ishay 93).

The reader should keep in mind that the European world's intellectual movement was "necessarily" hypocritical and cunning and Machiavellian. For example, to promote rights to life, civil liberty, and property "Enlightenment thinkers envisioned the spread of commercial enterprise and republican institutions, whose advance could also usher in an age of enduring peace [for white people]," according to Ishay. Locke, while one of the framers of the Constitution, also "owned…Royal African (Company) stock and had earlier invested in the Royal Adventurers" (50). The Royal African Company was involved in slave trade and stole gold from the mines off the west coast of Africa ("Royal"). Here, one of the framers of our U.S. Constitution, John Locke, is exercising the white man's rights to life, civil liberty and property, but traditional peoples' rights to life, civil liberties and properties were of no concern!

One might ask the question: how can the scientific method, industrialism and capitalism be methods for acquiring a prosperous and sustainable future for a nation when each devalues spirit? The answer: "Enlightenment produced the first modern secularized theories of psychology and ethics" (EncyclopediaBritannica, vol. 4, 2002)!! The white world was/is meticulous and calculating. The modern secularized theories of ethics and psychology have been used to desensitize the people to the insanities of their industrial-capitalistic lives. These two branches of knowledge, *modern ethics* and *psychology*, provided the needed psychological and ethical justifications for our industrial way of life.

"Moral purpose, as we have seen, had burned low in the 17th and early 18th centuries, and it was not to be exactly a devouring flame in the 19th. It was incomplete, easily compromised, apt (likely) to run to hypocrisy" (Cobban 180). According to the author of *Seven Bad Ideas: How Mainstream Economist Have Damaged America and the World*, "What really gave the impetus to the industry, and probably innovation as well…was the substantial enlargement of the domestic market (and the market)…mechanism's working depended on self-interest" (Madrick 22-23). In this nation's first planned city, the wealthy's self-interest was apparent.

> The City of Paterson, located on the Passaic River in New Jersey was once one of the mightiest industrial cities of the United States. It has a rich history as the Nation's first planned industrial city, as well as containing some of the country's oldest textile mills[iv] and businesses. In 1792, Alexander Hamilton formed an investment group called the Society of Useful Manufactures (the "SUM") whose funds would be used to develop a planned industrial city

in the United States that was later to become Paterson. ("Paterson, NJ: A History")

The first U.S. Secretary of Treasury Hamilton had proclaimed to the "SUM" that the national interest would be synonymous with the interest of the most economically energetic citizens—the wealthy. In time "...Paterson was also the site of historic labor unrest that focused on anti-child labor legislation, safety in the workplace, a minimum wage, and reasonable working hours" ("Paterson"). In short, from the very beginning, in Paterson, economic activity was arranged to benefit the greedy rather than the whole society. Herbert Abrams (36) writes, "In 1836, nearly 300,000 workers in the United States belonged to unions. The Medical Society of the State of New York took notice. In 1835, it proposed as a subject for its annual prize essay, 'The Influence of Trades, Professions and Occupations in the United States in the Production of Disease.'"

In 1884, Arnold Toynbee, the Britain historian who attended the University of Oxford, popularized the phrase "Industrial Revolution" in the English language and tried to point the American industrial experiment into the right direction by pleading, "It would be well if, in studying the past, we could always bear in mind the problems of the present and go to that past to seek large views of what is of lasting importance to the human race" (5). Toynbee continues: "...We must always apply the test: 'Does it fit in with the urgent present requirements of human nature?'" (103). His warning was a bit too late. The Machine had now built momentum.

An American lecturer, writer and political activist, Mary Elizabeth Lease also sent out a warning around the late 1880's. She declared, "This is a nation of inconsistencies. ...Wall Street owns the country. It is no longer a government of the people, by the people, and for the people; but a government of Wall Street, by Wall Street, and for Wall Street. The great common people of this country are slaves... Money rules... Our laws are in the output of a system which clothes rascals in robes and honesty in rags!" Even after being freed from the southern slave plantations and traveling north to the cities for work-for-pay, African-Americans were unconsciously walking into another form of slavery.

However, this time it was with the rest of the unknowing American working people. Although in terms of social status, African-Americans were still at the very bottom, and have been treated as such.

According to the *American Economic Review*, in 1900 union membership was 3 percent of the total civilian labor force, but in 1953 union membership was 26.8 percent of the total civilian labor force (Bernstein 302-303). This inferred that there were white Americans who did not welcome the Industrial Revolution with open arms. The resistance to the Industrial Revolution was due to the "stupidification of industrialization." The Industrial Revolution was increasingly creating human and environmental tragedies. For instance, automobiles were invented in the late 1800's. Early automobiles caused air pollution and respiratory health problems. Today (2018) automobiles are still a major source of our air pollution and respiratory health problems.

"The revolution in American technology could not have occurred had there not been equally revolutionary changes in American business laws" (Lerman and Schrag 734). This means legislators, lawyers and manufacturers were keys to the expansion of the Industrial Revolution. "The traditional American approach to law practice that is rooted in the Bill of Rights and in the autonomy (self-rule) and dignity of the individual is even more important in fearful times" (Freedman and Smith 355). Such sanctioned legal practice had advantages for competitive wealthy business owners. "The rise of the Wall Street lawyers was the most important event in the life of the (legal) profession during this period. ...By the end of the nineteenth century, hiring in-house counsel had become a common practice" (735). Armed with paid legal employees, the corporation and manufacturer were now better positioned to navigate through legal and political loopholes to pursue socially irresponsible ambitions for profits.

Eventually due to the rapid spread of innovations, commercialism and consumerism the "acceleration of social change...confronted governments with demands for services that heretofore had been accommodated by private sectors of society or not at all. ...No longer was personal experience in commerce, agriculture, law, or war sufficient to equip a congressman for almost every contingency" (Encyclopedia Americana, vol. 7, 2002: 573). "In 1945, when the nuclear bombs exploded, a whole new, yet familiar, set of environmental health concerns emerged…" (Abrams 73). At this juncture in American history, Albert Einstein was asked his view on man's overall progress up to this point, and he said: "'…everything had changed except our way of thinking'" (qtd. by Abrams).

Today, our way of life has contributed to an Arctic sea ice meltdown (NASA); a list of 1,456 *animals* [corals, reptiles, fishes, mammals, birds, snails, clams, insects, arachnids, amphibians, crustaceans] and 945 *plants* listed on the U.S. Fish and Wildlife Service: Environmental Conservation Online System's *endangered-threatened* list[v]; 72 percent of American adults stressed about money ("American Psychological Association Survey"); businesses and government formulating policies, legislation, and long-term plans based on unreliable economic forecast (Encyclopedia Britannica, vol. 4, 2007: 355); a paranoid nation who defense budget (in 2015/$631 billion) was more than the defense budgets of China, Russia, Saudi Arabia, France, United Kingdom, Germany, Japan, India, and South Korea *combined* ("National Defense"); worsening race relations (Sussman); and 16 million children living below federal poverty level ("Child Poverty,").

In conclusion, it has been shown that the Enlightenment has had a negative effect on every aspect of our lives and the biosphere and ecology. Thus, the "limits of reason" and the impact of the "Enlightenment" are concerns that must be given urgent attention in order to address the shortcomings of Western authoritative knowledge and its application in decision-making in government and human affairs.

~ ~ ~

Chapter 6
Introduction to a National Maat Public Policy

6.1 A Summation of Inventions:

According to Afro-Caribbean psychiatrist Frantz Fanon (315-316), "If we want to advance a step further, if we want to bring it (society) up to a different level than that which Europe has shown it, then we must invent and we must make discoveries. If we wish to live up to our peoples' expectations, we must seek the response elsewhere than in Europe. Moreover, if we wish to reply to the expectations of the people of Europe, it is no good sending them back a reflection, even an ideal reflection, of their society and their thoughts with which from time to time they feel immeasurably sickened. For Europe, for ourselves, and for humanity, comrades, we must turn over a new leaf..."

At the same time, it is useful for whites to take on the responsibility of being mindful that cognitive scientists have indicated reason tends to lead to shunning evidence that disconfirms one's beliefs of the world—and such occurrence leads to inaccurate personal and social judgments (Bassoff). This means that the white race must also "invent and make discoveries" on how to tap into and use their deeper spiritual resources within!

In this chapter, we will start with the fact that the Enlightenment thinkers envisioned the spread of inventions and commercial enterprise as a way to create enduring peace and prosperity. Let us look closer at the results. The Industrial Revolution began in the mid-1700s. According to the "U.S. Patent Activity Calendar Years 1790 to the Present," in 1790 there were only three utility patents issued for inventions by the U.S. government and there were no design (i.e., sketches/blueprints) or plant (i.e., vegetation/botany) patents ("U.S. Patent"). See Diagram 1. A utility patent protects new inventions and improvement on existing, functional inventions. Ten years later, in the year 1800 there were only 41 utility patents issued for inventions and, again, no design or plant patents.

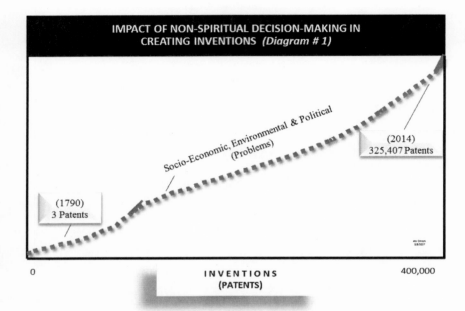

IMPACT OF NON-SPIRITUAL DECISION-MAKING IN CREATING INVENTIONS *(Diagram # 1)*

Socio-Economic, Environmental & Political (Problems)

(1790) 3 Patents

(2014) 325,407 Patents

0

INVENTIONS (PATENTS)

400,000

The figures forthcoming represent utility, design and plant patents combined. Starting in 1900 one hundred years later—there were a total of 26,414 patents issued for inventions. Fifty years later, in 1950, there were 47,847 patents issued for inventions.

In 1960, ten years later, 49,828 patents were issued. In 1970, a total of 67,695 patents were issued for inventions. In 1980, a total of 65,885 patents were issued. For 1990, the total was 98,707 patents issued for inventions. For the year 2000, a total of 175,455 patents for inventions were issued, and for 2010, the total was 243,394 patents. The number of patents issues by the U.S. government for inventions in 2014 was 325,407. Now, where is this enduring peace?

What we can safely believe here is that very many of these innovations came into being with little consideration to spirit. Such a mounting manifestation has been felt in a harmful way from deep in the ocean to mountain tops to deep outer space. "There is increasing evidence to suggest that noise pollution from modern shipping, military sonar activity and leisure boats is having an adverse effect on the way (blue) whales communicate (their communication range is thousands of miles) and how they act," according to National Geographic Magazine. [vi] "In the past 500 years, human activity has led to 500 species of land animals going extinct...a group of scientists now warn that rapid industrialization of the seas could spell a similar fate for marine life. ...Many scientists have identified the birth of the Industrial Revolution as one of the tipping points for increased extinctions on land. Desirable species were hunted to extinction. Demand for lumber and expanding farmlands and factories meant leveling forest habitats. Pollution and other factors killed other animals. ...Two hundred years later, the industrialization of fishing has ocean life facing similar pressures" (Carey). Also, high in the sky:

> *Far above the earth*, orbiting satellites play a crucial role in our everyday lives, powering countless services ranging from cell phones to banking, weather reports and navigation. Taken largely for granted, these modern conveniences are actually in constant peril due to potential collisions with *accumulating outer space debris left by defunct satellites and other spacecraft*. In 2008, countries at the UN adopted space debris mitigation guidelines to curb the pollution of outer space and promote international consensus on acceptable spacecraft operations so that outer space may be used in a sustainable way. ("Space Debris")

In his book *Sociopathic Society: A People's Sociology of the United States*, the author and sociologist Charles Derber has this to report:

> Let us be clear: the problem of surplus is the most glaring example of a systemic irrationality that is catastrophic in its consequences. Capitalist political economy creates not only a surplus crisis but also crises of inequality, militarism, and climate change that threaten the abilities of most people not just to find work but to survive with a civilized lifestyle on a habitable planet. (80)

Physicist Diop (365) explains that the "incapacity of language to embrace exactly the 'contours of the real' is often the cause of errors in philosophical, scientific, or even mathematical reasoning." This is to say that our current reason-based philosophical-scientific-mathematical knowledge has failed to help leaders create a suitable habitat for spiritual human beings. This is a problem that can be solved with a National Maat Public Policy. A National Maat Public Policy is a government administrative and management decision-making strategy that gives forthright consideration to the spirits of children, women, men, nature, and universe in addressing government and human affairs.

6.2 **What is Maat**?

Maat means right, true, truth, real, genuine, upright, righteous, just (trans. by Budge). "It is hard to translate or define Maat, the (universal spiritual) principle of truth, order, balance or justice. Ancient Egyptians believed that unless the king and his people preserved Maat (truth), forces outside creation would move in and destroy it" (Goldschmidt 17). African-American scholar Maulana Karenga, Ph.D., who holds two doctorate degrees, *one* in political science with focus on the theory and practice of nationalism and *the second* in social ethics with a focus on the classical African ethics of Ancient Egypt, has written "the first philosophical book that is based on a philologically (study of language in oral and written historical sources) and historically critical treatment of first-hand Egyptian material. It addresses current issues in African and Western philosophy" (xix), explains German Egyptologist Jan Assmann in the foreword of Dr. Karenga's book, *Maat, the Moral Ideal in Ancient Egypt: A Study in Classical African Ethics*. Karenga helps the reader to minimize her or his confusion about what Maat is, writing:

> The starting point for any serious discussion of Ancient Egyptian ethics is and must be the central concept of Maat. ...Maat was the foundational ideal of Ancient Egyptian... and ethics. Maat, however, is highly polysemic and apt to strike one unfamiliar with the conceptual elasticity of such ancient and central terms as lacking categorical

preciseness and thus, analytical utility. Actually, this conceptual elasticity which at first glance might seem problematic, on deeper inquiry proves promising due to... Maat's 'rich treasury of meaning.' ...Maatian ethics, before its recent revival, did not set forth any definitive or explicit moral theory or analysis of moral concepts. (4-5; 28)

"...Maat is actually one of the earliest...terms recorded in human history. By 3,000 BCE, Maat had evolved into a single philosophy of life that was based on the observation of the universe and the nightly procession of celestial bodies' proclaimed order. Such universal harmony appeared as a factor of existence that had to be mirrored on the Earth if the Egyptians were to prosper... Maat was the guiding principle for a national moral order and for human affairs" (Bunson 221). Maat is right order in nature and society as established by creation (Karenga).

This is to say, that Maat, the universal spiritual principle, is the sum of truth, justice, righteousness, balance, order, reciprocity, and harmony in our relationship with the Earth's ecology and universe. Maat is reflected throughout the universe. Research states that human beings are naturally endowed with a moral-spiritual disposition. This point is not necessarily remarkable when we consider the fact that even the cells in our bodies have an inherent disposition to function harmoniously (morally) in their relationship with the biological rhythms of our body, which promotes wellness. Furthermore, if we observe wildlife (i.e., birds, squirrels, raccoons, deer, and bears) and insects (i.e., ants and bees) in nature and their social interactions within their group, we can witness moral behavior amongst the members. This is evident by their "sense of meaningful purpose" and social order.

While it may be risky, it is nevertheless helpful to discuss the difference between religion and Maat, the universal spiritual principle. In putting forth this effort, this writer is mindful of our constitutional right to embrace a religion based on our personal preference. In offering a personal view on religion, there is no intent to offend anyone's religion. The church is a building used for public activities and worship. Religion is a belief in a particular teaching or doctrine. So here my focus will be general and on religion, not public activities and worship. It is assumed that the reader already knows that religion has been controversial in this country since its beginning. Case in point, in 1794 political activist and revolutionary English-American Thomas Paine published his work entitled, *The Age of Reason*. Some of his remarks concerning religion are given below.

> All national institutions of churches, whether Jewish, Christian or Turkish, appear to me no other than human inventions, set up to terrify and enslave mankind, and monopolize power and profit. ...Every national church or religion has established itself by pretending some special mission from God, communicated to certain individuals. The Jews have their Moses; the Christians their Jesus Christ, their apostles and saints; and the Turks their Mahomet as if the way to God was not open to every man alike.[vii]

Keep in mind that the goal of this paper is not to give an in-depth discussion on religion. Instead the goal is to prove we live in a reason-based society but should be living in a spirit-based society. This point should be kept in mind with other topics herein, such as money on which an appreciable amount of time is given. Being that Maat is a universal spiritual principle, the term "spirituality" will be substituted for the term "Maat" temporarily for our brief discussion on religion. It does help to know that Maat is NOT a religion! Religion is man-made. Spirituality is God-made. Religion is a belief. Spirituality is experience. Western religions are not known for supporting traditional people's spiritual ways. Western religions are known for destroying traditional people's spiritual ways.

Religion does not make people moral or spiritual. People are not moral or spiritual because of a religion. Spirituality comes from within; it must be a part of the genes (Hamer). Behavioral scientists agree that humans have an inborn disposition toward moral behavior. This truth is not readily apparent because we live in a reason-based society. Keep in mind that traditional people were moral and spiritual long before the invention of Western religions and Western civilization.

Religion is linked to a book. Spirituality is linked to the biosphere and all of its life forms, and the animated universe. The whole universe is an open holy book for all to observe, experience, and interpret within the range of his or her God-given genetic potential. Religion reasons about the supernatural. Spirituality is the Supernatural! Religion seeks money. Spirituality seeks harmony with the Universal Divine Oneness.

Some people think religion and spirituality are the same. If so, then why have the European and Arab world devoted so much time, resources and effort to **destroy** spiritual traditions in the name of religion? *Could it be lack of understanding?* This clearly should inform us, in this writer's view, Arabs and Europeans both are aware that there is some difference between religion and spirituality. This would be a good study: "Why do Arabs and Europeans prefer *religion* over *spirituality*?" Remember the United Nations (representing most of the world) has defined spirituality has a relationship with the universe.

During the 15th to the 19th centuries, there was an abundance of religious missionary work being done around the world to promote Christianity. This was accompanied by invasions, murder, thievery and destruction of spiritual traditions. In propagating Christianity, it would seem necessary to also defame and bastardize the word "spirituality" and anything affiliated with the word spirituality. Is the word "religion" a replacement for the word spirituality? Note today that the word "religion" is status quo—all while the word "spirituality" tends to be a low flickering flame. If the above is true, wouldn't the word religion be a neutered (castrated) version of the word spirituality? If so, the word "religion" is kind of like the name the white race gave to their intellectual movement—the Enlightenment. We saw that the Enlightenment was really a DE-ENLIGHTENMENT in the name of Jesus. The word religion has a similar effect as the word myth. The word religion diminishes and then blurs the concept of spirituality. Spirituality is not a *story*, *tale* or a *fable*— and traditional people's traditions and knowledge, which are passed from person to person and generation to generation by word of mouth, *are not myths*. Calling them such is an attempt to make their traditions and knowledge doubtful!

Metaphorically speaking, religion can have a chameleon/predator-like character. Religion can be very adaptive with the stealthy ability to change its color and form in order to blend nicely with a particular situation or culture. Religion can put on spiritual garments in order to approach, subdue, and control its prey (the people)—and even kill it—if needed. This process is done in a rather polite, nice, smooth deceptive way, during which the prey may start to develop trust or feelings for the religious predator (i.e., Stockholm syndrome[viii]).

Here are two examples. Native American Chief Pontiac (1720-1769) of the Ottawa Tribe had this to say, "They (whites) came with a Bible and their religion. They stole our land and *crushed our spirit* and now tell us we should be thankful to the 'Lord' for being saved" ("Native"). "In the paper, "Whose Land Is It Anyway? National Interest, Indigenous Stakeholders and Colonial Discourses," South African Bishop Desmond Tutu, a Nobel Peace Prize recipient, is quoted as saying, "When the missionaries first came to Africa, they had the Bible and we had the land. They said, 'Let us pray.' We closed our eyes. When we opened them…we had the Bible and they had the land" (qtd. to Banerjee 3).

The "truly genuine" acts of goodness by religious leaders are merely a reflection of the human temperament. This goodness can be displayed by most people under the right circumstances because we are spiritual beings. Religion has been used as sedative to relieve the mental and spiritual pain of victims of socioeconomic oppression and to control their impulse to retaliate against their oppressor. Karl Marx calls religion the "opiate of masses." An individual can make up a new religions. You cannot make up SPIRITUALITY! Remember, the United Nations stated, "Spirituality can be seen as an internal connection to the universe" (State 59-62).

Religion has shown its potential for cruelty that knows no limits. In times of insecurity and social unrest, we can see the 'unraveling' and **limits of religion**: "There can be a resurgence of suspicion and bias based on race and religion, and one's social class does not ensure protection or enjoyment of one's basic rights" ("Social Justice" 129). While it is true that people need moral instructions, it is truer that people need spirituality. Research states that the best way to develop morality is in a real-world ethical environment. This roundabout discussion on religion brings back memory of a conversation I had with a theologian a year or so ago. As our conversation was coming to a close, the theologian, as he hurried off made it a point to say to me regarding our conversation, "If you want to destroy a good idea, give it to the church!"

The comments below may help to clarify the theologian's well-intended comment. According to the *Columbia Guide to Religion in American History*, "Historically both 'religion' and 'politics' have been intertwined in American public life, mutually defining and at times placing checks on each other" (Harvey and Blum 137). For example,

> Particularly during ...early years, missionaries served political as well as religious purposes, sent out by their colonial governments to secure the friendship and cooperation of native people, and at times alliances against other tribes or nations. ...The early missions varied in style and method: Jesuits generally preferred venturing individually or in small groups into Native territories, where they lived among the people, learning the language and lifeways, with an eye toward building a mission in their midst, converting them to Christianity, and gradually reforming their moral lives to fit European expectation—including their approaches to family, marriage and gender roles. (70)

Harvey and Blum summarizes: "American religious idealism and greed propelled the expansion of the American empire across the west and then abroad" (2). Similar historical perspectives can be cited about Islam and Judaism. In the book *The Destruction of Black Civilization: Great Issues of a Race from 4500 B.C. to 2000 A.D.* by Dr. Chancellor Williams, the renown historian mentions that both Christianity and Islam underdeveloped the African continent economically and culturally,

> Africans who were neither Muslims nor Christians were classed as "pagans" and therefore required to disavow their whole culture and to regard practically all African institutions as "backward" or savage. The Blacks in their

own right became non-persons, members of a race of
nobodies, so hopeless that self-realization as personalities,
even in a subordinate status, could only be achieved by
becoming Muslims or Christians. (Williams 56)

Please note that Islam and Christianity are not traditional African
spiritual traditions. <u>They are the religions of the European and Arab
invaders</u>. From the book, *Jews and Judaism in the United States: A
Documentary History*, the author Jewish Rabbi Marc Raphael writes,

Jews also took an active part in the Dutch colonial slave
trade; indeed, the bylaws of the Recife and Mauricia
congregations (1648) included an imposta (Jewish tax)
of five soldos (silver) for each Negro slave a Brazilian
Jew purchased from the West Indies Company. <u>Slave
auctions were postponed if they fell on a Jewish holiday</u>.
In Curacao in the seventeenth century, as well as in the
British colonies of Barbados and Jamaica in the eighteenth
century, Jewish merchants played a major role in the
slave trade. In fact, in all the American colonies, whether
French (Martinique), British, or Dutch, Jewish merchants
frequently dominated. ...This was no less true on the
North American mainland, where during the eighteenth
century Jews participated in the 'triangular trade' that
brought slaves from Africa to the West Indies and there
exchanged them for molasses, which in turn was taken to
New England and converted into rum for sale in Africa.
(14, 23-25)

Historian Tony Martin, a former professor at Wellesley College,
while speaking at the 14th Conference of the Institute for Historical
Review had indicated that he had,

...discovered that according to the 1830 census, even
though Jews were a small proportion of the population
in North America, nevertheless they were inordinately

(largely) represented among the slave owners. Yes, they were a small portion of the population overall, but on a percentage basis that was significant. <u>Jewish historians who have analyzed the 1830 census have discovered that whereas something like 30-odd percent of the white population may have owned one or more slaves in the South, for Jewish households it was over 70 percent</u>. So according to an analysis of the 1830 census by Jewish historians, Jews were more than twice as likely, on a percentage basis, to own slaves.

In the study, "Religious Prosociality and Morality Across Cultures: How Social Enforcement of Religion Shapes the Effects of Personal Religiousity on Prosocial and Moral Attitude and Behavior," Dr. Olga Stavrova and Dr. Pascal Sieger reported the following:

> …analyses of data from (USA and) more than **70 countries** indicate that in countries with 'no social pressure' to follow a religion, religious individuals are more likely to endorse an intrinsic (innate) religious orientation (study 1), engage in charity work (study 2), disapproves of lying in their own interests (study 3), and are less likely to engage in fraudulent behavior (study 4) compared with non-religious individuals. Ironically, in secular context, religious individuals are also more likely to condemn certain moral choices than non-religious individuals (study 2). The effects of *religiousity* substantially weaken (and ultimately disappears) with increasing national levels of social enforcement of religiousity. (Stavrova and Sieger Abstract)

Stavrova and Siegers continues "our findings indicate that the association between religiousity (religious beliefs) and prosociality (kindness) is—in some sense—a reflection of societal processes" (330). It would seem that religious beliefs that are more compatible with our species' spiritual temperament (or) universal truth do not require strong enforcement. We need spirituality, not religion. The above research provides a perspective on why our growing religious world is becoming more violent and unethical—highlighting the need to restore spirituality in government and human affairs worldwide, see Diagram 2. Here is the list of countries involved in study: Albania, Andorra, Argentina, Armenia, Australia, Austria, Azerbaijan, Belarus, Belgium, Bosnia Herzegovina, Brazil, Bulgaria, Burkina Faso, Canada, Chile, Croatia, Cyprus, Czech Republic, Denmark, Estonia, Ethiopia, Finland, France, Georgia, Germany East, Germany West, Ghana, Greece, Guatemala, Hungary, Iceland, India, Indonesia, Iran, Iraq, Ireland, Italy, Japan, Jordan, Latvia, Lithuania, Luxembourg, Macedonia, Malaysia, Mali, Malta, Mexico, Moldova, Montenegro, Morocco, Netherlands, New Zealand, Northern Ireland, Norway, Peru, Poland, Portugal, Romania, Russia, Rwanda, Serbia, Slovak Republic, Slovenia, South Africa, South Korea, Spain, Sweden, Switzerland, Taiwan, Thailand, Trinidad and Tobago, Turkey, UK, Ukraine, Uruguay, USA, Vietnam, and Sambia (Stavrova and Siegers, ibid: 319-320).

Since we brought up the topic of slavery, it helps to also scrutinize Ancient Egypt in terms of slavery. "The Ancient Egyptian language used different words to express varying degrees of dependency that correspond to social roles like 'servant,' 'prisoner,' 'serf,' and 'dependent,' which makes it difficult to define 'slavery' as an autonomous social position. …In all periods of Egyptian history, military campaigns were the most important source for slaves. …Slaves were not mere objects, but people who could own property, be emancipated, and marry freewomen" (Rodriguez 243-244).

In Ancient Egypt, the two most important aspects of kingship were "divinity" and "unification" (Encyclopedia Americana vol. 10, 2000: 34). One of the king's most important rituals was the Presentation of Maat. In her work entitled, "The Presentation of Maat: Ritual & Legitimacy in Ancient Egypt," Egyptologist Emily Teeter writes, "Maat permeated ancient law and the administration of the state" (2). Maat is a universal spiritual principles.

The world's oldest spiritual instructions are the 42 Principles of Maat. Dr. Kwame Nantambu, a professor emeritus at Kent State University explains,

Moses was a Black-Afrikan man who was born in Ancient
Kemet (Egypt) during the reign of Pharaoh Harembab

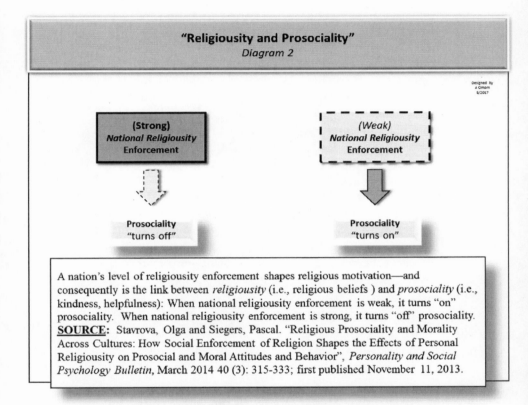

"Religiousity and Prosociality"
Diagram 2

(1340-1320 BC); he spent most of his life in Egypt…
The fact is that as a High-Priest… Moses was not only
familiar and knowledgeable with the '42 Negative
Confessions' (aka 42 Principles of Maat) but also with
the 10 categories of sins that existed in Ancient Kemet
(Egypt). …It was very easy for Moses to establish a new
religion…as a result of his spiritual education and training
in Western Kemet (Egypt). Moses then collapsed the '42
Negative Confessions' into the 'Ten Commandments'…
The fact of matter is that the original '42 Declarations

of Innocence' can be found in the sacred spiritual text inscribed on the walls of the Temple of Unas in Ancient Kemet. ...When the Egyptian Moses took these Ancient Kemetic laws to the Barbarians, he had to change them because he was speaking to a people who were living in the caves and hills of Europe and who had not lived a spiritual way of life. As such, Moses had to transfer the original Kemetic text "I have not..." to "Thou shall not..." that is, into Commandments. ...These 'Negative Confessions' represented the first moral code of ethics... These were developed before there was the Christian Holy Bible or an Islamic Quran. It took the Afrikans (Africans) fifty generations or 1,200 years to develop these moral, spiritual codes. In other words, the modern Euro-Christian Ten Commandments did not come nor were received from God above; they are Afrikan-Kemetic in origin. In this regard, it must be clearly understood that there is a vast difference between the original Afrikan spirituality and the derived Euro-Christian religion.

According to Ethiopian-born Egyptologist Dr. Yosef Ben-Jochannan, who is also a historian, engineer, cultural anthropologist, and author of the book *The African Origins of the Major World Religions*, the world's major religions borrowed from African traditional spiritual practices:

> **To speak of an Almighty God in the context used by Jews, Christians, and Moslems is impossible without going back to the roots of said belief... All eyes have to be centered on the indigenous African religions of the Nile Valley from whence all three derived, religions which are today called the Egyptian Religion and/or Mysteries.** (1)

Remember that by 3,000 BC, Maat was already a philosophy of life in Africa. Judaism was founded around 1500 BC, Hinduism was founded around 1500 BC, Taoism around 500 BC, Buddhism around 500 BC, Confucianism around 500 BC, Christianity around AD 1, and

Islam around AD 600, etc. Please note these dates tend to vary when you look at difference sources. Buddhism was also influenced by the indigenous African spiritual practices. In his article entitled "Ancient African Kings of India," Clyde Winters, Ph.D. writes, "Ethiopians have had very intimate relations with Indians (in India). In fact, in antiquity the Ethiopia ruled much of India. These Ethiopians were called Naga. It was the Naga who created Sanskrit." Sanskrit is an ancient language of India. Review a map to see the close proximity of Ethiopia to India.

Below are the 42 Principles of Maat (also known as the *42 Declarations of Innocence* and *42 Negative Confessions*), as translated by Egyptologist E.A. Wallis Budge from the Papyrus of Ani, Chapter CXXV, Plates XXXI and XXXII. Egyptologists are still debating the translation. See his book *Book of the Dead*, pages 576-582 for further information. The original Egyptian name for the *Book of the Dead* is **The Book of Coming Forth by Day and by Night**. This original title was changed by foreign invaders.

Please note the *italicized words* in the code are this writer's contribution to help clarify words. You may ignore this contribution. This code of ethics addresses relationships with self, human family, ancestors, nature, and the Divine (God). Keep in mind that Maat was common law. Please note below that number #20 and number #21 of the code were translated by Egyptologist Budge as the same. Also note the question marks (?) in number #19, #36 and #37 are Egyptologist Budge's work.

The reader is asked to slow down and read all 42 principles to be familiar with the high-ethical standards that regulated behavior of a nation for over three millennia through repetitive invasions and other domestic and foreign trials and tribulations. This code of ethics is an excellent guide for any world government because of its proven historical effectiveness in government and human affairs:

42 PRINCIPLES OF MAAT
(42 Declarations of Innocence)

1●- I have not committed sin.
2●- I have not committed robbery with violence.
3●- I have not stolen.

4●- I have not slain men or women.

5●- I have not stolen grain *(or property of others)*.

6●- I have not purloined *(misappropriated, embezzled)* **offerings.**

7●- I have not stolen the property of God.

8●- I have not uttered lies.

9●- I have not carried away food.

10●- I have not uttered curses.

11●- I have not committed adultery; I have not lain with men.

12●- I have made none to weep.

13●- I have not eaten the heart (i.e., I have not grieved uselessly, or felt remorse).

14●- I have not attacked any man.

15●- I am not a man of deceit.

16●- I have not stolen cultivated land.

17●- I have not been an eavesdropper.

18●- I have slandered [no man].

19●- I have not been angry without just cause (?).

20●- I have not debauched [*seduced*] the wife of [any] man.

21●- I have not debauched [*seduced*] the wife of [any] man.

22●- I have not polluted myself.

23●- I have terrorized none.

24●- I have not transgressed [the law].

25●- I have not been wroth *(intensely angry)*.

26●- I have not shut my ears to the words of truth.

27●- I have not blasphemed *(insulted anyone)*.

28●- I am not a man of violence.

29●- I have not been a stirrer up of strife (or a disturber of peace).

30●- I have not acted (or judged) with undue haste.

31●- I have not pried into matters.

32●- I have not multiplied my words in speaking.

33●- I have wrong none, I have done no evil.

34●- I have not worked witchcraft against the King (or blasphemed the king).

35●- I have never stopped [the flow of] water.

36●- I have never raised my voice (spoken arrogantly or in anger?).

37●- I have not cursed (or blasphemed) God.

38●- I have not acted with arrogance (?)

39●- I have not stolen the bread *(means of support)* **of gods** *(i.e., air, water, plants, earth, truth, man/woman, etc.)*.

40●- I have not carried away the khenfu cakes *(offerings made to ancestors)* **from the Spirits of the dead.**

41●- I have not snatched away the bread of the child, nor treated with contempt the god of my city.

42●- I have not slain the cattle *(property)* **belonging to the god.**

The next chapter will present a brief discussion on spiritual anatomy, and it will further aid the reader's appreciation of the *42 Declarations of Innocence* and its relevance to the self, human family, ancestors, nature, and the Divine (God).

~ ~ ~

Chapter 7
Introduction to Spiritual Anatomy

"With globalization and the growth of multiculturalism in many parts of the world, spirituality has become an important issue for the global village and our workplace everywhere. There is much support that the nonwestern countries have to offer in the domain of spirituality, yet this field of research is far from receiving the attention it deserves. Comparative religion or research on psychology of religion or religiosity hardly does justice to this field which is subjective and applied which runs against the grain of the positivist tradition that Western psychological research has vigorously pursued" (Bhawuk, xxi).

Medical doctor and acupuncturist Michael Greenwood states, "the human body has an energy field that...extends outward into space...with diminishing intensity the further out (it) goes" (27). Medical doctor Richard Gerber, author of the book *Vibrational Medicine*, states that the "human multidimensional anatomy" is the continuity of our physical system with higher nonphysical (invisible) energy systems. These subtle-energy systems play an important role in the total functioning of human beings. All of these invisible systems are superimposed upon one another in the same space. In other words, these higher subtle-energy systems are composed of matter with different frequency characteristics than that of the physical body. In other words, we also have auras, chakras, meridians, and nadis (119-161).

The picture to the right is a simplistic drawing of a human body with the seven chakras, which are indicated by the small white dots. The oval-shaped shaded area represents the seven auras that surround the human body. The meridians and nadis are not indicated in this drawing.

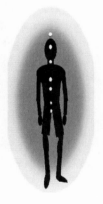

The seven auras are subtle energy extensions of the physical body, which interface with each other. *The auras are an invisible atmosphere that surrounds the body and interface with the environment.* Some people are capable of actually seeing auras. Auras are invisible light energy that surrounds the human body; each system contains consciousness, emotions and information that impacts how an individual sees the world and universe (Davies 43; Gerber 154, 157-62). The auras have been viewed as a reservoir of the thoughts and feelings surrounding the body (Brennan 109-110), and the invisible luminous auras correspond to the seven invisible chakras (spinning vortexes).

Chakras are the seven invisible centers of spiritual energy in the human body. The seven types are the root (base), sacral, solar plexus, heart, throat, brow/third eye, and the crown chakras. Each chakra corresponds to specific organs in the body. *The chakras, located along the region of the spinal column, act as transformers that step down incoming cosmic energy, which is processed through the endocrine and nervous system* (Iyengar 378-80). "Each of the seven major chakras is also…associated with a particular type of psychic perceptual functioning" (Gerber 130). For instance, "the heart chakra stands as a mid-point between the two worlds of spirit and matter" (277). This is the point where the experiences of the spirit and physical world merge, integrating and transforming the body, psyche, and personality of the individual (Beinfield and Korngold 111; Gerber). The first step to transformation involves unconditional love for others; this opens the heart chakra and develops higher consciousness (Gerber 378). **The "true nature of reality is beyond the scope of our ordinary sensory channels"** (162). This statement spotlights the limitations of the scientific method and Western authoritative knowledge, which devalue spirit! "The ability to activate and transmit energy through one's chakras is a reflection of a rather advanced level of consciousness development and concentration by the individual" (132). The crown chakra is associated with union with the universe, the highest state of consciousness, Universal Mind.

We also have meridians. *"The meridian system is also a part of the subtle-energy bodies, which is a specialized type of electrolytic fluid system that conducts certain types of subtle energy (chi) from the external environment to deeper internal organ structures"* (Capra 126). Meridians are used in the profession of acupuncture.

We have the ability to feel subtle spiritual energies. *We have "nadis," which "parallel the bodily nerves in the abundance"* (131; Gerber 119-120). Nadis are 72,000 channels for the flow of consciousness associated with the chakras. See also Maheshwarananda.[ix] In summary, the "spiritual dimension is the energetic basis of all life because it is the energy of spirit which animates the physical framework" (Gerber 44). In Yoruba psychology, consciousness originates from lae-lae (eternity), the mystical source of creation (Oxford, 953).

The spiritual anatomy (human multidimensional anatomy) is the facility for extrasensory perception (ESP), which is beyond the five senses and scientific understanding. Forms of ESP include astral travel (ability to spiritually separate from the physical body and travel vast distances), clairvoyance (ability to see without use of the five senses or technology), telepathy (ability to communicate with others minds), pre-cognition (ability to foresee events), bilocation (ability to be in two places at once), psychokinesis (ability to move objects with the mind), etc. As a child I astral traveled.

Cultural relativity could be a conceptual limitation in understanding extrasensory perception (Irwin 4). "In some societies, for example, ESP is regarded as a human skill that falls entirely within the natural order, yet in our society it generally is thought of as paranormal." In a racially and culturally diverse society, this gives further meaning to the importance of cultural relativism in America and to physician Reginald Crosley's declaration that the "public is not interested in being only a rational, left-brain being, living by the tenets of an academic dogma, a dogma imprisoned behind the bars of Euclidean-Newtonian dimension [European Enlightenment]. The public wants to live in the universe with its alternate pathways" (229). **The U.S. Congress must learn how to legislate on the behalf of spiritual people.** Those who are competent in proceeding with good judgment should be highly valued. Notice that reading about spirituality will not make one more spiritual. Acupuncture, herbals, nutrition, therapeutic massage, chi gong, yoga, tai chi chuan, meditation, moral reasoning, and other holistic traditional healing practices can stimulate spiritual consciousness flow in our spiritual anatomy to promote physical, mental, and spiritual healing. When the spiritual eye opens, the physical eyes close!

The spiritual anatomy is not taught in the elementary, middle, and high schools, colleges, universities, and professional schools in America— despite the fact that everyone has spiritual anatomy. Parapsychology has been studied in Europe since February 1882 when the Society for Psychical Research was officially constituted (Irwin 13). That's more than a hundred and thirty years ago. The U.S. Department of Health does have a National Center for Complementary & Integrated Health. Its mission is to "define, through rigorous scientific investigation, the usefulness and safety of complementary and integrated health interventions and their roles in improving health and health care." Holistic medicines have been used successfully by traditional people for thousands of years—long before Western medicine existed. Holistic healing practices used to be a *modus operandi* (well-established) cultural practice worldwide! So we must ask the question, "How much more rigorous scientific investigation is needed before these holistic spiritual practices impregnates society's daily activities again?"

While teaching tai chi chuan at a small private religious school, with the approval of the principal, this writer successfully taught students in the fifth, sixth, and seventh grades about the auras, chakras, and meridians. After a week or two, these bright African-American children were able to go the blackboard in front of the class and draw a basic sketch of the spiritual anatomy: an outline of the human body and the auras with lines around the body; chakras (indicated by a big dot) at the top of the head, mid-brow, throat, heart, solar plexus, sacral, and the root (gonads) regions of the body; and the meridians with (intentional scribbling) lines indicating that the meridians ran internally throughout the body. They were also able to articulate the basic function of the auras, chakras, and meridians. The nadis were not discussed. They also enjoyed the pleasant relaxed feeling of energy (chi) they experienced while practicing tai chi chuan. Some students commented on how the tai chi helped them in their relationships at home and in the classroom.

Activity to emphasize the presence of the chakras: The students had an opportunity to experience the presence of some of their chakras by standing and relaxing and slowly moving the hand continuously (without touching) up from the center of the back of the head, over the top of the head, and down the center of the forehead, face, throat, chest, abdomen, and pubic area slowly. No student could feel all seven chakras. However, most of the students admitted that they could sense/ feel some chakra(s) as their hand slowing moved over them. This would occur each time they repeated the exercise.

Activity to emphasize the universality of energy: The students had the opportunity to experience the pleasant energy (chi) radiating from trees without touching the trees. They were only instructed to stand (about a foot away) facing the tree, calm the mind, relax, and just be with the tree. Four or five trees were selected. All students admitted they experienced the energy (chi) from the trees. Some raised the palm of their hands to the trees (without touching); some just stood. Good spirit is everywhere. It's in us and all around us in the natural environment. Truth is everlasting. We live in a vital energetic universe. America must learn how to tap into the good spirit and its rich treasures that exist in our biosphere and ecology.

All energies are not good energies. Some emotions and energies are good, and some are bad. Healthy emotions/energies are a sense of wellbeing. Unhealthy emotions/energies are a sense of *dis-ease*. Both healthy and dis-ease energies can advise and reveal. This too is culturally subjective.

In the study "The Role of Positive and Negative Emotions in Life Satisfaction Judgment Across Nations," the authors' results showed "how emotional aspects of the good life vary with national culture and how this depends on the values that characterize one's society. Although to some degree, positive and negative emotions might be universally viewed as desirable and undesirable, respectively, there appears to be clear cultural differences in how relevant such emotional experiences are to quality of life" (Kuppens et al. 66). In the next chapter, we will explore this point further.

~ ~ ~

Chapter 8
A Perspective on Policy Implementation

8.1 <u>Reversing the Industrial-Capitalistic Cultural Assimilation</u>

In writing this section, this author clearly understands that the federal government already has a legislative process in place for making laws that are suppose to improve life satisfaction in America. Generally, the process follows this sequence: introduction and referral of proposed bill, committee consideration, calendars and scheduling (bill eligibility), House floor (debate), Senate floor (debate), executive business in the Senate, resolving differences, and Presidential actions.

The process may require legislators' collaboration with scholars and experts from diverse backgrounds and the general public. Any vagueness and feasibility concerns of any part of this proposal would be resolved through the legislative process. Before implementation, each social institution may examine its activities in relationship to other social institutions and relevant constitutional laws, regulations, case precedents, and customs. So, while it is not possible to speak definitively on the legislative process or implementation process as it relates to this proposal, this analyst seeks only to offer some thoughts that may be helpful.

After review of Chapters 4, 5, 6, and 7, it may be clearer that advocacy for positive social change must begin immediately. It is also true that the process must be positive. This means there is a need for a new philosophy of life. Knowing that the mission of Enlightenment laid the foundation of our contemporary society and that the institution of white supremacy permeates the entire industrial world is only one part of the story.

You see, it is also still true that the "Machine" was even resisted by workers in Europe when the Industrial Revolution first began. This resistance was based on human rights concerns. The following illustrates what is being said: "<u>A cultural polarity gradually emerged between Englishness</u>, identified with the pastoral vision ('green and pleasant land'), <u>and industrialism</u> (the 'dark satanic mills'). The vision was felt to be precarious (delicate) as the pastoral vision was being eroded bit by bit by the advance of industry. The power of the Machine was invading" (Wiener 81).

In the book *Rebel Against the Future: The Luddites and their War on the Industrial Revolution*, the author describes the workers' reaction to the Machine. <u>There were riots by a band of English workers called the Luddites</u>. These workers made a courageous attempt to preserve working people's livelihoods by destroying machines with hammers and burning down factories. "Indeed, the Luddites were for a while real heroes...and, if measured by their deeds as well as their impact on the psyche of a nation, should be well remembered today...they represented something quite new in England history" (Sale 4). The author Kirkpatrick Sale continues,

> The stream engine...was the iron heart of the industrial revolution. ...(I)t was the first manufacturing technology in human history that was—in a sense—independent of nature, of geography and seasons and weather, of sun or wind or water or human or animal power. ...(T)here is then, a kind of technological logic connected to this iron monster with a pulse of steam...called the logic of industrialism, which they say is why all industrial societies look pretty much alike. (27-28)

In France, there was a similar view and reaction to the Machine. Frank Manual, Ph.D., author of the paper entitled "The Luddite Movement in France" explains,

> Normandy (France) was the first center to be invaded by machines from England, and its petitions were bitter. The workers of the parish of Ocqueville-en-Caux cried: If the project of these men with systems, who wish to introduce the usage of machines, through which a single man will supplant the labor of twenty, ever succeed, let them build poorhouses for us and our children! These fine machines will enrich a few individuals and will ruin a whole country. Let them not proclaim before us the interests of commerce

in general! As long as the artisan remains unemployed, misery will be fixed in France! (Manuel 181)

So today when the urban dwellers complain and protest the quality of life in an industrial-capitalistic society, it is not their desire to be troublemakers. People have a nervous system. The human temperament is speaking out in these cases. Members of Congress may want to carefully ponder the question raised by Wiener (88): "If industrialism were not natural to Europe's spirit, to whose was it?" Would it be the psychopaths??

If immoral whites had confidence in creating a *world* of falsehood, surely ethical people of *all races* have confidence in their ability to create a *nation* of truth! "The most effective way of creating a strong sense of efficacy (effectiveness in this matter) is through 'mastery experiences'" (Bandura 71). "A resilient sense of efficacy requires experience in overcoming obstacles through perseverant effort!" "The more we practice crafting and speaking our values and developing our own voice, the more likely those scripts will become our default (i.e., automatic) positions when we face conflict. We are more likely to say those words when we have pre-scripted ourselves and have rehearsed in front of our peers, inviting supportive feedback and constructive coaching" (Gentile 47).

Moral action is needed now! However, we cannot overlook historical truths when we act. As it has been shown in this proposal, "Europe invented a global solution to its locally produced problems—and by doing so, forced all other humans (in the world) to seek, desperately and in vain, local solutions to (Europe's)…globally produced problems" (Bauman 229). In summary, it must be clear that the solution to the problem cannot be based on the logic that created the European globally produced problem.

From this point on in this chapter, there will be a brief discussion on: (a) racial diversity, (b) the prerequisite for moral decision-making, (c) U.S. Cabinet, (d) cultural relativism, and (e) economic development. These topics are viewed as important considerations. The second part of this chapter will discuss "*the law and emotions.*"

8.1.1 Racial Diversity

The U.S. Census for 2010 indicates that whites represented 72.4 percent of the American population. According to the U.S. Census "Projections of the Size and Composition of the U.S. Population: 2014 to 2060," in the year 2014 whites represented 62.2 percent of the American population. Observe the decrease in the percent of white population from 2010 to 2014. For the year 2060, "whites" are projected to represent 43.6 percent of the American population while for the same year "non-whites" are projected to represent 56.4 percent of the American population. "The majority of us understand that where the survival of our planet and the health of our people are concerned, the only race that matters is the human race" (Cummings A-3).

Questions: With the above national population shift, how do whites want to be treated if such a racial composition becomes a reality? Or better stated: How do whites want their children and their children's children to be treated as a minority group in the future? What type of legacy will today's white Americans leave for future generations? What will it be?

According to the United Nations "World Population Prospects: The 2017 Revision": "From 2017 to 2050, it is expected that half of the world's population growth will be concentrated *in just nine countries*: India, Nigeria, the Democratic Republic of the Congo, Pakistan, Ethiopia, the United Republic of Tanzania, the United States of America, Uganda and Indonesia (ordered by their expected contribution to total growth)" ("World Population").

8.1.2 Prerequisite for Moral Decision-Making

The scholarly data herein has indicated that the white race's intellectual movement devalued humanity's spiritual traditions in order to take leadership in the world. It is, therefore, recommended that Members of Congress observe that the United Nations' 2009 State of the World's Indigenous People report announced that "spirituality is the relationship to the universe." This means, in the twenty-first century, it is political parties' responsibility to select candidates, mobilize voters, and help organize the legislative process in a manner that guarantees the revival of a way of life that is based on a spiritual relationship with the universe.

Tanzanian Laurenti Magesa, who holds a Ph.D. in moral theology and a Ph.D. in sacred theology; has taught in universities in East Africa, Europe and the U.S.; and published several books, declares that the "agent for moral action…are vital forces of the entire created universe, both visible and invisible worlds" (58). The above UN report adds: "Spirituality is the relationship human beings create with the spirit world in order to manage forces that seem overpowering…"

By reviewing the definition of the National Maat Public Policy, the reader can see that this proposed policy encourages a relationship with the spirit world because the policy is a government administrative decision-making strategy which gives forthright consideration to the spirits of children, women, men, nature, and universe in addressing government and human affairs. This is consistent with the worldview of indigenous people.

8.1.3 United States Cabinet

It is suggested that the legislative process begin with a national dialogue on the policy. Then, social institutions (i.e., family, education, health, economic, politics/law, religion) should explore creative ways during this time to align their missions with the proposed policy. Obviously the National Maat Public Policy is actually foremost applicable to the three branches of the federal government: Legislative Branch, Judicial Branch, and the Executive Branch, which includes the U.S. Cabinet. The Cabinet is composed of senior appointed officers of the executive branch and the *U.S. Vice-President.* The three branches of the federal government set and regulates national behavior.

Each senior officer heads one of the following federal executive departments: *Department of State, Department of the Treasury, Department of Defense, Attorney General, Department of the Interior, Department of Agriculture, Department of Commerce, Department of Labor, Department of Health and Human Services, Department of Housing and Urban Development, Department of Transportation,*

A CONCEPTUAL VIEW OF POLICY IMPLEMENTION
Diagram 3

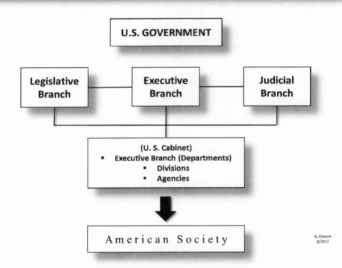

Department of Energy, Department of Education, Department of Veterans Affairs, Department of Homeland Security.

This also means the proposed policy is applicable to all divisions and agencies of each federal executive department. See Diagram 3. For example, the divisions of the U.S. Department of Health & Human Services are: Administration for Children & Families (ACF), Administration for Community Living (ACL), Agency for Healthcare Research & Quality (AHRQ), Agency for Toxic Substances & Disease Registry (ATSDR), Center for Disease Control and Prevention (CDC), Centers for Medicare & Medicaid Services (CMS), Food & Drug Administration (FDA), Health Resources & Services Administration (HRSA), Indian Health Services (HIS), National Institute of Health (NIH) and Substance Abuse & Mental Health Services Administration (SAMHSA).

Each of these divisions, along with their subordinate <u>agencies,</u> would manage in the context of the proposed policy. When consideration is given to all three federal branches of government, one can begin to see the far-reaching potential of the National Maat Public Policy into areas such as international peace, economic prosperity, national defense, law and order, environment, agriculture, homeland security, science and technology, commerce, labor, healthcare, housing & urban development, education, transportation and essentially into the lives of the American people in a positive way. What elected official, Democrat or Republican, wouldn't want this?? Would it be the psychopaths??

For further illustration of how the policy can have a far-reaching impact on society, we can turn to the National Center for Charitable Statistics (NCCS), which is the national repository of data on the nonprofit sector in the United States. Its mission is to develop and disseminate high-quality data on nonprofit organizations and their activities for use in research on the relationships among the nonprofit sector, government, the commercial sector, and broader civil society ("Quick Facts about Nonprofits"). NCCS reports there are 1,532,250 tax-exempt organizations, which include 1,061,916 public charities; 102,055 private foundations; and 368,279 other types of nonprofits organizations, including chambers of commerce, fraternal organizations and civic leagues. These organizations under the new proposed policy would be required to administer with forthright consideration of spirits in children, women, men, nature, and the universe in decision-making. Tax-exempt organizations would know to formulate their vision and mission to complement the new policy.

It is recommended that all businesses be mandated to administer according to the policy. In 2012, there were 5.7 million firms (i.e., large businesses); and 7.4 million establishments (i.e., small businesses) in America with 115,938,468 full-time employees (Caruso 7: appendix table). So it is true that a multitude of our national, state, local, community, and personal problems can be simultaneously impacted positively by a National Maat Public Policy. In this regard, radical activism for social justice becomes a societal initiative rather than just an individual's or an organization's initiative. It becomes a non-violent, socially-sanctioned ethical revolution with the goal of establishing a balanced ecology.

Finally, the National Maat Public Policy can be the U.S. Congress' sword and shield for engaging and dismantling those transnational corporations that continue to commit corporate crimes and are socially irresponsible (via false advertisement, embezzlement, tax evasion, market manipulation, human-trafficking, labor corruption, environmental pollution, racism, sexism, genocide, drug-trafficking, murder, theft, bribery of public officials, starting wars, etc.).

8.1.4 Cultural Relativism

It is recommended that Members of Congress consider and debate this proposal with consideration to "cultural relativism." Cultural relativism is important in social interactions. Cultural groups tend to have a distinctive ways of viewing the world that may differ from other cultural groups. From a multicultural perspective, social interaction has been shown to be good-natured when cultural relativism is valued.

As a species, we should turn the page and start by bringing forth our inherent goodness. We have spent an enormous amount of time and energy demonstrating that we know how to be demonic criminals and cosmopolitan savages! We get an A-plus here. Now it is time to aspire to get an A-plus in being civilized and morally elegant humans.

Cultural relativism is understanding the norms and values of another culture from the view of the members of that culture. This is not an easy task for an outsider. Specifically, looking back we learned that:

A. <u>Our diverse ways of viewing the universe are reflections of our biological differences, which are due to heredity and environment</u>.

B. <u>Our ability to be attentive to subtle divine energies in our surrounding environment is a prerequisite in cultivating moral understanding</u>.

C. <u>We tend to consciously and/or unconsciously show favor or disfavor to the range of stimuli and events in our environment based on our genotype</u>.

D. <u>Our degree of openness to these experiences and sensations are both determinants in whether or not we are inclined to acknowledge the supernatural</u>.

In essence, these points appear to be the context from which a people's culture naturally emerges—if left alone! If we are looking at nature, we can find some commonality with the above point. For example, in the book *Light: The Visible Spectrum and Beyond*, the authors Kimberly Arcand, who specializes in image and meaning research at NASA, and Megan Watzke, who specializes in communication, also at NASA, states "mammals aren't considered to have the widest range of visual sensitivity in the animal kingdom. Rather, many kinds of insects, such as bees, wasps, dragon flies, and butterflies, have a broader range. Butterflies… can detect parts of the <u>infrared</u> band" (77). "Because ultraviolet falls just beyond violet in the visible light band, most humans can't detect <u>ultraviolet</u> light with our eyes… Certain animals (i.e., reindeer) and insects, however, can" (113, 117). The main point here is that all living things have a prescribed—yet limited—range of genetic potential that is dictated by our genotype and environment. Historically, traditional people made progress in learning how to interact with and live amongst the diverse genetic potential in our planet's ecology.

What causes racial prejudice? Racial prejudice is formulating beliefs about a certain race without sufficient information about that race. "Do people who undergo training usually shed their biases? Researchers have been examining that question since before World War II, in nearly a thousand studies" (Dobbin and Kalev 54). Harvard sociologists Frank Dobbin and Alexandra Kalev state that:

> <u>The positive effects of diversity training rarely last </u>
> <u>beyond a day or two</u>, and a number of studies suggest
> that it can activate bias or spark a backlash. …Research
> from the University of Toronto reinforces our findings:
> In one study whites read a brochure critiquing prejudice
> toward blacks. When people felt pressure to agree with it,
> the reading strengthened their bias against blacks. When

they felt the choice was theirs the reading reduced bias. (54-55)

This research should help us to see that one race forcing its beliefs and values upon another race is poor race relations. If the Grimaldi Negroid (black race)—*with the rest of animal kingdom (i.e., mammals, reptiles, fish, birds, insects)* and *plant kingdom*—was here on Earth for 180,000 years learning, maturing, surviving and striving in quest of living harmoniously with the Earth's diverse mysterious ecology long before the appearance of the white race (Cro-Magnon man), yellow race (Chancelade man), and the yellow Semites, then history has been witnessing a form of unimaginable evil by *nonblack* races that see fit to oppress black people just because they are black people, and never giving thought to the fact that black people are the "original" people of this planet! Again, African people were the ORIGINAL HUMAN SPECIES. Why are black people enduring racism around the world from *nonblack* people? Black people are more than fully qualified to administer their own affairs without the supervision of nonblack people!!

But wait! Nonblack races have also shown their ability to learn, mature, survive and strive through many challenging circumstances for thousands of years, striving in quest of living harmoniously with the mysterious diverse ecology too. Nonblack people are more than fully qualified to administer their own affairs without the supervision of another race too. Each race has the ability to self-govern. Each race ALREADY HAS the human right to self-govern! We need race-based sovereignties. We may be so inclined to conclude that under such circumstances the "complexity of human behaviors provides unending challenges for legal systems…," states Attorney Owens Jones (1706) who specializes in the intersection of law and behavioral biology.

In spite of the legal challenges that might arise from multiracial sovereignties, these legal challenges can be minimized by valuing the importance of cultural relativism. Case in point, indigenous people of each race must be viewed as prestigious consultants and partners in the establishment of these proposed race-based sovereignties. After all, subtle exposure to a group can influence our morals. Industrial people have acquired a large number of false beliefs and need persistent introspection and counsel of indigenous sages—rather than capitalists. With that said, the research herein informs us that each race is inclined to design its legal system in a way that is compatible with their genotype and cultural preferences "—just as beaver dams, despite their differences, all reflect the effects of evolutionary processes on beaver brains, the legal systems, despite their differences, all (will) reflect the effects of evolutionary processes on human brains. That is, it will be possible to view at least many of the largest-scale features of legal systems as reflections of human neural architecture." A national cultural landscape that is a reflection of all of the diverse racial and neural architecture—under a National Maat Public Policy—will indeed be a natural, beautiful and scenic cultural experience to behold! The field of *cultural anthropology*, which studies cultural variations of human societies, can validate this point! <u>The complexity of ethnicity, nationality and language are resolved with the particular race-based sovereignty</u>.

There are many benefits from having race-based sovereignties. Case in point: "More than 52% of white working-class Americans believe discrimination against whites is as big a problem as discrimination against blacks and other minorities. However, at the same time the "white working-class Americans are roughly as likely as Americans overall to believe many minority groups face substantial discrimination in society" (Cox, Lienesch and Jones).

Sociologists Dobbin and Kalev have indicated that resolving racial prejudice requires more than training or coercion. If this nation is serious about solving the race relations problem we would see how race-based sovereignties have their value in terms of being an appropriate cultural sanctuary where the particular person can be assured that he or she is not pressured to assimilate into a society that is hostile to his or her genotype and psychosocial needs. This highlights the importance of race-based sovereignties.

Next, the biosphere and ecology have been a friend indeed. Industrialism has been an enemy. We cannot eat the Machine and survive, however we can eat the diverse nutrients and use the natural resources provided by the biosphere and ecology for our survival. The Machine promote control and destruction. The biosphere and ecology give and promote life. We must remember that industrialism was forced upon humanity. We must remember that most people preferred a way of life that is in harmony with the natural environment rather than a way of life that is hostile to the natural environment. This fact should be seen in a positive light as such preference means that each race-based sovereignty is inclined to function as caretaker and protector of the biosphere and ecology—if the corporations and psychopaths do not intervene. For example, race-based sovereignties can address the air pollution problem by decreasing car usage. Because the sovereignties are cooperative-communities there will be a lesser need for long-distance travel to and from corporate entities. This means people would pollute less. The concept of a job will be no more. A "job" will instead be "community responsible" where the individual takes care of the moral sovereignty and the moral sovereignty takes care of the moral individual. When we look at today's communities there is pretentiousness regarding this practice contributing to crime, violence, and health problems and lack of moral development within communities. In the race-based sovereignty work is done to benefit the whole sovereignty.

The human development within these racial sovereignties, from babyhood to childhood to adolescence to adulthood, would observe the National Maat Public Policy in conjunction with cultural preference. This would help to eliminate many antisocial behaviors (i.e., racism, criminality). In other words, these racial sovereignties' (a) institution of *family*, which determines kinship; (b) institution of *health*, which oversees healing and spiritual traditions; (c) institution of *education*,which transmits knowledge from one generation to the next generation; (d) institution of *economics*, which regulates the distribution of goods and services; and the (e) institution of *politics/law*, which regulates personal and government powers, would all function according to preferred cultural traditions and the National Maat Public Policy.

In the article "Global Extinction Rates: Why Do Estimates Vary So Wildly?," which was published at the Yale School of Forestry & Environmental Studies, Fred Pearce, an award-winning environment author, reports that "by concentrating on global biodiversity, <u>we may be missing a bigger and more immediate threat—the loss of local biodiversity</u>. That may have a more immediate and profound effect on the survival of nature and the services it provides… Ecosystems are profoundly local, based on individual interactions of individual organisms." Race-based sovereignties would become experts on the local biosphere and ecology.

Being receptive to the subtle energies of the local biosphere and ecology helps us to bond and understand how to be with the environment. This wisdom will help to prevent further local environmental degradation and extinction of local endangered animal and plant species. The inauguration of racial sovereignties under a National Maat Public Policy should be seen as simply a much needed humanitarian and ecological initiative. People would have the right to live and work wherever they want with regard to the proposed national policy and sovereignties' laws and customs. As a species we all have SURVIVED epidemics, famines, natural disasters, social revolutions, wars, European Enlightenment, and the Industrial Revolution (hopefully). Race-based sovereignties are not new, not rocket science, and we have done this before!!

If the issue of land rights is a concern, we should think in terms of being a protector and caretaker rather than "the owner." If we use the same inductive reasoning that many non-blacks use to justify their racist claims, we can arrive at the following logical conclusion: Since black Africans are the "First People on Earth" hundreds of thousands years before any other race (and in Africa, Asia, Australia/Oceania, Europe, North America, South America, everywhere)—the Africans are the true owners of the WHOLE WORLD! This includes the whole biosphere (air, water, land) and the whole ecology and you too!? Actually, the "First People on Earth" were protectors and caregivers of Mother Earth. For European-Americans, Native Americans, and Mexican-Americans who are of the opinion that they are the original Americans, it is helpful to know that ground-breaking research has revealed that the "true" original first Americans were black Africans. When we consider the fact that black Africans were the sole representative of the human race for 180,000 years, this makes good sense!

In his book *The First Americans Were Africans: Documented Evidence*, Dr. David Imhotep who is the first person to hold a Ph.D. degree in Ancient African Studies, reports that "There is evidence of Africans in South America 56,000 years ago, and in North America 51,700 years ago" (62-63). The "presence of modern humans in Mexico as early as 40,000 years ago" has been well documented (64). "These first Americans remained black complexioned until 3000 B.C., when the first Asians entered and began to mix blood with the Protoamerican Africans" (66). Keep in mind there were no yellow or Asian people in existence 40,000 years ago. The Mongolians did not enter into America until 3000 BC (8-9). "The mixing of blood with the Mongolians had an effect on the proto-Americans and their physical appearance began to change" (10). "Proto" means the foremost, earliest, first. "A major ethnic group among the ancient Egyptian/Nubians were the Manding people" (80). There is evidence that shows "the high civilizations of Mexico (Maya and Aztecs) had acquired many of cultural and religious [spiritual] traditions of the Malinke-Bambura (Manding people) of West Africa" (83).

Nevertheless, despite overwhelming evidence of African presence and influence some Native Americans Nations ignore, hid, and/or destroy this factual evidence that ties present-day Native American people to their black African ancestors (the First People). We can find many similar cases of such occurrences around the world. Here, we will look at the Southeastern Indians (Native Americans), in particularly the Muscogee (Creeks). The Five Civilized Tribes (Cherokees, Chickasaws, Choctaws, Creeks, and Seminoles) are Southeastern Native American tribes that survived war with the white man and were relocated to the Mid-West. "Muscogee (Creek) people are descendants of a remarkable culture that, before AD 1500, spanned all the region known today as the Southeastern United States. Early ancestors of the Muscogee constructed magnificent earthen pyramids along the rivers of this region as part of their elaborate ceremonial complexes" (Muscogee "Nation").

Christopher Haveman, Ph.D., professor of history and specialist in the history of Southeastern tribes, has examined "the removal of approximately twenty-three thousand Creek Indians from Alabama and Georgia to present day Oklahoma between 1825 and 1838. At its height, the Creek Nation encompassed most of the present states of Alabama, Georgia and Florida" (iv). The Muscogee (Creeks) had three branches of government: (1.) a civil administration branch, (2.) a military branch, and (3.) a branch that was dedicated to the sacred (Ortiz, 26). "It was a vibrant, multi-ethnic and multi-lingual society. But, the Creek Nation increasingly found itself under siege by white settlers and state and federal politicians who wanted to open up the Creeks' land for white settlement" (iv). "A majority of the emigrants were forced from their homes and marched west under the supervision of the United States military in 1836 and 1838. The hardships faced on the 'Creek Trail of Tears' were legendary" (2). The removal from Creek ancestral lands to the Indian Territory is one of America's greatest tragedies.

Cow Tom (aka "Cow Mikko" and probably Cow-e-to-me-ko) is of Yamasee descent (Muscogee 'Band'). "Yamasse Indians were Africans." "Cow Tom was born in the Seminole Nation and it is said that he had derived his name by being related by blood to members of the Cowkeeper Dynasty of the Seminole Nation" (Cow "Keeper"). In the book, *Africans and Creeks*, author Daniel Littlefield indicates, "Creek, Seminole, Yamacraw, and Yemasee Indians were all tribes of the Creek Confederacy" (Muscogee "Band"). His wife was Amy Cow Tom. "Grandchildren of Cow Tom described him as 'a jet black'" [person] (Cow "Keeper"). In his early years Cow Tom worked as a cattle man and interpreter for Chief Yargee of the Upper Creeks. "After arrival in the Indian Territory... Cow Tom became the chief within the Muskogee (Creek) Nation. Being among one of the few persons who spoke Muskogee fluently, as well as English, all depended upon Cow Tom...." (African 'Cow Tom'). "He assumed leadership in the manner through which other Creeks chiefs were occasionally elevated, by a combination of capacity and necessity" (Greenberg 23). Cow Tom is not the first or only Black Native American chief.

With the goal of further weakening and dividing the Five Civilized Tribes, the U.S. government continued furthering the mission of white race's intellectual movement by encouraging tension and racism within the tribes. For example, historically the U.S. Gov't has been negligent in paying its debts (money) owed to the tribes from use or consumption of natural resources, i.e., land, timber, oil, and other minerals, and grazing leases (Brinkley). Withholding money from the tribes has contributed to health and socio-economic problems, and therefore further straining race relations within the tribes.

Case in point, "After the civil war freedmen (African people) were granted their citizenship in the Creek Nation, the Creek Indians refused to recognize the rights of the freedmen. Ketch Barnett, with Harry Island and Cow Tom went to Washington DC as a representative committee of

(Creek) freedmen..." (Buchanan). Harry Island's wife was Maggie Cow Tom-Island. In the book, *The Road to Disappearance* author Angie Debo described Harry Island as a "shrewd Creek Negro who served as interpreter and apparently looked after the interest of his race" (African 'Island'). "Harry Island, a black Creek, acted as interpreter at both the Fort Smith and Washington (D.C.) negotiations" (Chang, 101).

According to Richard Thornton, who is one of the nation's leading experts on Southeastern Indian: "Mako [strong-Itza Georgia Creek word for king]-the word became meko in Muscogee" (Thornton, 'Meso'). The website, Children of the Sun: Native Culture states that the Creek word for chief is mekko. Please note the two spellings for "Chief" mekko and meko. The main point, however, is while both Cow Tom (Cow Mikko) AND Harry Island negotiated and signed the official Creek Treaty of 1866: Cow Mikko's SEAL is also stamped on the Treaty, being that he was the Chief of the Muscogee (Creek) Nation.

In negotiating the Creek Treaty of 1866, it was Harry Island who is said to have helped to secure the essential mandate that: "...inasmuch as there are among the Creeks many persons of African descent...shall have and enjoy all the rights and privileges of native citizens, including an equal interest in the soil and national funds, and the laws of the said nation shall be equally binding upon and give equal protection to all such persons, and all others, of whatsoever race or color, who may be adopted as citizens or members of said tribe" (see Article 2, Creek Treaty).

Two decades later, there was still a sizable population of persons of African descent in the Creek Nation. According to the *Seventh Annual Report of the Commission to the Five Civilized Tribes to the Secretary of the Interior for the Fiscal Year Ended June 30, 1900*: the number of enrolled Creeks in 1890 was 9,463; and the number of enrolled freedmen (Africans) in 1890 was 4,228 (21). Remember thousands of Creeks died on the Creek Trail of Tears. Today (2018) the Muscogee Creek Nation has a population of 83,570 Creek citizens. Race relations were still unsatisfactory. "It took more than a hundred years...for the Creek tribe to undo what Cow Tom had achieve. In 1979, the Creek leaders rewrote their constitution, excluding Freedmen (African men and women), and inter-married couples, as well as their descendants from the tribal roll" (Greenberg 33). For example, there are African

Creeks who were active citizens and still loss their Creek citizenship. There are many who continue to be denied citizenship even with family history documentations proving their ties to the Creek Nation, such as this writer's family on my father's side of the family. Case in point, Cow Tom is my 3X great grandfather, and Harry Island is my 2X great grandfather.

Because of the senseless persistence in violating citizenship rights of thousands of African Creek descendants, four astute African Creeks decendants: Jeffery D. Kennedy, Sharon Lenzy-Scott, Rhonda Grayson, and Ron Graham stepped forward and founded the 'Muscogee Creek Indian Freedmen Band:' "to educate the public regarding the African Creeks' political rights as citizens of the Creek Nation, as defined by Creek Treaty of 1866, Article 2." The national headquarters of the National Association for the Advancement of Colored People "supports the Muscogee Creek Indian Freedmen Band Association as they petition the Office of Federal Acknowledgement in becoming a 'federally recognized' Indian Tribe" (NAACP Resolution). On July 20, 2018, the Muscogee Creek Indian Freedmen Band, Inc., along with their attorneys: Damario Solomon-Simmons (3x great grandson of Cow Tom), David Riggs, Don Bingham, Kris Koepsel, Melvin Hall, Graham Zorn, John Guttmann, Nessa Horewitch Coppinger, and Matthew D. Schneider; filed a lawsuit in the Federal District Court for the District of Columbia demanding that Creek citizenships be restored.

The above ongoing tradegies nationwide highlights the importance of having race-based sovereignties, and especially a MANDATED National Maat Public Policy!! Land is priceless and of great value in a people's quest to be free! It is, however, delusional to believe that land "alone" is the ultimate solution to being free. Look carefully at the State of the World! **When a people are regulated by a government that shows preference to the rich and corporations, and INTENTIONALLY disregards the spirit of children, women, men, nature, and universe; then land (which is submerged in such a country) will not guarantee any people long term freedom. That is why we need a National Maat Public Policy.**

Returning to our earlier point, race-based sovereignties that embrace the traditional ways of our wise pre-colonial ancestors under the National Maat Public Policy are of real value to the fight to 'Save the

Planet.' Does it help to know that in 2011 the U.S. Department of State, under Pres. Barack Obama, announced support for the United Nations Declaration on the Rights of Indigenous People? Could this be a sign for future generations? The announcement states:

> The United States supports the Declaration, which—while not legally binding or a statement of current international law—has both moral and political force. It expresses both the aspirations of indigenous peoples around the world and those of States in seeking to improve their relations with indigenous peoples. Most importantly, it expresses aspirations of the United States, aspirations that this country seeks to achieve within the structure of the U.S. Constitution, laws, and international obligations, while also seeking, where appropriate, to improve our laws and policies. (Announcement)

Isn't the thought of creating a natural cultural landscape inspirational?? Is it enough to motivate such organizations as the United States Congress, National Governor's Association, United States Conference of Mayors (USCM), National Congress of American Indians (NCAI), Mexican American Legal Defense and Educational Fund (MALDEF), Asian Americans Advancing Justice (AAAJ), National Council of La Raza (NCLR), Rainbow/PUSH Coalition, Muscogee (Creek) Nation, Friends of the Earth USA, Physicians for Social Responsibility (PSR), The National Latino Health Organization (NLHO), National Association of Colored Women's Clubs (NACWC), National Education Association (NEA), Ujima People's Progress Party (UPPP), National Hispanic Medical Association (NHMA), The American Public Health Association (APHA), Nation of Islam (NOI), Anti-Defamation League (ADL), Republican Party (RP), Muscogee Creek Indian Freedmen Band (MCIFB), U.S. Supreme Court, The Association of Black Psychologists (ABP), American Civil Liberties Union (ACLU), Ku Klux Klan (KKK), Historically Black Colleges and Universities (HBCU), American Association of State Colleges and Universities (AASCU), National Association for the Advancement of Colored People (NAACP), Greenpeace USA, Democrat Party (DP),

Descendants of Freedmen of the Five Civilized Tribe Association (DFFCT), Cherokee Nation, National Medical Association (NMA), The National Black Lawyers (NBL), U.S. Homeland Security, Egbe Omo Yoruba Association of Yoruba Descendants in North America (EOYNA), American Medical Association (AMA), U.S. Department of Health &Human Services (USDHHS), and all other professional, civil rights, human rights, and environmental organizations—to rally in support of the National Maat Public Policy!? With a mandated National Maat Public Policy it ties the whole nation together under a political framework that the people will find highly desirable and will want to preserve it!

Humans have a spiritual beauty that has been suffocated by the industrial-capitalistic matrix. A "review of the study of self in India reveals that indeed the core of Indian self is metaphysical, and it has been the focus of study by philosophers as well as psychologists. There is general agreement that the metaphysical self, Atman, is the real self" (Bhawuk 65). Metaphysical is related to things that cannot be seen. An American Psychological Association report entitled "Intelligence: Knowns and Unknowns" quotes Dr. Wade Boykin, professor and director of the Graduate Program in the Department of Psychology at Howard University, who states: "… (African-American) culture includes an emphasis on such aspects of experience as spirituality, harmony, movement, verve (vigor), affect, expressive individualism, communalism, orality, and a socially defined time perspective. While it is not shared by all African Americans to the same degree, its accessibility and familiarity gives it a profound influence" (qtd. to Neisser 95).

> The conventional idea is that there is only one, superior way of knowing. That is rational and scientific knowledge, which is considered to be universally applicable because it is based on rational theoretical concepts and robust methods of research characterized by, amongst other features, objective methods, quantification, randomizing, replications, statistical analyses, logical reasoning and controlled experiments. Yet, across the globe, people perceive reality in different ways, and the resulting worldviews lead to different ways of learning and different

ways of knowing. Within the many distinguishable knowledge communities on the globe, people interact according to their perceptions, interpretations and lessons learned and between themselves come to a certain consensus about what is valid or acceptable knowledge. (Haverkort and Reijntjes 12)

In the paper "Maat and Order in African Cosmology: A Conceptual Tool for Understanding Indigenous Knowledge," the author Denise Martin informs us that "Traditional knowledge is polyrhythmic because it simultaneously negotiates human, familial, communal, earthly, and celestial rhythms" (963). Thinking in terms of our spiritual anatomy can add meaning to the above. Physicists and spiritualists agree that everything in the Universe is energy and that there is only One Consciousness in the universe (Singh 480; Dossey 116, 274). Hence, it is fundamentally dangerous for any living thing (whether a single-cell organism, plant or animal) to separate from this One Consciousness!

A "cross cultural study of the characteristics of traditional knowledge and science in Latin America, Africa, and India was carried out by the Comparing and Supporting Endogenous Development (COMPAS) programme. COMPAS is an international cooperative programme founded in 1995 by NGOs and universities from <u>Africa</u>, <u>Asia</u>, <u>Europe</u> and <u>Latin America</u> with some ten years of action research and learning from local knowledge," states Haverkort and Reijntjes (17). They continue:

Between 1998 and 2006 more than 50 case studies were made to describe traditional worldviews of learning and ways of knowing. ...The most important lesson is that traditional ways of knowing are holistic. Even with the immense diversity in the ways local knowledge is phrased and expressed, <u>a common feature is represented by conceiving life in terms of three interrelated and inseparable domains: the natural world, that social world, and the spiritual world</u>. ...An important feature is that none of these domains exist in isolation. In many

> traditional ways of knowing a notion of unity exists according to which the natural, social and spiritual worlds are considered to be inseparable and integrated. …The spiritual domain includes knowledge and beliefs about the invisible world, divine beings, spiritual forces, ancestors, and translates into values and sense-giving and related practices such as rituals and festivals. (18, 19)

"Recent advances in several areas of psychological science demonstrate that a significant amount of decision-making and cognition is largely automatic and unconscious" (Van Slyke 212). Could this mean since our nature is moral that Americans—regardless of the race—already have an evolved "moral sense" for re-kindling that harmonious relationship with the social, natural, and spirit worlds??

There is "scientific evidence of a universal human tendency toward moral judgment" (Cohen 344). This would mean that we do have an evolved moral sense for rekindling our traditional spiritual way. The problem has always been that we live in a reason-based society. We just need to be in a spirit-based society. Case in point, in an exploratory survey in downtown Baltimore, Md., involving approximately 25-30 multiracial respondents (citizens), this analyst asked the respondents "Do you have the right to be ethical in your daily affairs?" About ninety percent of this small group of respondents initially said "yes". However, after giving further thought to the question, most of those respondents added that if they were ethical (in the workplace), they might or would get into trouble.

How widespread is this fear of expressing ethical behavior on a national scale? Why should American citizens have to suppress their moral tendencies to satisfy an insensitive, egoistic, greedy irresponsible individual or individuals? Why? <u>Shouldn't ethical people have a constitutional right to be ethical</u>?? From a cultural relativism standpoint, this predicament can be resolved with race-based sovereignties under a National Maat Public Policy. **Haverkort and Reijntes have just stated that people tend to interact according to their perceptions and experiences, and among themselves they come to a consensus about what is valid or acceptable knowledge.**

British-American anthropologist M.F. Ashley Montagu's summary below gives us an inform explanation regarding Haverkort and Reijntes' above point:

> The full discussion of the principles of the genetic approach to the study of evolution of the variety of mankind cannot be attempted here; all that can be done is to present a condensed statement of the genetical theory of "race." The conception of "race" proposed here is based upon the following fundamental postulates: (1.) That, the original ancestral human species (African) population was genetically relatively homogeneous (i.e., similar). (2.) That, by migration away from this original ancestral group or population, individual families or groups of families, became dispersed through space. (3.) That, some of the groups thus dispersed became geographically isolated from one another, and remained so isolated over more or less considerable periods of time. (4.) That, upon (the occurrence of) all of these isolated groups several of the following factors came into play as conditions leading to evolutionary change: (a.) the inherent variability of genetic material composing each individual member of the (particular) group, (b.) physical change in the action of a gene associated...with a particular character (i.e., physical, mental, and spiritual characteristics) that is, gene mutation. (The random variation of a particular group) in gene frequencies will...in time, come to exhibit certain differences from other isolated groups. (Montagu 371)

8.1.5 Economic Development

This section puts economic development into agreement with the "contours of the real" (Diop). This means that it is suggested that the Economic Development Administration (EDA) of the U.S. Department of Commerce "lead the federal economic development agenda" to coincide with the mandates of a National Maat Public Policy. Stuart Hart, a Cornell professor and a leading authority on the implications of environment and poverty for business strategy indicates:

> It is critical to think in terms of creative destruction rather than continuous improvement (of our current economic paradigm) when it comes to the pursuit of sustainability. Often this means turning the existing technology and business model on their heads. That, in turn, means getting outside the current corporate straightjacket of central research and development. (288)

When we have millions of individuals making the decision to start a business based upon *personal interest* and *profit* with minimal regard to the human family and natural environment—this is a recipe for a crisis. This sequence of events has been further complicated by competition. In summary, the activities of our free-market economy has contributed to over-consumption of natural resources, an increasing income gap between the upper class and the working class, and a global socio-economic and environment crisis. This is un-sustainable!

Hart continues, "The next sustainability challenge…is to become indigenous. By incorporating the true voices of those who have previously been bypassed by globalization and learning to co-develop technologies, products and business models with nature and local people, companies can become native to the places where they operate. This requires a healthy dose of humility and respect" (282). Possessing humility and respect is very important to the traditional way of life. Anthropologist Jomo Kenyatta, Ph.D., who in 1964 became the first president of the Republic of Kenya in East Africa, provides us with an excellent example of "humility and respect" in economic development in his anthropological study of traditional practices of the Gikuyu People in Kenya, where he grew up. In doing so, he has provided us with a real-world glimpse at a pre-colonial economic way of life linked to the social, natural, and spiritual worlds. It is an extremely valuable practice that has been displaced by industrial-capitalistic values. Kenyatta writes:

Gikuyu People...maintain a close and vital relationship with spiritual entities. Their daily lives, both individuals and groups, are influenced at all points by belief in the supernatural ...When a sacrifice is made to the High God on an occasion of national importance, the ancestors must join in making the sacrifice. ...Sacrifice to Mwene-Nyaga (God) for rain is made if rain fails to fall at the usual time; when people, after preparing their fields for planting, see that the rain has failed... When the rain...has fallen, the elders of the sacrificial council...immediately arrange for a short planting ceremony. This is to bless the seeds in order to ensure good crops ...The (purifying) ceremony is performed about two or three moons after the planting of seeds. ...The elders meet and prepare for ceremony which purifies the fields. ...When the crops have ripened and are almost ready for harvest, it is time to offer a sacrifice to Mwene-Nyaga for his generous gift of rain, which has now brought prosperity to the community. (222- 247)

The above rituals are not empty. Language, rituals, and symbols alone will not satisfy. This appears to be an example of sincere and compassionate hearts open to the social, natural, and spirit worlds.

8.2 The Law and Emotions

This is Part Two. In this part, the goal is to further our understanding about the role of emotions in human affairs while offering some insight into why it is important to give consideration to the spirits in children, women, men, nature and the universe in government decision-making and human affairs.

Did you know that there is no legal definition for the term "evil?" Here are two psychiatrists' opinions on the absence of that definition. Psychiatrist M. Scott Peck has an explanation regarding the nonexistence of a professional definition for evil, saying, "There are a *variety of reasons* we have not yet developed a psychology of evil.

Psychology is a very young science, as it is, and cannot be expected to have accomplished everything in its short lifetime" (255-257). What do you think??

Forensic psychiatrist Michael Welner (420) reports in his paper, "Response to Simon: Legal Relevance Demands That Evil Be Defined and Standardized," "Evil behavior bedevils the law and the behavioral sciences, <u>and it will not go away</u>. Defining evil is only the latest frontier where psychiatry, confronting the challenge of ambiguity, will bring light out of darkness." Now, what do you think??

In this proposal, it has been shown that as the European world developed its social and material industrial world with the use of artful rhetoric and dazzling intimidating theoretical philosophical lies, which were used to distort and argue away historical truths, all while purifying, legitimizing, and advancing their new theoretical philosophical lies. For example, "Bacon (had) commenced his general perambulation (survey) of learning by dividing learning into three basic categories (history, poetry, and philosophy), corresponding respectively to the three faculties of the human understanding (memory, *imagination*, and *reason*)," according to historian Zagorin (61).

Enlightenment also created a new mode of conversation called — argumentation! Today, we can see industrialized people really know how to argue (intellectually masturbate). This is inductive reasoning. <u>Inductive reasoning tends to be *speculative*, yet inductive reasoning is the distinguishing characteristic of the European intellectual movement</u>. My point: deep within we all have a sense of what evil is! So how come the legal profession doesn't have a legal definition for evil? We can say that the reason the legal profession does not have a legal definition is because psychiatry has not provided one. However if we stop here we will overlook something that is more significant. In my opinion, there is no legal definition for evil because a reason-based society "necessarily" does not value emotions. Emotions can brings us to the stairway of moral reasoning which can lead to a face-to-face confrontation with truth.

Case in point, remember that the rapid spread of industrialism was the result of corporate and legal cooperation. Since the rise of Wall Street, big corporations and lawyers have established a healthy working relationship. Today corporate crimes inflict more harm on society than all street crimes combined! So we must turn our attention to the profession of law to see what underlies this occurrence. This is an important area to examine since it is the legal path that this proposal must travel for approval and implementation. In doing this, it helps to turn our attention to the topic of emotions.

Emotions are behavioral adaptations that have evolved during our evolutionary development and that have played a central role in our survival. Remembering this will help the reader to better assess the legal approach. "The role of the emotions is much neglected in legal theory," explains Eric Posner (1), a professor of law at the University of Chicago. Attorney Posner continues...

> One reason for the neglect of emotions in legal theory may be that the dominant strains of normative legal theory—economic analysis, moral-philosophical analysis, constitutional analysis—rely on methodologies that are not well suited for analyzing emotion, or at least, for reasons of intellectual history, have simply not yet focused on the emotions. Another reason may be the primitive state of the psychology literature on the topic. Psychologists themselves admit that they do not have a good theory of the emotions, in part because research in this area is relatively new. Yet a review of that literature reveals a number of insights that are sufficiently well-developed to be of value for legal theory. (1-2)

Professor David Pizarro of Cornell University offers an opinion on the relationship between law and emotions, saying...

> One of the standard instructions given by judges to members of the jury is that they should not allow any emotions of sympathy influence their judgment. The instructions reflect a fundamental assumption on the part of our legal system that the presence of emotions in the deliberation process works against the goal of accurate

judgments concerning moral blame. This assumption is by no means restricted to our legal system. Historically, many theorists have shared the view that emotions are detrimental to moral reasoning and moral judgment. This view stemming from a philosophical tradition [Enlightenment] traceable to the writing of Kant (1785) has had a profound influence on the psychological study of morality.

It is true that emotions may get the best of us at times and mislead us. However, it is also true that emotions keep our thoughts consistent with reality, and their instantaneous origin is deeply linked to *something* very relevant as <u>emotions</u> are "behavioral adaptations that have occurred during evolutionary development" (Campbell 9th ed.). **Furthermore, behavioral scientists have stated that morality and emotions are linked** (Cameron et al.). This makes sense when emotions (energies) are the mediums of moral actions. To ignore our emotions is to ignore or marginalize the *Self* since emotions along with the mental and moral characteristics "make up the core of someone identity" (VandenBos *see spirit*).

Exactly what influence did Immanuel Kant have on the <u>psychological study of morality</u>? Recall that Kant is also known for his <u>theoretical philosophical justification of superior-inferior classification of race</u>. "Kant (sought to legitimate) the practical use of the concepts of freedom, moral law, and the categorical imperative by tracing their origin in the faculty of reason" (Hiller 65). What may the "categorical imperative" be? "<u>The fundamental principle of morality—the Categorical Imperative—is none other than the law of an autonomous (self-determining) will</u>. ...All specific moral requirements, according to Kant, are justified by this principle" (see "Kant" 1st paragraph).

According to Jeppe von Platz, Ph.D., who is an assistant professor of philosophy, Kant believed that "<u>autonomy is the supreme principle of morality</u>" (369). Keep in mind that autonomy "means" self-rule, self-determination, independence. A maxim is a short statement expressing a rule, motto or proverb. It is said that for Kant, "A will whose maxims necessarily coincide with the laws of autonomy is holy will, good absolutely" (Crocker, 168). When we consider the historical climate in which the term "categorical imperative" emerged (i.e., Age of Discovery, Age of Enlightenment, Transatlantic Slave Trade), it is possible to form a creditable opinion on why Kant may have considered "autonomy" as the supreme principle of morality. The categorical imperative made it moral for whites to do whatever they wanted to do including evil. This is to say, psychiatry is not the main reason there is no legal definition for evil. There no legal definition because of the goal of the white world which is: *to change the way people think and to take and sustain leadership in the world*! The categorical imperative morally legitimize whites' criminality and savagery and therefore made their antisocial behaviors socially acceptable amongst whites. As Alfred R. Hall, a historian of science declares, "Conquest, like missionary effort, was an aspect of the boundless energy of the west" (710).

Returning to our discussion about what seems to be the basis to the controversy surrounding emotions and law, we can get even further authoritative insight from the *Wolters Kluwer Bouvier Law Dictionary*, which states:

> Law is only what is recognized by officials as the rules of law. Legal positivism is the study of law as a system of rules created from rules that are inherent aspects of a state. ...At its core, legal positivism rejects the idea that law is recognized or created by morality or justice, contending instead that while law may reflect morality or an idea of justice, what makes it law is the action of the creation of laws according to rules for their creation. (Sheppard 591)

Now, social worker Vanessa Jackson has made available historical data that gives insight into the benefit of legal positivism for white America. This information also gives us a perspective on why emotions tend to be downplayed in a court of law, why there is no legal definition for "evil," and the historical value of the "Categorical Imperative" for the white race:

> In 1851, Dr. Samuel Cartwright, a prominent Louisiana physician and one of the leading authorities in his time

A Perspective on Policy Implementation

<u>on the medical care of Negroes</u>, identified two mental disorders peculiar to slaves. *Drapetomania*, or the disease causing Negroes to run away, was noted as a condition, 'unknown to our medical authorities, although its diagnostic symptom, the absconding (running) from service, is well known to our planters and overseers.' Dr. Cartwright observed, 'The cause in most cases, that induces the Negro to run away from service, is such a disease of the mind as in any other species of alienation, and much more curable, as a general rule.' Cartwright was so helpful as to identify preventive measures for dealing with potential cases of *drapetomania*. Slaves showing incipient *drapetomania*, reflected in sulky and dissatisfied behavior should be whipped-strictly as a therapeutic early intervention. Planter and overseers were encouraged to utilize whipping as the primary intervention once the disease had progressed to the stage of actually running away. Overall, Cartwright suggested that Negroes should be kept in a submissive state and treated like children, with 'care, kindness, attention and humanity, to prevent and cure them from running away.

It seems legal positivism was at work in the following national and international televised court case. On April 12, 2016, Freddie Gray was arrested in Baltimore City, Md., and placed in a police van to be transported to the police station. Eventually it was discovered that he was injured. He was taken to the hospital. He was diagnosed with a spine injury and hospitalized. Later while hospitalized, Gray died as result of his injury. The medical examiner ruled that his death was a homicide. This triggered daily protests and a riot. Six Baltimore City police officers were charged in the death of Freddie Gray, who was a 25 years old African-American male. As the trials progressed, eventually charges against the police officers were dropped.

In explaining the management of the trial, the presiding judge explained that under Maryland law, it was his responsibility to find facts and render a verdict without emotions or sympathy. The *Maryland Reporter*, a daily news website, stated, "He (judge) remains faithful to

89

the law, not emotions or social movements of the moment" (Rascovar). "He ruled only on the basis of facts and the law."

Journalist Barry Rascovar persists, "Indeed, the next time U.S. Sen. Ben Cardin is asked to recommend a name to the White House for a federal judicial post, (Judge) Williams should be on Cardin's short list. And the next time Gov. Larry Hogan is in the market for an appellate judge from Baltimore, Williams should get top consideration... Williams has been a sparkling example of how a judge is suppose to act in trials large and small." Attorney Marilyn Mosby (Baltimore City's State Attorney) should receive accolades for her warrior emotional spirit in her quest to seek justice on the behalf of Freddie Gray.

While not questioning or critiquing the judge's decision, it looks like the Maryland law is in conflict with neurobehavioral science, which indicates that emotions can be a positive asset as they help to keep our thought in contact with reality. We can better understand the confusion here if we remember that during the Enlightenment it was firmly established that historical truths and emotions (spirit) were not a part of the equation for calculating the truth—unless of course it was favorable to whites! Remember Bacon's words concerning truth. "Truth, he said is 'rightly called the daughter of time, not of authority,' and he therefore condemned 'those enchantments of antiquity and authority,'" stated historian Zagorin earlier. In spite of this, we must still adhere to the fact that: "Sociobiologists point to the preeminence of heart over head at... crucial moments (and) ...they conjecture about why evolution has given emotions such a central role in the human psyche. Our emotions, they say, guide us in facing predicaments and tasks too important to leave to intellect alone" (Goleman 4).

This suggests that if departments of justice (on the federal, state, and local level) do not value emotions in interpreting and enforcing the laws, they *cannot administer* true justice throughout the nation and ensure public safety against domestic and foreign threats. Additionally, if the U.S. Senate and the House of Representatives do not value emotions in making laws, they simply *cannot make* just laws! Posner openly admits that current (1.) constitutional analysis, (2.) legal theory, (3.) economic analysis, and (4.) even moral-philosophical analysis have given little attention to emotions. Certainly Democrat and Republican legislators want to address this shortcoming in government with a mandated National Maat Public Policy.

The forthcoming provides important info that can help us to appreciate the value of emotions in legal decision-making. It will also answer the question above about <u>why evolution has given emotions a central role in the human mind</u>. Psychologists Ana Seara-Cardoso and Essi Viding (733) inform us that individuals who show low responsiveness (in relevant areas of the brain) to emotional stimuli may have psychopathic traits. According to the article "Focus on Psychopathy," from the July 2012 edition of the FBI Law Enforcement Bulletin,

> Psychopaths, perhaps 1 percent (3.2 million people) of the general (American) population...are manipulative (controlling); deceptive (calculating liars); self-centered (preoccupied with self); lacking in empathy (inability to relate to others' feelings); lacking in guilt (inability to feel that they did something wrong); callous (insensitive disregard for others); and remorseless (heartless, coldhearted, without regret). They present a serious challenge to everyone involved with criminal justice, including officers and investigators; judges, prosecutors, and defense attorneys; probation officers, corrections personnel; and psychologists, psychiatrists and social workers. (Hare 2)

While all psychopaths are not criminals (Slater and Pozzato 1), "Psychopathy is the most dangerous of the personality disorders," according to "Psychopathy: An Important Forensic Concept for the 21st Century" (Babiak and Hare 3). The authors of the study "Anti-sociality and the Construct of Psychopathy: Data from Across the Globe" summarize their research results: "The overall findings indicate... that anti-sociality is a core component of the psychopathy construct" (Neumann et al. 678).

Birbaumer et al. in the article "Deficient Fear Conditioning in Psychopathy: A Functional Magnetic Resonance Imaging Study," write: "Psychopaths belong to a larger group of persons with antisocial personality disorder and are characterized by an inability to have emotional involvement and by the repeated violation of the rights of others. It was hypothesized that this behavior might be the consequence of deficient fear conditioning [lacking fear]."

The authors of the book *Snakes in Suits: When Psychopaths Go To Work* state, "**The premise of this book is that psychopaths do work in modern organizations; they often are successful by most standard measures of career success**, and their destructive personality characteristics are invisible to most of the people with whom they interact" (Babiak and Hare xiv).

Robert Hercz states that criminal psychologist Robert Hare and others have confirmed that psychopaths' brains work differently from ours, especially when processing emotion and language. Hercz adds that, once, Hare illustrated this for Nicole Kidman, an Australian actress and film producer. She had invited him to Hollywood to help her prepare for a role as a psychopath in the movie *Malice*. How could she show the audience there was something fundamentally wrong with her character, she wondered? Hercz shares Dr. Hare's comments below:

> "I said, 'Here's a scene that you can use,'" Hare says. "'You're walking down a street and there's an accident. A car has hit a child in the crosswalk. A crowd of people gather round. You walk up, the child's lying on the ground and there's blood running all over the place. You get a little blood on your shoes and you look down and say, "Oh shit." You look over at the child, kind of interested, but you're not repelled or horrified. You're just interested. Then you look at the mother, and you're really fascinated by the mother, who's emoting, crying out, doing all these different things. After a few minutes you turn away and go back to your house. <u>You go into the bathroom and practice mimicking the facial expressions of the mother.</u>'" <u>He (Hare) then pauses and says,</u> "**That's the psychopath: somebody who doesn't understand what's going on emotionally, but understands that something important has happened.**" (qtd. by Hercz)

~ ~ ~

Chapter 9
Morality versus Money

S ure, money is important in a capitalistic society. But do we really need money to establish a National Maat Public Policy? It is widely known that corporations and wealthy people use their money to influence the language of legislation. In the 21st century the world must start thinking of a global economy that is not based on money! I mean, what if legendary investor and former Duke Energy CEO Jim Rogers is correct in forecasting a major market crash in a few years?[x]

What is money? Money is a system of exchange. Money is a circulating medium of exchange. Barter is a circulating medium of exchange, too. Bartering has proven to be an effective system of exchange for millennia. While struggle for survival has always been an inherent part of the human story, humanity and the natural environment's struggles have intensified since the arrival of money.

If the American economy collapsed right now for a long period, the universe, our solar system, planet Earth and its mountains, oceans, seas, rivers, wetlands, grasslands, flowers, forests, fish, reptiles, ants, bees, birds, squirrels, rabbits, wolves, deer, bears, mountain lions, etc., and even indigenous people would not be critically affected by the economic collapse. However, industrialized people would tend to panic due to the unraveling of a world of money, consumerism, overconsumption and greed that is the source of our mental stability (ego construct). We would have concerns because the occurrence would spotlight our moral nakedness, savagery, and disconnect from nature.

Like religion, for centuries capitalism has been controversial. Capitalism has always benefited the rich and has been oppressive to the common man and woman. Economist Alan Blinder, who served on the Council of Economic Advisors under Bill Clinton, had this to say about capitalism: "Having looked at monetary policy from both sides now, I can testify that central banking in practice is as much art as science. Nonetheless, while practicing the dark art, I have always found the science quite useful."[xi] Did he just call capitalism a 'dark art' that is benefited by science? Isn't this clearly saying that science is used to legitimize a dark art? As early as 1922, wealthy American industrialist and founder of the Ford Motor Company, Henry Ford is known for the following quote regarding our monetary system: "It is well enough that people of the nation do not understand our banking and monetary system, for if they did, I believe there would be a revolution before tomorrow morning."[xii]

While speaking to Congress in 1997 as chairman of the Federal Reserve Board, Alan Greenspan gave a list of some things people despise about capitalism. Greenspan's list "includes such charges as responding to short-term opportunities to the neglect of long-term effects, dispensing power without responsibility, promoting material values over spiritual ones, commoditizing human relations, monetizing social values, corrupting democracy, unsettling old communities, institutions, and arrangements, and rewarding aggressiveness and—yes—greed" (qtd. by Appleby 422-23). Money has been said to originate in the sixth century BC in Lydia, Western Asia Minor (Diop "Precolonial" 28). "Capitalism began when private investments drove the economy, and entrepreneurs and their supporters acquired power to bend political and social institutions to their demands" (Appleby 118). So we can see that there has been a long unbroken relationship between the rich and politicians. Since capitalism is "an economic system in which individuals or private businesses own most of the nation's means of producing goods and services" (World Book, vol.3, 2009: 194), it is reckoned that it is appropriate for government to have authoritative oversight over such businesses. This authoritative oversight, however, should be consistent with the mandates of the proposed National Maat Public Policy.

Bill Gates defines creative capitalism as "an approach where government, nonprofit, and business work together to stretch the reach of market forces so that more people can make a profit or gain recognition for doing work that eases the world's inequities" (McElhaney ix). Spreading and stretching the reach of capitalism is not creative; instead, it is ecologically irresponsible. Sure, money is *very* important and *very* nice to have in a capitalistic society. However, as a species, as a nation, we have arrived at an epoch in our evolutionary journey where we need to stop this money foolishness!! Capitalism doesn't work for the majority of the people. It never did. Money is not and will not be the solution to mankind's problems!

Before giving full attention to morality, shall we quickly look at mathematical reasoning? Why? Because mathematical reasoning underlies money and monetary decision-making. Mathematical reasoning can involve evaluating and describing situations, drawing conclusion, and solving problems with mathematics. In general, mathematical reasoning is used to assist us in determining what makes sense. Mathematical reasoning involves the use of arithmetic values expressed by figures, forms, notational symbols, numbers, and words to analyze and solve problems. Mathematics is the study of number, quantity, structure, and space. Mathematics has been around for many millennia, long before Western civilization and Western mathematics.

However, it was only after Isaac Newton's *Philosophiæ Naturalis Principia Mathematica* came out in AD 1687 that "numbers became the measure of real life" (Morris 470). "His most famous book, in which planetary orbits were explained by his gravitational theory, was entitled *Mathematical Principles of Natural Philosophy* (English spelling). It was not entitled Mathematical Principles of Natural <u>Science</u>" (Brooke 7). Observe that his work was a <u>philosophical</u> perspective.

"<u>On the surface Newton would seem to have had a full blown concept of divine providence; but in effect he did no more than substitute the word dominion for the providence</u>; and as Newton defined 'dominion' he manifestly did not mean direct and immediate governance. God's 'dominion' was His arbitrary freedom in shaping matter and promulgating laws at the original creation" (Westfall 202). We have discussed the limits of reason—and this limit is applicable to Western mathematical reasoning.

For evidence, we can simply turn to Dr. George E. P. Box, who is one of the world's greatest statistical minds of the twentieth-century. Statistics is the science of collecting and analyzing numerical data. Box served as president of the American Statistical Association in 1978, president of the Institute of Mathematical Statistics in 1979, and in 2003 was a recipient of the George Box Medal from European Network of Business and Industrial Statistics in recognition for outstanding contributions to industrial statistics.

Dr. Box shocked the profession of statistics with his now famous statement, noted in the book *Empirical Model-Building and Response*

Surfaces: "…essentially all (statistical) models are wrong, but some are useful" (424). Several years earlier in an issue of the *Journal of the American Statistical Association* in the article "Science and Statistics," Box wrote, "Since all models are wrong, the scientist cannot obtain a correct one by excessive elaboration. On the contrary…he should seek an economical description of natural phenomena. Just as the ability to devise simple but evocative models is the signature of the great scientist, so overelaboration and overparameterization is often the mark of mediocrity" (792). Box continues, "Since all models are wrong, the scientist must be alert to what is importantly wrong. It is inappropriate to be concerned about mice when there are tigers abroad."

The above claim is further supported by French physicist Bernard D'Espagnat, who was the winner of the 2009 Templeton Prize for his work that confirms that "science is unable to fully explain the nature of being." He states,

> We are no longer unaware that a theory grounded in some given concepts has every chance of, at some time or other, being superseded by another theory, grounded in different concepts. If we really view science as being aimed at describing facts and objects, knowing that much may legitimately render us skeptical concerning it. (158)

What about mathematical reasoning as it relates to economics? Economic consultant Jeff Madrick states, "The pretense that economics is a science is harmful in that it gives economics ideas more credibility than they often deserve. Policymakers—and U.S. citizens—are unaware of the questionable underpinning of much of the advice offered by economists, which has time and again led to gravely incorrect policy decisions" (189). In summary, while addressing the Prussian Academy of Science in Berlin on 27 January 1921, Albert Einstein had this to report to the scientific community: "As far as the laws of mathematics refer to reality, they are not certain; and as far as they are certain, they do not refer to reality" (Shapiro 228).

Now with that said, we can now turn our discussion to money vs. morality. In doing this, the importance of emotions in human affairs will be further spotlighted. Thomas Jefferson was an American founding father, principal author of the Declaration of Independence (1776), and the third President of the United States. One of his famous quotes is "Money, not morality, is the principle commerce of civilized nations." What do you think?

According to an article entitled "Legal History of Money," money is "like cartoon characters who run over a cliff—they never fall until they look down. If a law regarding money is sufficiently contested, it will no longer be the law of money because whatever the money was will have ceased being a medium of exchange" (Kreitner 416-417). It is this writer's stance that the replacement for money must be compatible and flexible with our species' temperamental disposition. Therefore, morality should be the principle commerce of a civilized nation for the following justification:

- God created everything! Everything is God's property. Everything in the universe is a form of energy. There is One Consciousness in the universe. Energies are the mediums of moral action. Therefore moral action is God's property. Hence, morality must be the principle commerce of a civilized nation because morality is God's property—and moral actions promote life, humanitarianism, and a balanced ecology.

Now the above logic may seem like mere foolishness when compared with current economic analysis, but this is not foolishness! Here numbers are NOT given the opportunity to be the measure of real life. Instead moral reasoning has replaced numbers. By substituting moral reasoning for mathematical reasoning it allows for possibility of creating a situation and reality that is complementary to human's spiritual nature and the biosphere/ecology. Furthermore, one of the codes in the 42 Declarations of Innocence states "I have not stolen the property of God!" This means this logic has historic significance. With a slight adjustment here and there the above logic can fit very well within a familial, communal, regional, national, and global economic analysis because we are all spiritual beings. This logic calls on us to reevaluate the concept of individualism in an animated spiritual world and to bring forth our higher "truer" self in economic analysis. It is an empowering concept as it addresses the deficit of emotions in economic analysis, and this logic can help to save the planet. The above logic is more creditable and reality-based than Immanuel Kant's theoretical philosophical justification for the superior/inferior classification of races and Sir Francis Bacon's empiricism. This includes Isaac Newton's Philosophiæ Naturalis Principia Mathematica in which he merely "substituted the word dominion for providence" and *arbitrarily shaped matter* and popularized laws at the origin of creation to HIS satisfaction (Westfall).

To say the above differently: being that most of humanity has a moral disposition, and being that moral action is the byproduct of the resulting repercussion of openness to invisible and visible forces in the entire universe [within the limits of one's genetic potential], then moral action (not money) must be the principle commerce of a civilized nation because moral action is linked to an inexhaustible and procreative Universal Divine Source. When our spiritual eyes open, the physical eyes close—and money runs off the cliff and looks down— because there is nothing to monetize (express as currency) because everything is God's property!

"Over the past two centuries...the moral argument for capitalism became less prominent. The case for capitalism was more often made on efficiency grounds alones" (Forster 40). However, as one dissolves his or her ego into that which is of greater Universal Divine significance, the view of capitalism being efficient is permanently swept far away. Some suggest that money is more efficient than bartering, stating the limitations of bartering are "there needs to be a double coincidence of wants; there is no common measure of value; indivisibility of certain goods; lack of standards for deferred payments; and the difficulty in storing wealth" (Wright and Quadrini). However, these reflect the requirements for capitalism. These are not the requirements for bartering! Bartering's requirement is moral reasoning! Moral reasoning is like Maat; it is universally flexible.

Lastly, it is understood that traditional people do not have difficulty storing wealth. They have a way of life that is in harmony with their local natural environment. They are not concerned with excess accumulation and profits. Traditional people are very efficient in using natural resources. They are not preoccupied with lying, competition, exploiting, killing or digging miles into the earth for gold, silver, diamonds, oil, etc., for excessive profits. They focus on cooperating with Mother Nature. Moral bartering never generated an ecological crisis for the whole planet. Capitalism (money) has done just this. In this sense, capitalism is a form of terrorism. Terrorism is the use of intimidation and violence to achieve a political goal. The American people are intimidated into supporting capitalism in order to survive. If the American people don't support or participate in the capitalistic system to a sufficient degree, they will die on the industrial-capitalistic streets, and people will walk by unconcerned because they, too, are trying to avoid a similar fate. So most people support capitalism out of fear!!

Based on the international research by Haverkort and Reijntjes on indigenous people's way of knowing, it seems safe to be of the opinion that traditional bartering is very efficient and successful because the natural, social and spiritual worlds are given consideration as one. Earlier, anthropologist Kenyatta gave us an example of this. Medical doctor Eric Strach in a speech "Astronomy and Medicine," did likewise declaring that:

> The common denominator of astronomy and medicine is quite different in the modern era from that of ancient and medieval times. ...Right up to the eighteenth century the link between astronomy and medicine was astrology. To be a good astrologer, you had to know a good deal about the motions of the Sun, the Moon, the planets, the Zodiac and the constellations. Astrologers played an important role in public life: they were advisers to kings and politicians, they determined propitious hours to sign treaties and they made predictions. The study of medicine was intimately linked with the study of the motions of the Sun, the Moon and the planets. In particular, the motion of the Moon was thought to influence the normal physiological rhythm

and such terms as "lunatic" have survived and are still in use today. ...A man's character, his temperament, his success or failure depended on where the planets and the Sun were at the moment of his birth. ...Right up to the seventeenth and eighteenth centuries medicinal herbs had to be gathered on certain nights and remedies administered according to the planetary configuration. By observing the stars a doctor was supposed to be able to tell whether a patient was likely to recover... Only a good astronomer, it was believed, could possibly become a good physician. (164)

Keep in mind that astrology was the (link) between medicine and astronomy prior to the 1800's. Even in Europe, during the Renaissance in 1575 (or 1475*) Jean d'Indgine, a professor and author of a chiromancy and physiognomy textbook that was used by his students, had this to say, "That which many physicians could not cure or remedy with their greatest and strongest medicine, the astronomer hath brought to pass with one simple herb, by observing the movement of the stars. ...The physician who does not understand astronomy cannot be a complete physician" (qtd. by Ball 237-238). In this context, we can see that moral bartering would involve consideration to more than just numbers or profit.

"Magic and medicine were often in the same melting pot. ... <u>Effective treatment required that the body be in a receptive state (for) beneficial forms of spirit, which could remedy deficiencies resulting from temperament or life-style. The powers residing in herbs, stones, and aromas were both natural and divine. As a gift of divine origin, there was nothing sacrilegious (disrespectful) in their use</u>" (Brooke 64).

So, because everything in the universe is energy (and interrelated), no race has the right to monetize or commoditize or own any part of this universal Oneness. We should be caregivers and protectors of this Oneness. Traditional societies saw the gifts of nature as divine. For example, only "five hundred years ago, the most sophisticated society in South America, the Inca Empire, was moneyless. The Incas appreciated the aesthetic qualities of rare metals. Gold was the 'sweat of the sun,' silver the 'tears of the moon'" (Ferguson 20). "In 1532, however the Inca Empire was brought low by a man who, like Christopher Columbus, had come to the New World expressively to search for and monetize precious metal." This man was Francisco Pizarro, a Spanish conqueror.

Even today when traditional people see the commoditization and monetization of the gifts of nature, their hearts are saddened. An example is indicated by Chip Brown, contributing editor of the National Geographic Magazine. The traditional Kayapo people in Brazil live in "one of the largest tracts of intact tropical rain forest in the world" (41).

> The first Kayapo encounters with the grimy (colonialist's) Brazilian banknotes led to the coining of their evocative word for money: *pe-a-caprin*, or "sad leaves." More and more sad leaves were a part of Kayapo life, especially in villages close to towns on the Brazilian frontier. In the Kayapo village Turedjam, near Tucumã, pollution from clearing-cutting and cattle ranching had wrecked the fishing grounds, and it was not uncommon to see Kayapo shopping in supermarkets for soap and frozen chicken. (49)

After many generations of being stupefied by assimilating into the industrial-capitalistic world, we see money as "happy leaves" instead of "sad leaves." These fake "happy leaves" keep us blinded to the fact that we (white, yellow, red, brown and black) are all real authentic slaves. The sad leaves have impacted how we psychologically and morally interact on a daily basis. In a study entitled "Seeing Green: Mere Exposure to Money Triggers a Business Decision Frame and Unethical Outcomes," the researchers from Harvard University and University of Utah concluded:

> Considering the significant role of money in business organizations and everyday life, the idea that subtle reminders of money elicit changes in morality has important implications. Our findings demonstrate that the mere presence of money...can serve as a prompt for

immoral behavior operating through a business decision frame. These findings suggest that money is a more insidious corrupting factor than previously appreciated, as mere, subtle exposure to money can be a corrupting influence. (Kouchaki et al. 61)

This research offers insight into why the wealthy, influential politicians, both Republicans and Democrats, may be having problems deciding to do the right thing for the American people and the environment. In research by Markus Quirin, et al. entitled "Giving or Taking: The Role of Dispositional Power Motivation and Positive Affect in Profit Maximization," they found that "individuals with a high power motive don't care about the outcome of the other, which means that they do neither attempt to diminish the other's outcome…nor to increase the other's outcome" (120). In other words, there is "a positive relationship between power motive and selfishness" (121).

In the study entitled "Wealth and the Inflated Self: Class, Entitlement, Narcissism," social psychologist Paul Piff, Ph.D. concludes: "Research documents increasing narcissism in society. … (R)esearch reveals that recent rises in narcissism may be most pronounced among upper-class individuals and less accelerated, if increasing at all, among lower-class individuals" (41). In another study, "Higher Social Class Predicts Increased Unethical Behavior," the researchers at University of California at Berkeley and University of Toronto had this to say:

Seven studies using experimental and naturalistic methods reveal that upper-class individuals behave more unethically than lower-class individuals. In studies 1 and 2, upper-class individuals were more likely to break the law while driving, relative to lower-class individuals. In follow-up laboratory studies, upper-class individuals were more likely to exhibit unethical decision-making tendencies (study 3), take valued goods from others (study 4), lie in a negotiation (study 5), cheat to increase their chances of winning a prize (study 6), and endorse unethical behavior at work (study 7) than were lower-class individuals. Mediator and moderator data demonstrated that upper-class individuals' unethical tendencies are accounted for, in part, by their more favorable attitudes toward greed. (Piff et al.)

The above research findings offer some clarity about the self-centered, manipulative, and cold-hearted nature of the capitalistic societies. By the way, at the time of the 113th United States Congress (2013-2015), the majority of the Congressional members were millionaires.[xiii]

This is not to say *all* wealthy people are unethical, but it is clear that capitalism is definitely not the solution to advancing a truly civilized nation. Bill Gates' creative capitalism, in long terms, will not work because capitalism breeds competition, unethical decision-making, greed, and corruption. It appears, without a doubt, that morality is the best option for easing the world's inequities and advancing humanity!

Regularly we read in the newspapers and hear on television how corporations tend to be willing to do anything to make a profit: lie, steal, and indirectly or directly kill. In an article published in Forbes Magazine on Feb. 8, 2016, journalist Matthew Herper reported that "All drug companies make price increases in the U.S. on their medicines, often at rates much higher than inflation" (85). For instance, Martin Shkreli, a former pharmaceutical executive of Retrophin, Inc., raised the price per-pill for the drug Daraprim from $13.50 to $750.00 (82). The drug is used to treat a rare infection called toxoplasmosis in patients.

Shkreli was arrested by the FBI in December 2015 and charged with securities fraud. "When asked (by the U.S. House Committee on Oversight and Reform Committee) whether he would have done anything differently, he replied, 'probably would have raised the price higher is probably what I would have done...which is my primary duty. Again, no one wants to say it. No one's proud of it. But this is a capitalistic society, capitalist system, and capitalist rules. My investors expect me to maximize profits.'"

Martin Shkreli's point is further clarified by an article posted in the New York Times on Feb. 3, 2015, entitled "New York Attorney General Targets Supplements at Major Retailers."

The New York State Attorney General's office accused four major retailers… of selling fraudulent and potentially dangerous herbal supplements and demanded that they remove the products from their shelves. The authorities said they had conducted tests on top-selling store brands of herbal supplements at four national retailers —**"GNC", "Target," "Walgreens," and "Walmart"** (the world's largest retailer)—and found <u>that four out of five of the products did not contain any of the herbs (listed) on their labels</u>. The tests showed that pills labeled medicinal herbs often contained little more than cheap fillers like powdered rice, asparagus and houseplants, and in some cases substances that could be dangerous to those with allergies. (O'Connor)

Just when you would think environmentalists would be more concerned about saving the environment than money, we find the director of the Center for the Blue Economy and chairman of the International Environmental Policy Program saying, "'There's a really interesting paradox, the things we think are precious and most sacred are actually the things that need price tags the most.' …Blue economy proponents argue that policymakers would be more apt to protect wetlands and other oceanic and coastal features if they were assigned a monetary value" (Cirino). Then, we have the president of the Earth Policy Institute in Washington, D.C., who believes that "If the world is to move onto a sustainable path, we need economists who will calculate indirect costs and work with political leaders to incorporate them into market prices by restructuring taxes" (184). Mother Nature would never cooperate with such foolishness!! The world can move onto a sustainable path, if corporations stop their greed and corruption.

For example in developing countries: "People at the top of government—or those who have significant control over the government, but who are not government officials (<u>often wealthy individuals and corporations</u>)—can and do obtain resources coming into the government. Government revenue is often not devoted to beneficial services, but instead siphoned off by those in control of government"

(Vanderslice 318). *Newsweek Magazine* in a March 24, 2017 issue reported, "...*Latin America* is now the most dangerous place in the world for environmental activists, according to a 2016 report by Article 19, a British human rights group. More than *122 activists* were killed in the region in 2015, one of the deadliest years on record, according to the most recent study from Global Witness, another nongovernmental organization" (18). When there is "conflict between TNCs (transnational corporations) and Indigenous peoples over the appropriate use of land arise, governments have tended to favor the former's interests over the latter's human rights. There is presently inadequate accountability for the human rights abuses perpetrated by TNCs upon Indigenous peoples, which often occur with the acquiescence (acceptance) or even the active assistance of host governments, in either international or municipal law" (Joseph 82). It appears that the wealthy should not have a leadership role in planning or administrating intervention into addressing climate change.

In 2015, an APA study found that 72% of Americans are stressed about money. Even religious institutions are preoccupied with getting some fake happy leaves. "Each (religious institution) claims that the function of money is to fulfil the advancement of general human welfare" (Pentland 96-99). We must come to terms with the fact that money is not a long-term solution to the advancement of human welfare. The advancement of human welfare long ago had spiritual correspondence with the powers of the gods/goddesses (vital forces) who "through their actions and interaction, created, maintained, and continue to maintain the universe" (Gadalla 66).

It is said that even when money first appeared, money had some linkage to the spirit realm. "In his book *Magic, Money, and Myth*, William Desmonde states that in some ancient cultures money was used as a symbol to replace food in sacrificial communion rituals" (Pentland). Desmonde was also of the opinion that "from a psychological point of view, the first form of money is mother's milk" (Collas 112).

If we viewed ourselves as caregivers, protectors, and a part of the planet's ecology rather than "the Owner," and if we used morality as the principle commerce, we could still construct buildings, bridges, homes, roads, etc.; make clothes, shoes, jewelries, etc.; grow fruit, vegetables, etc.; have education, health care, domestic and international trade etc., without money. Since we already know how to build, make, grow, educate, and heal, we need only to engage into these activities in an ecological friendly way as care-givers and protectors. Money is a double-edged sword. While money helps us, it can hurt us, too. Here is an angle on how money unravels religious institutions to their core:

> A study of the growth of the Christian church, from its first three centuries through the Middle Ages to the present day, is needed to show how this separation between the spiritual practice and the attitude towards money has increased and hardened. At first supported by voluntary gifts, demands for tithes and fresh fruits are added. Endowments and vacant benefices (of bishops) are sold, absolutions (forgiveness) and dispensations (exemption) are granted at a price, taxes are levied by the Vatican, church courts raise money by fines, fees, and the sale of icons, or by permits to view sacred relics. In other words, as money needs are faced, spiritual leaders are apt to lose sight of the primary purpose of their ministries. They exploit the religious conviction of their followers in order to support the institution. The institution, rather than being a means to a higher end, becomes an end in itself. (Pentland)

It seems as if money (the cartoon) may be slowly running off the cliff…but it has not looked down yet! The principal investigators for the Equality of Opportunity Project, Dr. Raj Chetty at Stanford and Dr. Nathaniel Hendren at Harvard, have indicated that middle-class college students today are less likely to earn more than what their parents did. Chetty states, "It's basically a coin flip as to whether you'll do better than your parents." Also in 1940, 90% of children earned more than their parents; in 1950, about 80%; in 1960, about 65%; in 1970, about 60%; and in 1980, 50% (Chetty). This trend applies to both low and high income families.

An investigative report by *USA Today News* dated Dec. 9, 2016 announced that "Overall, young men's prospects are worsening at a quickening pace than young women's. Sons born in 1984 are only 41% likely to earn more than their fathers, compared to 95% of sons born in 1940. Still, they're better off than daughters born in 1984, who are only 26% likely to earn more than their fathers, down from 43% of daughters born in 1940. The study did not compare daughters to their mothers" (Bomey). The reader should know that there is a decline in the income potential as the *number of innovation patents increase*. For example, in 1940, there were <u>48,467</u> invention patents issued by the U.S. Patent Office, and in 1984, there were <u>72,350</u> invention patents issued ("U.S. Patent Activity").

Florence Jaumotte, et al. reported in their research "Rising Income Inequality: Technology, or Trade and Financial Globalization?" the following: "<u>Estimates using a new and more reliable dataset on inequality and detailed measures of globalization suggest that the observed rise in inequality across both developed and developing countries over the past two decades is largely attributable to the impact of technological change</u>" (16).

Erik Brynjolfsson and Andrew McAfee, director and co-director of the Massachusetts Institute of Technology (MIT) Initiative on the Digital Economy, both "foresee dismal prospects for many types of jobs as these powerful new technologies are increasingly adopted not only in manufacturing, clerical, and retail work but in professions such as law, financial services, education, and medicine. ...They believe that rapid technological change has been destroying jobs faster than it is creating them, contributing to the stagnation of median income" (qtd. to Rotman).

The above occurrence brings back to mind the concerns that the English and French workers had when the Industrial Revolution first started. Remember the Luddite movement in England and France. Remember the French workers' cry: "If the projects of these men with systems, who wish to introduce the usage of machines, through which a single man will supplant the labor of twenty, ever succeed, let them build poorhouses for us and our children! These fine machines will enrich a few individuals and will ruin a whole country." Jean-Jacques

Rousseau, one of the most influential Enlightenment thinkers in AD 1750, warned in his first major work, *A Discourse of the Sciences and Arts*, that science caused corruption.[xiv]

With the aid of the Enlightenment, science, Industrial Revolution, and capitalism, the greedy transnational "corporations have taken possession of human consciousness...to evoke the deepest of psychic compulsions toward limitless consumption. This invasion of human consciousness has brought about deleterious effects throughout the moral and cultural life of the society as well as the impoverishment of the Earth. Yet the corporations are so basic to contemporary life that a central pose of contemporary education from high school through college, and even through professional training, is to prepare younger persons for jobs within the corporation context" (Berry 120). Berry continues: Corporations "in alliance with the governments of the world, are now related to or organized into such establishments as the World Bank, the International Monetary Fund, the World Trade Organization, the International Chamber of Commerce, the World Business Council for Sustainable Development, and the International Organization for Standardization. Bonding of common interests has become so coordinated that it is increasingly difficult to escape not only their influence but their control over the various nations and cultures of the world. So influential is the present commercial-industrial order that our dominant professions and institutions are functioning in this context; not merely our economic system, but government, jurisprudence, the medical profession, religion, and education. Every aspect of life has been absorbed into the commercial-industrial context. We seem not to know how to live in any other way" (109). Now, wouldn't you rather have morality as the principle commerce??

~ ~ ~

Chapter 10
The Porcupine Climbs Trees
Since It is a Monkey!

I t is useful to point out that "Bacon's (science) philosophy went far toward the very unorthodox conclusion of *abolishing the distinction* between art and nature, the natural and artificial. The artificial, accordingly, did not differ from the natural in its form and essence but only in being the effect of human knowledge and intervention" (Zagorin 223). Does this mean that because reason is a mere belief that makes the irrational rational, the boundaries between the artificial and natural can be blurred? Is Bacon saying that the boundaries between a lie and truth can be blurred?

In this chapter, we will look at the significance of emotions in reasoning from a clinical perspective. Keep in mind that normally the left and right hemispheres of the brain work together under normal conditions. Each hemisphere controls different types of thinking. The left hemisphere of the brain is rational (analytical, logical). The right hemisphere of the brain is intuitive and emotional.

Most of the information in this chapter was taken from the clinical research entitled, "Divergent Thinking Styles of the Hemispheres: How Syllogisms Are Solved during Transitory Hemisphere Suppression," by Vadim Ivovich Deglin, M.D., and Marcel Kinsbourne, M.D. (285-307).

In their study, the patients were asked to solve syllogisms[xv] while their left hemisphere and right hemisphere were temporarily alternately suppressed by electroconvulsive therapy (ECT).[xvi] Each syllogism was composed of a major premise, minor premise, and a question. <u>The premises were familiar or unfamiliar, true or false.</u> The respondents' task was to answer the question of the syllogism. Syllogism #15, #13 and #14 are presented below in the same order as shown in the research article. The information that you are about to read was taken from pages 297 and 300-302 of the research article. Please note that the respondents' responses are in bold letters. The interviewer's remarks are *italicized* without the parentheses.

In the three dialogues, the reader will note that with <u>right-hemisphere suppression</u>, the syllogisms are solved by the patient theoretically [*guessing*]—even when the facts were known, leading to [*false statements*] and an [*absurd conclusion*]. With left-hemisphere suppression, the syllogisms are solved by the patient applying their [*prior knowledge*]—and if the syllogism content was unfamiliar or false, they did not answer the question but instead [*emotionally*] declared the question as unfamiliar or false.

SYLLOGISM (N15)

Major Premise:

(**N15**) Winter is cold in tropical countries. (This premise is false.)

Minor Premise:

Equador[xvii] is a tropical country.

Question:

Is it cold in winter in Equador, or not?

** Extracts from the Records of Patient F

Control Investigation: (before electroshock)

-- Please read what is written here and answer the question (syllogism N15 is presented):

-- **Probably not.**

-- *Why do you think so?*

-- **According to what is written here, the answer should be positive, but I think that Equador is in Africa and it is always warm there.**

Investigation following [Left-Sided Electroshock]

(The same syllogism is presented; the patient shrugs her shoulder, reads again):

-- **Winter is not cold in tropical countries! It's a lie!**

Investigation following [Right-Sided Electroshock]

(The same syllogism was presented. The patient read it quickly and answered it immediately):

-- **It's cold in winter in Equador because Equador is a tropical country.**

-- *Oh, is winter really cold in tropical countries?*

-- **I think so. Winter is cold there and summer is warm.**

-- *Are you sure of this?*

-- **No, I am not.**

-- *Equador is a tropical country; then, can it be cold there?*

-- **No, it can't be since it is a tropical country.**

(Continued in 5 min):

-- *Is it cold in winter in Equador?*

-- **No, Equador is a tropical country.**

(The same syllogism is presented):

-- **It is cold in winter in Equador because Equador is a tropical country.**

-- *But you do know that it is not so?*

-- **But it is written here.**

* * *

SYLLOGISM (N13)

Major Premise:

(**N13**) Northern limits[xviii] often are seen in Africa. (This premise is false)

Minor Premise:

Uganda is in Africa.

Question:

Are northern lights seen in Uganda, or not?

** Extracts from the Records of the Investigations of the Patient S

Control Investigation: (before electroshock)

Syllogism N13 is presented

-- **Northern lights occur in Uganda because Uganda is in Africa.**

Investigation following [Left-Sided Electroshock]

(The same syllogism is presented):

-- **Oh, what nonsense?! What is it, Uganda? There is no such country.**

-- *There is such a country in Africa.*

-- **All the same, northern lights can't occur in Uganda. Northern lights do not occur in Africa.**

Investigation following [Right-Sided Electroshock]

(The same syllogism is presented):

-- **They happen, because Uganda is in Africa.**

-- *Do you know where northern lights occur?*

-- **I do, at the North Pole.**

-- *And do they occur in Africa?*

-- **Probably not.**

(The syllogism [N13] is presented again):

-- **Northern lights occur in Africa since that is written on the card.**

* * *

SYLLOGISM (N14)

Major Premise:

(**N14**) All monkeys climb trees.

Minor Premise:

The porcupine is a monkey. (This premise is false)

Question:

Does the porcupine climb trees or not?

** Extracts from the Records of the Investigations of the Patient K

Control Investigation: (before electroshock)

Syllogism N14 is presented

-- **It does not climb; the porcupine runs on the ground.**

-- *And how does it look?*

-- **It is prickly.**

-- *It is like a monkey?*

-- **No, it is not.**

Investigation following [Left-Sided Electroshock]

(The same syllogism is presented):

-- **Porcupine? How can it climb trees? It is not a monkey. It is prickly like a hedgehog. It's wrong here!** (She is speaking with indignation [emotional displeasure]).

Investigation following [Right-Sided Electroshock]

(The same syllogism is presented):

-- **The porcupine climbs trees since it is a monkey.**

-- *But is the porcupine a monkey?*

-- **No, the porcupine is prickly, like a hedgehog.**

-- *Can it climb trees?*

-- **No, it can't; trees, it can't.**

** (The same syllogism is presented again):

-- **Since the porcupine is a monkey, then it climbs trees.**

-- *But you do know that a porcupine is not a monkey?*

-- **It is written so on the card.**

"The subjects...showed **pronounced emotional responses** to <u>false premises</u> under left hemisphere suppression" [*right-hemisphere is active*]—however, with a *right-hemisphere* suppression the subjects "performed formal–logical operations quite calmly, with confidence, and remained unmoved by the absurdity of the information offered by the premises" (300). The researchers have shown that the latter is due to the subjects' inability to access the emotional right-hemisphere under the experimental condition.

This work was accomplished with subjects who were sufficiently mentally ill to require the benefits of ECT. Can the results (of this study) be generalized to the general population, it being obvious that normal people cannot be subjects for similar observations? It is reassuring in this respect that in the control condition (Experiment 1), responses were in line with the normative data in the literature. The subjects' responses in the experimental conditions, though not without inter-individual variability, showed common, systematic effects of the conditions and the nature of the tests materials. **We see no evidence that psychopathology biased subjects' attitudes to the test. Nor is there any evidence that the fundamental design characteristics of the hemispheres differ as between mentally normal and mentally ill people.** (302)

It is my subjective view that the effect of suppressing the emotional right hemisphere offers a perspective on how the *European intellectual movement* works. We saw how suppression of the emotional right hemisphere impairs our ability to reason in the context of reality. Thus by suppressing historic truths with a barrier composed of an *array of falsities*—we are lesser able to mentally penetrate and access historic truths for a comparative analysis with our present state of being. Therefore, we reason in the context of the falsities and as a result remain "unmoved by the absurdity" of our predicament.

~ ~ ~

Chapter 11
With A Lie You Can Go Very Far, But You Can Never Go Back![xix]

11.1 <u>A Need for "National" Moral Leadership</u>

In this chapter, there will be a discussion on *some of the challenges* in the advocacy for a National Maat Public Policy. The importance of properly identifying challenges helps us to formulate effective strategy for overcoming these challenge. Here we will open with the assertion that there is a need for national moral leadership. Without national moral leadership a nation's future does not look too pleasant.

For instance, if we look back in time to AD 1948 when nations from around the world signed an agreement that was just as important as the recent 2016 Paris climate agreement, you may get a little concerned. This agreement was called the United Nations Universal Declaration of Human Rights. It was signed three years after World War II. The first article of this UN Human Rights Declaration states, "All human beings are born free and equal in dignity and rights. They are endowed with '<u>reason</u>' and '<u>conscience</u>' (moral sense) and should act towards one another in a spirit of brotherhood."

I am sure after the world war hopes for world peace were very high. Yet, over a half a century later, human rights violations are still a major problem in the U.S. and around the world. Former President Jimmy Carter wrote the following in an issue of the *New York Times* on June 25, 2012:

> With leadership from the United States, the Universal Declaration of Human Rights was adopted in 1948 as 'the foundation of freedom, justice and peace in the world.' ...It is disturbing that instead of strengthening these principles, our government's counterterrorism policies are now clearly violating at least 10 of the declaration's 30 articles... At a time when popular revolutions are sweeping the globe, the United States should be strengthening, not

weakening, basic rules of law and principles of justice enumerated in the Universal Declaration of Human Rights. But instead of making the world safer, America's violation of international human rights abets (assists) our enemies and alienates our friends.

In the book *Human Rights in Our Own Backyard: Injustice and Resistance in the United States*, the authors indicate that in response to increasing human rights violations in the U.S., a number of organizations are collaborating to bring human rights home, and they have formed the "U.S. human rights movement" for this purpose (Armaline et al. 242). This book was awarded the 2013 Hirabayashi Book Award by the Human Rights Section of the American Sociological Association.

It is my belief that the persistence of human rights violations after the signing of the Universal Declaration of Human Rights is directly linked to the world's inattentiveness to the importance of moral development. This is extremely problematic when moral action is now desperately needed to solve the world's human rights and environmental problems! At the Headquarters of the United Nations in New York City on April 22, 2016,

> World leaders from 175 countries signed the historic Paris climate accord (agreement)... using Earth Day as a backdrop for the ceremonial inking of a long-fought deal that aims to slow the rise of harmful greenhouse gases. 'We are in a race against time,' U.N. secretary-General Ban Ki-moon told the gathering at the United Nations headquarters in New York. 'The era of consumption without consequences is over. **The poor and most vulnerable must not suffer further from a problem they did not create,**' Ban added. '...Today is a day for our children and grandchildren and all generations to come.' (Rice)

The U.N.'s human rights and climate agreements must succeed! Success is dependent upon a high-burning moral flame in industrial societies. There is a need for *moral ambitious* leadership to put the world upon its proper foundation again. Joseph Thomas, a military professor of leadership at the U.S. Naval Academy and author of the paper "Four Stages of Moral Development in Military Leaders," writes that the stages of moral development are: (1) compliance, (2) moral understanding, (3) moral maturity, and (4) *moral ambition.*

"The most important transitory step from the role of follower to that of leader is the step from *compliance* to *moral understanding*," he writes. As a society we seem to be stuck at the compliance level. "...*Moral maturity* is not an end-state; rather, it is the product of continuous evaluation." While we may be morally mature, we have not preoccupied ourselves with continuous self-evaluation; thus we have fallen back to the compliance level, in my view. It's like developing a strong muscle, and due to lack of use of the muscle the muscle cells degenerate making the muscle weak again. "...*Moral ambition* is the final and ultimate stage of moral development." Professor Thomas explains,

> It (moral ambition) represents the pinnacle of self-actualization. **Moral ambition is the active...pursuit of virtuous (high moral) behavior not only in self, but in all members within the individual's sphere of influence.** ...It is a quality that few are capable of achieving, for it demands reflection, willingness, courage, and constancy of purpose. In matters of day-to-day life, moral ambition may cause an individual to impact situations that are little known to others (returning a lost wallet, aiding a stranded motorist, etc.). **In certain situations, moral ambition, on the part of influential people, can change the world.**

We must make sure that all of our social institutions are propagating and motivating the display of moral ambition in society. Without *moral ambitious* national leadership America will continue to decline into a land of the industrialized criminals, savages, racists, psychopaths and sociopaths. We are assured to lose sight on what it means to act like an intelligent and *morally refined human being.* We can see trends of this in our universities and colleges. Sororities and fraternities can be the gateway to academic support, internships, mentoring, networking, and nice careers in the corporate sector, politics, etc., and leadership roles. Still these organizations have a reputation of engaging "secretly" in immoral conduct (sometimes criminal conduct). For example, journalist John Hechinger who is the author of *True Gentlemen: Broken Pledge of America's Fraternities*, states that fraternities "embody many of the unresolved conflicts still plaguing the United States" (249). He adds that the evidence suggests that the wealthy fraternity alumni have a part in this occurrence (254). The lesson to ponder here is what good is it to loose your soul for a piece of silver or gold? There is another sociological concern that we rarely give our attention to as we go about our daily affairs. Here are a couple of things to ponder:

In her book *The Sociopath Next Door*, Dr. Martha Stout, who is a psychologist states, "People without conscience (moral sense) provide endless examples of such stunning 'I've done nothing wrong' statements" (49-50)! Stout continues, alerting us to a social challenge that is being overlooked by the general population:

> We feel that if someone is bad, he (or she) should be burdened with knowledge that he (or she) is bad… **In fact, a refusal to see the results of one's behavior as having anything to do with oneself**—'consistent irresponsibility' in the language of American Psychiatry Association—**is a cornerstone of the antisocial personality diagnosis**.

In the book she reports that 4% of the American population "secretly has no conscience and can do anything at all without feeling guilty" (9, 82). Using U.S. Census data, in the year of 2005 because of the copyright date of her book, 4% of the American population at this time was represented by the figure 11,856,416 people. For the year 2015, 4% of the national population was represented by the figure 12,856,752 people. So, in 2015, there are an estimated 13 million *sociopaths* living in America.

In comparison, according to 2015 Census data, there were only 5.4 million American Indians and Alaska Natives, including those of more than one race representing a mere 2% of the U.S. population.

In summary, the 13 million sociopaths outnumber the 5.4 million Native Americans! In the publication *Psychology Today*, in the article, "The Ice People," Dr. Stout writes the following:

> Some cultures contain fewer sociopaths than do others. Sociopathy appears to be relatively rare in certain East Asian countries. Studies conducted in Taiwan have found a low prevalence of antisocial personality disorder, ranging from .03 percent to .14 percent—impressively less than the Western world's average of 4 percent. ... Robert Hare, a professor emeritus of psychology at the University of British Columbia writes, 'Our society is moving in the direction of permitting, reinforcing, and in some instances valuing some traits such as impulsivity, irresponsibility, lack of remorse.' Other theorists propose that North American culture, which holds individualism as a central value, tends to foster the development of antisocial behavior, and also to disguise it. In America, the guiltless manipulation of other people "blends" with social expectations to a much greater degree than it would in more group-centered societies. (76-78)

If that is not enough, what about the 3.2 million psychopaths mentioned earlier? Add these 3.2 million psychopaths to the 13 million sociopaths. Psychopaths have [no fear]! They have no conscience and are classified as the most dangerous of all personality disorders, representing 1% of the U.S. population. Some of the psychopath's personality attributes are valued in companies. "...(S)ome psychopathic individuals manage to achieve high corporate status," according to the article "Corporate Psychopathy" (Babiak, Neumann and Hare 189).

Time Magazine in the article, "Which Professions Have the Most Psychopaths? The Fewest?" reveals in descending order the *top ten professions* with the most *psychopaths*: 1-**CEO**, 2-**lawyer**, 3-media (TV/radio), 4-salesperson, 5-surgeon, 6-journalist, 7-police officer, 8-clergyperson, 9-chef, and 10-civil servant (Barker). Could there be any kind of relationship between the Industrial Revolution and the two top professions with psychopaths, since it has been shown that *business* and *law* were indispensable to the advancement of the Industrial Revolution (Lerman and Schrag)?

In the March 14, 2012 issue of *Harvard Business Review*, the article, "Psychopaths on Wall Street," written by Ronald Schouten, MD, JD, indicates that it has been conservatively estimated "that 10% of people in the financial services industry are psychopaths." As of June 2016 there were 6.1 million people employed in the "Finance and Insurance Industry," according to U.S. Department of Labor/Bureau of Labor Statistics. Ten percent of the 6.1 million people would be 610,000 people. So there are an estimated 610,000 psychopaths—who have no fear—working in financial services industry.

In the article "Treatment of Psychopathy: A Review of Empirical Findings," cognitive-psychologists Dr. Grant Harris and Dr. Marnie Rice concluded the following:

> We believe there is no evidence that any treatments yet applied to psychopaths have been shown to be effective in reducing violence or crime. In fact, some treatments that are effective for others offenders are actually harmful for psychopaths in that they appear to promote recidivism. We believe that the reason for these findings is that psychopaths are fundamentally different from other offenders and that there is nothing 'wrong' with them in the manner of a deficit or impairment that therapy can 'fix.' Instead, they exhibit an evolutionary viable life strategy that involves lying, cheating, and manipulating others. Although no therapy has yet been shown to reduce the likelihood of future violence or crime among psychopaths, this does not mean that nothing can help. The best available evidence for effective intervention comes from the application of social learning principles in the form of behavioral programs... We can also conceive of societal changes that might reduce the behavioral niche for psychopathy, but such changes inevitably carry some

negative impact with respect to the personal liberty of all citizens. ...It is to be expected...that psychopaths will attempt to subvert harm reduction strategies employed by non-psychopaths. (568)

11.2 Institutional Racism

In the book *The Half Has Never Been Told: Slavery and the Making of American Capitalism*, the author presents evidence on how the slavery industry has influenced the making of the industrial-capitalistic society (Baptist). "The idea that the commodification and suffering and forced labor of African Americans is what made the United States powerful and rich is not an idea that people necessarily are happy to hear. Yet it is the truth" (xxi-xxii). In the article "Modern Slavery as a Management Practice: Exploring the Conditions and Capabilities for Human Exploitation," the author Andrew Crane writes, "Modern slavery represents one of the worst possible forms of human exploitation. However, despite its persistence in the global economy, it has received relatively little theoretical attention among management scholars" (65).

Institutional racism is a systematic discriminatory practice that is directed at a particular race or races by the social institution(s) of a society. These discriminatory practices involve unfair and unequal treatment of a particular race or races. While white people are indeed subject to the general exploitative forces of industrialism and capitalism, they do not experience these exploitative forces *plus* racial discrimination on a daily basis.

For example, despite the fact the U.S. Constitution was ratified in 1788 and the 15th and 14th Amendments added to the Constitution in order to limit the power of the federal and state governments to discriminate; discrimination against historically black colleges and universities (i.e., Morgan State University, Howard University) continue. According to the Higher Education Act of 1965 (P.L. 89-329), Part 1 General Higher Education Programs, Title III-Institutional Aid, Part B-Strengthening Historically Black Colleges and Universities, Sec. 321 [20 U.S.C. 1060] Findings and Purposes [*As Amended Through Public Law 113–67, Enacted December 26, 2013*]:

The Congress finds that—(1) the historically Black colleges and universities have contributed significantly to the effort to attain equal opportunity through postsecondary education for Black, low-income, and educationally disadvantaged Americans; (2) States and the Federal Government have discriminated in the allocation of land and financial resources to support Black public institutions under the Morrill Act of 1862 and its progeny, and against public and private Black colleges and universities in the award of Federal grants and contracts, and the distribution of Federal resources under this Act and other Federal programs which benefit institutions of higher education; (3) the current state of Black colleges and universities is partly attributable to the discriminatory action of the States and the Federal Government and this discriminatory action requires the remedy of enhancement of Black postsecondary institutions to ensure their continuation and participation in fulfilling the Federal mission of equality of educational opportunity... (138-139)

Second, Trinidad professor emeritus Tony Martin (1942-2013) was the founding member of the Africana Studies Department at Wellesley College with over thirty years of teaching in this department. At the 14th Conference of the Institute for Historical Review in Irvine, California in June 2002, Martin addressed the audience concerning a puzzling personal controversy. He states,

The first thing I should do by way of introduction is just to basically summarize precisely what my controversy was. ...For many years I've taught a survey course in African-American history. ...In 1993 I introduced to this course a book, which is on sale here, a book which then was fairly new... This book, which is published by the historical research department of the Nation of Islam, is entitled

The Secret Relationship between Blacks and Jews. And what that book did, relying primarily on sources written by Jews and Jewish sources of a variety of types, is to try to sort of synthesize the existing information on Jewish involvement in the slave trade, the bringing of Africans as slaves from Africa to the so-called new world. …All the information, practically, was secondary information, which had been already published, although hidden away to a large extent in very esoteric Jewish journals, which the average Jew, I discovered later, had no idea about.

What I discovered was…Jewish role in that slave trade had been very cleverly camouflaged for many, many years. Where Jews were involved, usually they tended not to be identified as Jews, whereas where Christians were involved, or where Muslims were involved, there was ready identification of such persons by their ethnicity, by their religious affiliation, and so on. In the case of Jews, they would be called other things—Portuguese, Spanish, Brazilian, whatever. But…that crucial identification tended to be obscured. …So I was…fascinated by this new information, and decided to add a few readings from this book in my class. And that's when…all hell broke loose.

Here is a brief on some of the things that happened to Dr. Martin for his efforts to meet his legal, ethical, and contractual obligations as a historian and scholar. Jewish organizations got involved!! One Sunday morning on the ABC TV program *This Week With David Brinkley*, the whole section was about Dr. Martin's teaching that the Jews were involved in the slave trade. A professor colleague of Martin at the college alleged that he pushed and physically assaulted a white student; Martin file a libel suit and lost even though his colleague admitted she was in wrong. Misinformation was sent to a student about Martin. Jewish groups were able to call a special press conference, which included Roman Catholic, Baptist, Protestant and Jewish leaders and the city mayor, who assembled an entire coalition of religious and, apparently, civil rights organizations with the intent to further discredit Dr. Martin. Once, a Jewish man came on the college campus, stating that he had come "to get" Dr. Martin. This individual was escorted off campus by college police. Returning to Martin's address to the conference audience, he continued...

> ...Then there was the <u>American Historical Association</u>. Three Jewish historians actually went to the American Historical Association and got it to decree (rule)—that's the only term I can use—to decree, by executive fiat, that the Jews were not involved in the slave trade. [Audience Laughter] ...This is totally antithetical to the way that academia operates. Who's ever heard of such a thing: historical fact being determined by presidential decree from the American Historical Association...? [Audience Laughter] It is absolutely amazing, but they actually succeeded in having this done. (Martin)

The strategy used by the white race to take leadership in the world involved the suppression of humanity's historical truths worldwide and replacing them with lies and white supremacy in order TO COMPENSATE for their now mutation disposition (i.e., white-skin, personality change) caused by being trapped unexpectedly in uninhabitable and brutally cold glacial climate for an estimated "twenty-thousand years" in Europe! This time span under such harsh conditions proved to be significant in race relations between whites and melanated people, especially African people who whites use to look like and be like. Generally speaking, the separation between whites and nonwhites' personalities is NOT white people's fault AND it is NOT nonwhite people's fault. It was an act of Nature. Nevertheless, we are ecologically charged with the duty of finding a remedy to our global race relations predicament!

One thing for sure, hate will not solve a NATURE-INDUCED DILEMMA. And hopefully we see now that supporting the white race's mission of white domination is not the solution. Certainly just getting a job, making money, becoming famous, obedient to status quo, boot-licking, and going along just-to-get-along does not solve a nature-induced dilemma that can have long-term durability. It is solved with moral reasoning, moral understanding and moral action.

Hence, there are three actions that I believe will help to "initiate" the remedy for the race problem: (1.) whites publicly acknowledge that they have been and continue to be an ecological problem; (2.) whites establish a long line of history that serves as precedential evidence that whites are sincere about making amends for past wrongdoings due to whites sadly NOT having a historical period of moral civility (or) a cultural tradition that could be used as creditable evidence to prove the likelihood; and (3.) whites begin to courteously relinguishing their leadership and domination over melanated people by way of race-based sovereignties under a MANDATED National Maat Public Policy. This way each race can have, without racial discrimination, its own cultural values, languages, beliefs, artifacts, symbols, and norms to establish their own social organization, customs, traditions, literatures, arts, economic system, and form of government according to their relationship with the supernatural forces (goddesses and gods) that regulate aspects of the universe, spirit world, nature, and/or human societies. Melanated people are obligated to reciprocate respectfully.

11.3 The American Empire

Yes, America is a superpower empire! **Yes, with lies white America has gone very far, and very reluctant to go back!** American domestic and foreign affairs are intertwined to varying degrees, and domestic and foreign policies can be driven by the transnational corporations' interest. This means that our government is in a struggle with corporate influence. America is an imperialistic empire.

Imperialism is the military, economic, political, and cultural influence by one country over another country or countries! John Flynn, a journalist, who was best known for opposing President Roosevelt on America's entrance into World War II, describes American imperialism: "The enemy aggressor is always pursuing a course of larceny, murder, rapine and barbarism. We are always moving forward with high mission, a destiny imposed by the Deity to regenerate our victims, while incidentally capturing their markets; to civilize savage and senile and paranoid peoples, while blundering accidentally into their oil wells."

Case in point, Libyan President "(Muammar) Qaddafi (also spelled Gaddafi) was not killed for humanitarian purposes but for the oil and for money. His ideas of an African gold-backed currency were his major undoing" (Gwaambuka). "In 1967 Colonel Gaddafi inherited one of the poorest nations in Africa; however, by the time he was assassinated, Gaddafi had turned Libya into Africa's wealthiest nation. Libya had the highest GDP per capita and life expectancy on the continent" (Chengu, "Global Research").

An article in *Foreign Policy Journal* entitled, "Hillary Emails Reveal True Motive for Libya Intervention" states, "…historians of the 2011 NATO war in Libya will be sure to notice a few…truly explosive confirmations contained in the new emails: …Western nations jockeying for access to Libyan oil…and concern over Qaddafi's gold and silver reserves threatening European currency" (Hoff).

According to Chancellor Williams, Ph.D., who is a highly respected historian, "Caucasians will wage frightful wars against other Caucasians, but will quickly unite, as though by instinct, against non-whites, not only in wars but in international policies. They have developed a kind of built-in solidarity in their relations with non-Caucasian peoples. This fact, as much as anything else, helps to explain their position as masters of the world" (298). According to Andrew Bacevich, professor emeritus of international relations and history and author of *American Empire: The Realities and Consequences of U.S. Diplomacy*, our nation's agenda is:

> …to preserve and…expand an American imperium (sphere of control). Central to this strategy is a commitment to global openness—removing barriers that inhibit the movement of goods, capital, ideas, and people. Its ultimate objective is the creation of an open and integrated international order based on the principles of democratic capitalism, with the United States as the ultimate guarantor of order and enforcer of norms. In

the eyes of American policymakers, an open world that
adheres to the principles of free enterprise is a precondition
for continued American prosperity. (3)

"…The [myth] of the 'reluctant superpower'—Americans asserting
themselves only under duress and then always for the noblest purposes—
reigns today as the master narrative (lie) explaining the nation's exercise
of global power" (8). As the heart and soul of this superpower empire,
the American people have the power to transform our superpower
empire into an "Empire of Civility and Goodwill" by exercising our
voting power to get the federal branches of government (legislative,
judicial and executive branches) to work together cooperatively to
establish a mandated National Maat Public Policy.

11.4 **Self-efficacy**

With all of the above in mind, what are the chances that we will ever
have a National Maat Public Policy? Living in a superpower empire
where low morals, materialism, capitalism, racism, sexism, sociopathy,
and psychopathy are "common" influences at all levels of the society,
we cannot just be calm and unmoved by the absurdities of our times
anymore! While all of the above social pathologies are a concern, it is
the *low morals* that are viewed as our biggest challenge. The fact that
moral development has NEVER been a high priority—in a standard
customary way—in the United States, it makes the advocacy for a
National Maat Public Policy even more important. Actually it is very
easy to accomplish!!

Here is one quick illustrative point: If the government simply
pivot its point-of-reference away from the commands of the rich and
corporations to the directives of the people, biosphere, ecology and the
universe, this would be the foundation for facilitating the flowering of
an "Empire of Civility and Goodwill!"

~ ~ ~

Chapter 12
Summary:

At the heart of the world's problems today is the disappearance of spiritual societies. The industrial societies have replaced spiritual societies:

- We began this proposal with the fact that modern woman/man originated 200,000 years ago as a black people in Africa.

- Nubia is the mother of the longest lasting human civilization known in the world, Ancient Egypt, which originated around 3100 BC in the Nile Valley region in Africa.

- Using the above dates, it means that human civilization is 5,117 years old: [from 3100 BC to AD 2017 = 5,117 years]. It also means that starting from the time of modern humans' origin, it took up to 194,883 years before modern woman/man was able to achieve civilization [200,000 yrs. minus 5,117 yrs. equals 194,883 years].

- The above calculation is something to notice. Traditional people's spiritual ways of knowing and being were derived from hundreds of thousands of years of evolutionary experience of Black African people. They endured a divinely-prescribed, turbulent evolutionary process that led to achieving authentic civilization!

- Another way of looking at the above is to note that of the total time that modern humans have been in existence, it took 97 percent of that time for the *black race* to achieve civilization. (If we use Ta-Seti's date 17,700 years ago, it still took 91 percent of the time.) And when the *black race* finally achieved civilization, "Maat" was the regulating principle in government and human affairs. This occurrence spotlights the moral-spiritual disposition of traditional people—African people for sure!!

- Of the short time that human civilization has been in existence, the white race has broken humanity's divine spiritual bond with the biosphere, ecology, celestial heavenly bodies, and universe—through reason which "has no aim and no inherent goodness" (Calne)—and replaced our divine bond: with a heartless and unfeeling world that is based on falsehood and Machines.

Below we will continue summarizing our discussion from the standpoint of the following topics: (1.) lying, (2.) defense mechanism, (3.) where is western knowledge taking us?, (4.) industrialism is an anti-ecological defense mechanism, (5.) morality, melanin, biosphere, and universe, (6.) and beyond the world of materialism: re-embracing the spirit world.

12.1 Lying

One might wonder why a particular racial group of our species wants to do harm to the natural environment and its own species to the extent that has been demonstrated. Why would the white race be so obsessed with making billions of people uncomfortable, confused, poor, and culturally and economically disempowered through the spread of falsehood, industrialism, capitalism, and imperialism? There are three anti-social behaviors that have emerged from this proposal that were resourceful in helping the white world's intellectual movement to have long durability: avoiding historic truths, lying, and pretending to be sincere and of goodwill.

It has been mentioned that people tend to avoid truth that may challenge their view of the world. Enlightenment scholars struggled to understand traditional people of the world (Wilder 190). Spirituality was a factor. In fact, whites have even struggled to understand how to make clear their own made-up Christian theology, that is based on misinterpretation of the Ancient Egyptian Mysteries (Ben-Jochannan). This struggle has lasted through Christianity's first one thousand years of existence and beyond. The struggle is due to "reason" and "politics" being more or less the sole mediums of Christian theology. For some evidence review the history of the "Catholic Ecumenical Councils" and "Great Schism of AD 1050." Briefly, in general Church dignitaries met and struggled about how to falsify world history and make religious imagination appear to be God's word (Ben-Jochannan). It is therefore concluded that because of whites' lack of understanding of many of the spiritual cultures they confronted during the Age of Discovery, whites preferred to *avoid assimilating into these spiritual cultures* and thus classified them as unimportant and a hindrance to the progress of our species. Please note that the word veracity means truth. In a study entitled "People Lie for a Reason: Three Experiments Documenting the Principle of Veracity," the researchers found that "people usually do not lie when goals are attainable through honest means" (Levine, Kim, and Hamel 271). In other words, people are more likely to lie when goals are not attainable through honest means.

Anthony Gottlieb, in his book *The Dream of Enlightenment: The Rise of Modern Philosophy*, offer some evidence of the claim that whites tend to be *over-confident pompous liars*. Of course, real world evidence has been the best evident. He writes:

> The notion that there was something ultimately discreditable or foolish about Enlightenment...was so widespread in the twentieth century that it was written into the Oxford English Dictionary. From 1891 until 2010, the dictionary contained the following entry for 'Enlightenment': ...<u>philosophers of the 18th century or others whom it is intended to associate with them in the implied charge of shallow and *pretentious intellectualism*, unreasonable contempt for tradition and authority</u>. (242)

In a general sense, it is this writer belief that before contact with the white world, most of humanity was preoccupied with truth-telling, as they had the enormous task of learning the importance of communicating truth in order to live safely and productively within their challenging local natural environment. In short, there was little room for tolerating lies. Under such circumstance, doesn't it seem that truth in communication had to be highly valued as it increased their chances of survival. Sociologist John Barnes argues that "people are inclined to tell the truth, but mostly to deal with things sensibly and realistically for practical purposes."

In the research paper "Why do People tell the Truth? Experimental Evidence for Pure Lie Aversion," the authors indicate that "results suggest that pure lie aversion (which means **strong dislike for lying**) is a widespread motive, possibly influenced by beliefs...and have implications for understanding behavior" (Lopez-Perez and Spiegelman 233). "Being hardwired to be trusting makes us intrinsically gullible" (Bhattacharjee 47). People "who tell the truth are more likely to believe that others will tell the truth as well" (Lopez-Perez and Spiegelman).

It is believed that this assumption made traditional people vulnerable to the white race. In his paper "Active Deception Detection," Timothy Levine, Ph.D., concludes: "Without the aid of technology, human lie detection was little better than a coin flip" (127). However, Levine does go on to say that *background history* is useful in lie detection. Traditional people had never seen or experienced white people before. So, traditional people did not have a background history on white people. Today, the world does have a background history on the white race.

From an ecological and public health perspective, it is imperative for all races to acknowledge the existence of this cultural trait (lying) of the white race. It is a very serious matter as lying has been shown herein to be at the foundation of Western authoritative knowledge and culture! In general, the different forms of lying: (i.e., personally, socially, economically, environmentally, educationally, historically, religiously, politically, legally, medically, scientifically, technologically, astronomically, etc.); are generated by white fear and the need to control in order to sustain authoritarian-leadership in the world. Thus perpetual lying is a defense mechanism to hid. It has worked successfully, for 500 years, as a veil, mirage, and camouflage. This brings to mind a need for an effective "defense mechanism" for dealing with this *over-confident pompous lying* in the 21st century.

All living things have a defense mechanism. A defense mechanism is a particular defensive reaction of ANY living organism to threats in its environment to help it to survive. For example, for people of color one aspect of this defense mechanism should involve a mental process that triggers intimate memories of "life experiences" with the white race. This way healthy decision-making strategies are possible. Herein scholars have repeatedly stated that past experience keeps our thoughts consistent with reality. Earlier Bouchard mentioned in his paper "Genes, Environment and Personality," that a "people help to create their own environments based on their genotype" if left alone! It is an ecological necessity! Today people of color must emphasis this point in their struggle for freedom.

12.2 Defense Mechanism

Out of ecological necessity, it is important for all of us to reacquaint ourselves with the history of Ancient Egypt in order to guide us in the right direction as a species, being that it is the most respected and *longest-lasting human civilization known in the world*. As spiritual beings who are spiritually linked to the natural environment, we must establish an "ecological defense mechanism" that is consistent with guaranteeing our bonding with the human family, nature, and universe. "The world as a sacred abode (habitation) of the life forces of God, the ancestors, and diverse spirits (and our interconnectedness with it) is what gives (moral) human action its necessarily sacred character" (Magesa 57).

When the UN concludes that spirituality is the relationship to the universe and that traditional people created a relationship with the spirit world for the purpose of managing forces that seem overpowering, we know that our **ecological defense stance** should be based on a relationship with universal truth.

Zagorin helps us to see why it would be hypocritical not to strive to react to our ecological danger in a wise manner. He does this by offering a historical overview of what has been removed from human affairs:

> ...one of the two essential features of the scientific revolution was the distinction of the old conception of the cosmos which meant that the world ceased to be thought of as an infinite, hierarchically ordered and qualitatively and ontologically differentiated whole. ...This...implied the disappearance...of all considerations based on *values, perfection, harmony, meaning,* and *aim*, **none of which could have a place in the new ontology**. (127-128)

In other words, our western philosophical perspective on the "nature-of-being" which is our new ontology is void of a conventional moral value, meaningful aim, and harmony. Zagorin continues using a late-1500's poetic analysis. This poetic analysis spotlights the fact that very early in the intellectual movement, some saw the movement as an unjustifiable evil. "...Sir Philip Sidney's 'An Apology for Poetry' (1595) compared history (*his-story*) unfavorably with poetry not only because it fell short of truth in its dependence on hearsay and conjecture (guessing) but **because of its inferiority in teaching virtue** (morality). Because history was tied, according to Sidney, 'not to what should be... it often discouraged well-doing and encouraged wickedness'" (206).

Physician Gerber has already mentioned that the spiritual dimension is the energetic basis of all life as it brings to life the physical world. Because of our preoccupation with reason without Gerber's point in mind, we have been UNABLE to achieve a moral civilization. Why? Because the spiritual dimension also underlies moral action. So, we have created a simulated-civilization.

The illusion that we have of living in a real civilization is due to our reasoning in the context of *materialism* and *Western authoritative knowledge*, which is our "new" ontology that has been unfairly thrust upon traditional people. The white society will reward this type of reasoning. However, the white society will not reward reasoning in the context of the *spirit of the biosphere, ecology* and *universe*, which is our "old" ontology.

Since the demise of their cultures by the European world people of color have sought strategies to re-embrace their old ontology. In the book entitled *Negro Plot: An Account of the Late Intended Insurrection Amongst A Portion of the Blacks of the City of Charleston* (1822), the author Joseph Ingraham gives insight into the elaborate and largest slave revolt attempted in America. The plan was led by an African slave named Denmark Vesey. During court proceeding a witness stated: "'I know Denmark Vesey, on one occasion he asked me what news? I told him; none. He replied: We are free, but the white people here won't let us be so; and the only way is, to raise up and fight the whites'" (Ingraham 36). Of course, the revolt did not succeed and Vesey was executed for wanting to be free! The point here, however, is that our "defense mechanism" must return us to our "old" ontology. The United Nations has reported that spirituality is the relationship to the universe that helps us to construct social relationships and give meaning, purpose and hope to life ("State" 59-62).

Because we now view the irrationality of our "new" ontology as rational and normal—industrialism is not only a mere trophy for the white race, but more so it is the "Crown of the White Race" as the underlying logic, scripts, blueprints, and innovations of our industrial society are directly or indirectly influenced by the Enlightenment philosophies and theories. This Crown has been effective in ensuring that whites do not have to return to their historic past (i.e., Dark Ages). This memory of their past seems to be a driving force behind the construct of the "Crown of the White Race." Couldn't it be said, that because of the whites' astuteness of their historic truths their thoughts are in the context of their true reality. And because industrialized descendants of traditional people are *not* astute about their historic truths their thoughts are not in the context of their true reality.

Nevertheless, with climate change we now know that the Crown must be dethroned in order to save our planet. To address the fear of such an occurrence the defense mechanism of white, yellow, red, brown and black people must unravel the underlying logic, scripts, blueprints and innovations—through a *mandated* National Maat Public Policy—using the 42 Declarations of Innocence as a guide. In this regard, the race-based sovereignties prove they're significant!! In other words, the unraveling of the logic, scripts, blueprints, and innovations of industrialism will not cause widespread "panic" or "terror" because the race-based sovereignties will naturally seek to return to the "old" ontology of traditional people.

Within these sovereignties, the environment would be most suitable for cultivating our "old" ontology. For further clarity, consider the fact that experiential knowledge is "the understanding and expertise that emerge from life experiences, rather than professional training" (VandenBos). It is experiential knowledge that keeps us in touch with our particular reality. Notice that the white world prefers that we rely foremost on professional training because professional training is the "*nut*" and "*bolt*" that holds together the industrial-capitalistic matrix! However, professional training does not value our experiential knowledge that has emerged from life experiences living under white supremacy. There is minimal opportunity *to express this acquired wisdom* to liberate ourselves to participate harmoniously in our animated universe. This is a problem that race-based sovereignties can successfully solve under a mandated National Maat Public Policy.

12.3 Where is Western Knowledge Taking Us?

The "Crown of the White Race" was achieved by ignoring historical truth, lying, and pretending to be sincere and caring—worldwide! In an issue of the *International Journal of Law and Psychiatry*, Lana Muzinic, M.D. et al., affirms that a "delusion is 'a false belief based on incorrect inference about external reality, and the delusion is firmly held in spite of evidence to the contrary'" (90). Then it is safe to conclude that under such circumstance many of us are experiencing *delusions*, and because of this fact we have been unable to address many of our problems as a people.

Deglin & Kinsbourne (285) and Shuren & Grafman (917) have explained that we tend to not be alarmed when we are unable to remember past experience for comparison with an existing experience. We just accept the existing experience until we fully experience the experience and then evaluate accordingly; however with a delusion our evaluation has high probability of being flawed. Is it because reason is simply and solely a tool without any legitimate claims to moral content (Calne) that the American Psychological Association now concludes: "Although at one time reason was considered a MENTAL FACULTY, this is typically NOT intended in current usage" (Vandenbos 774)? This seems to be one of the considerations.

To traditional people, *knowledge is truth*. **"In 1620 Francis Bacon published a scientific manifesto titled 'The New Instrument.' In it, he argued that '<u>knowledge is power</u>.' The real test of 'knowledge' <u>is not whether it is true</u>, but whether it empowers us.** ...<u>The real test is utility</u>" (Harari 259). Remember statistician George Box's famous statement: "Essentially all models are wrong, <u>but some are useful</u>" (424). Typically, the usefulness of knowledge in industrial societies is "shaped by economic, political and religious interests" (Harari 271). *In other words, truth is not necessarily the determining factor in the usefulness of knowledge in our society today.*

"Science is unable to set its own priorities. It is also incapable of determining what to do with its discoveries" (274). For instance, "science, industry and military technology intertwined only with the advent of the *capitalist system* and the *Industrial Revolution*. Once this relationship was established... it quickly transformed the world" (264). Remember that "Capitalism began when private investments drove the economy and entrepreneurs and their supporters acquired power to bend political and social institutions to their demands" (Appleby 118).

Because of these types of circumstances surrounding Western knowledge, wouldn't it be wise to re-evaluate all branches of Western knowledge through the diverse lenses of cultural relativism and antiquity's historical truths? Additionally, what about the fact that Western knowledge came into being in a white supremacist climate? See Diagram 4.

What about the fact that to Sir Bacon "of the twenty-five hundred years of recorded history, little more than five centuries or so were propitious (favorable) for the progress of knowledge. These comprised the period of the **Greeks**, that of the **Romans**, and most recent past of the **nations of Western Europe**" (Zagorin 203). How does one not deem the history of Nubia and Ancient Egypt as favorable for the progress of knowledge?

"The form of (Ancient Egypt's) government was unique, quasi-divine kingship, the desirability of which to the Egyptians is evident from its perpetuation throughout the period and later" (Clark 837). If Africa re-writes its history, it will reveal a glory that Africa will inevitably seek to recapture (Chengu 5). "After all, the greatest threat towards Africa having a glorious future is her people's ignorance of Africa's glorious past." This point would also be true for other people of color. Let us glance at the descendants of Mesoamerican civilizations in Mexico (i.e., Maya, Olmec, and Aztec). It is widely acknowledged that the Catholic Church played a leadership role in the destruction of Mesoamerican civilizations and throughout Mexico. In 2015 Pope Francis apologized to indigenous people of the Americas stating: "'I humbly ask forgiveness, not only for the offense of the church herself, but also for crimes committed against the native peoples during the so-called conquest of America'" ("Pope").

A Proposed Visual of
Traditional People's Reasoning Processes Before
& After Contact with the White Race (Diagram 4)

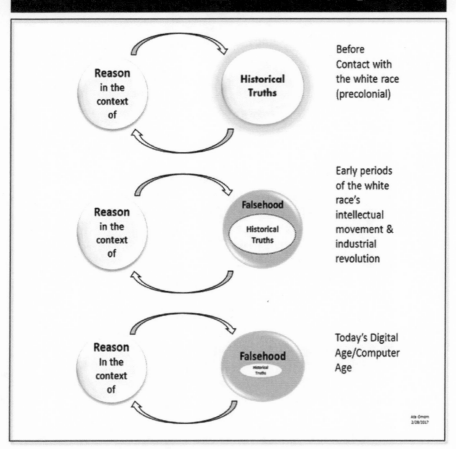

However, because of what seems to be memory loss of their ancient historical truths we find that, according to the United Nations Data/Statistics: Population by Religion, Sex, and Urban/Rural Residence, in the year 2010 Mexico had an estimated 120 million Catholics??! There are similar problems like this around the world, and one was brought to light by Prof. Molefi Asante who has "traveled extensively" on the continent of Africa, and has written over 70 books. Asante reported, to an astute audience that had the ability to assess his assertion, that: "I have never seen an *African* **city**...I have never seen an *African* **university**...I have never seen an *African* **government** ("Revival").

Keep in mind that all living organisms have a constitutional (inborn) nature to react to their environment in a particular way. This particular way of reacting to the environment is due primarily to our genetic constitution. When someone is preoccupied with controlling how we react to our experiences, that someone is interfering with an aspect of the evolutionary process. This cannot be tolerated. That someone is "not" a friend.

Maybe it is helpful to remember that the American and European universities and scientific societies played a central role in: (1) suppressing humanity's historical truths, (2) making up lies to replace historical truths, (3) legitimizing these lies, and (4) providing the context in which these lies could be "develop and communicated" from one generation to the next generation (Berry 187; Black).

For example, for traditional people astronomy was participatory. Traditional people gave human and animal characteristics to the Earth, Moon, planets, and stars according to their daily, seasonal, and annual biological, mental and spiritual experiences with them. The behaviors and influences of these celestial bodies helped to shape traditional people's self-concept, cultural rhythms, norms, values, languages, rituals, and symbols. Does it help to know that stars play a role in the creation (of the content) in the universe. Again, "every object in the wider universe, everything around us, and everything we are, originated from stardust" (Schrijver, 8). We have something in common with everything in the universe because we are made from stardust. Remember by 3,000 BC Maat was a philosophy of life based on the observation of the celestial order in the universe—which guided national moral order (Bunson).

The above astronomical participatory practices were interrupted with help from the Enlightenment pioneers. Since Isaac Newton, the field of astronomy has become a non-participatory study of the universe for traditional people. Newton, metaphorically speaking, helped to collapse and subdue traditional people's energetic participatory relationship with the universe into a mathematical-logical observational practice. In doing this, numbers emerged as the measure of real life (Morris 470)— starting with the universe! Today, modern astronomers "take great care to distinguish their field from astrology... (But) the definition between astrology and astronomy has not always been as rigid as it now stands" (Peek and Yankah 11). Astronomy now is the branch of knowledge that deals with the "*physical*" universe—and not the *animated* universe.

Astrology, while "not" considered a branch of knowledge, is the study of celestial bodies' (i.e., planets', stars') movements and influences on human affairs and the natural world. "Most traditional African societies perceive the universe as an entity that encompasses pervasive (widespread) vital powers. These powers, or forces, are hierarchically ordered and exist in a state of equilibrium. The conceptually perceived harmony among the elements of the universe ensures the well-being of humankind" (247). Of course, the European and American universities would have none of this!!

"The difference in the intellectual approach of the African and European researcher often causes...misunderstandings in the interpretation of facts and their relative importance. ...The African scholar distrusts the "scientific" activity, the aim of which seems to be the fragmentation of the collective historical African consciousness into minute facts and details (Diop "Origin" 275).

So, for African and nonwhite people exactly where is Western knowledge taking us? We must ask ourselves this question. Historian Sanjay Subrahmanyam, Ph.D., emphasizes that "knowledge must always be understood in relation to the concrete circumstances of its production." We have discussed the concrete circumstances that have produced Western authoritative knowledge. We have learned that Western knowledge is tainted with falsehood and white supremacy!!!

For example, psychology is a branch of knowledge. Psychology is the study of the mind and behavior. Western psychology was founded

1879. This field is preoccupied with standardizing what a healthy mind and social behavior is in an industrial-capitalistic society! The standard criteria for this healthy mind and social behavior in an industrial society are established by whites. <u>Today, we rarely think about how dysfunctional our industrialized mindset and social behaviors are to traditional societies, the natural environment and universe</u>! We tend to think we are smarter than traditional people—even while we are destroying the entire planet! This proves Deglin & Kinsbourne and Shuren & Grafman's point about how we respond to insanity with calmness when we are unable to retrieve past experience (historical truths) to compare with our present experience. In such case, we tend to "reason" through the insanity using the logic of our society and thereby reason and conclude that the "industrial experience" is sensible, intelligent, and sane.

Sociology is a branch of knowledge. Sociology is the study of relationships between two or more individuals and human interactions. Sociology was founded in the mid-1800s. Its purpose initially was for studying social behavior in relation to our rapidly growing and expanding industrial environment *as traditional people gradually surrendered their traditional social behaviors*. In this regard, the goal of sociology is to make the administration of the industrial-capitalistic societies more efficient for the ruling class. Social behavior is expected to promote the advancement of western science, technology, and social values that benefited whites foremost. Shouldn't we be more concerned about learning and applying knowledge that would help us to interact and live harmoniously and rhythmically with the human family, natural environment, and especially the heavenly celestial bodies?

For a brief perspective on religious knowledge we turn to Charles C. Jones (1804-1863), educator, clergyman, missionary, planter and author of *The Religious Instruction of African Americans & the History of Their Church in the United States*:

> If a people are to be instructed orally, let the instruction
> be communicated to them in early life. It will then do
> them most good; they will learn to use their memories
> and their reasoning powers and be prepared to profit by
> more elevated services of the sanctuary. The amount of

religious knowledge which may be communicated orally, can be conceived of by those only, who have made the experiment. (171)

Keep in mind these are just a few of the branches of knowledge. There is a branch of knowledge called "behavioral ecology," which is the study of animal behavior and adaptation strategies due to *ecological pressures*. It appears whatever knowledge that has been acquired from this branch of knowledge is not being used to save animals (i.e., fish, birds, humans, whales, bees, etc.). The Machine Culture has *pressured* many animals to become extinct or an endangered species. Where is Western knowledge taking us?

The branch of knowledge called cybernetics, according to Wikipedia, is the study of "control of any system using technology." Cybernetics is not being used in an ecologically friendly way to promote a balanced ecology. For example, bees are disappearing, and this adversely impacts the pollination of flowers, trees, and agricultural crops. Harvard University's Wyss Institute for Biologically Inspired Engineering and Harvard's School of Engineering and Applied Sciences is developing *robotic bees*, called RoboBees. "The 3-centimeter (1.2 in) wingspan of RoboBee makes it the smallest man-made device modeled on an insect to achieve flight" ("RoboBee").

RoboBees can be used to collect pollen from agriculture crops as a tactic for addressing the bee shortage ("Autonomous Flying"). It is my understanding that there may be billions or trillions of bees in the world. Do we really want billions or trillions of tiny little robotic machines (bees) flying around if bees continue to vanish? Wouldn't it be wiser for us to change our wasteful way of life since the shortage of bees is linked to our industrial activities? Then we can let Mother Nature replenish the bees! After all, Mother Nature knows a little bit about this kind of thing!! Where is Western knowledge taking us?

Then, cybernetics presents the "nano-satellites," which can weigh a mere two pounds. "India's space agency has announced the successful launch of a record-breaking 104 nanosatellites into orbit" (Safi): Ninety-six nanosatellites belong to U.S. companies; three belong to Indian companies, and the rest belong to companies in Switzerland,

Netherlands, Kazakhstan, Israel, and United Arab Emirate. The motive: to explore markets in outer space for private enterprise. <u>Are we going to establish social and economic systems based on money and the Machine throughout the animated universe without careful consideration of the "proven" cancerous effects of industrialism and capitalism</u>? If people with "moral ambition" do not intervene quickly, probably so!

Traditional people would not keep doing something that is proven to be destructive to the entire ecology of our planet and then take that practice into deep outer space. In the near future, young people might get tricked into finding themselves walking around on a waterless and barren planet in outer space—in a spacesuit, looking for a money-making opportunity rather than learning how to live harmoniously with the planet on which God placed us. Oh by the way, in case you pack a lunch to go, astronaut Scott Kelly, who spent a year aboard the International Space Station, wants you to know the following, writing from outer space: "Fruits and vegetables seem to rot much faster here than on Earth. I'm not sure why, and seeing the process makes me worry that the same thing is happening to my own cells" (70). Do you think it's just a joke. According to *Newsweek* magazine: "Astronaut Scott Kelly's DNA 'was' altered by a year in space, results from NASA's Twins Study have confirmed. Seven percent of his genes did not return to normal after he landed, researchers found" (Hignett).

Since this chapter is the summary, it is helpful to revisit Chapter 10 and the interviewer-respondent dialogue in syllogism N14. In this instance, there has been a slight revision in presenting the dialogue, due the writer's added comments. Please note that the basic structure of the interviewer-respondent dialogue in syllogism N14 is unchanged from what is seen in Chapter 10. Again the syllogism was written on a card and reads as follows:

-All monkeys climb trees;
-The porcupine is a monkey (This premise is intentionally false).
-**Question:** Does the porcupine climb trees or not?

As the interview begins, with no electroshock, the respondent is asked to read and answer the above syllogism. The respondent answers by saying, **"It does not climb; the porcupine runs on the ground."** Notice that it is clear that the respondent knows the difference between a monkey and a porcupine. The interviewer asks, "And how does it look?" The respondent says, **"It is prickly."** Prickly means thorny. The interviewer asks, "It is like a monkey?" The respondent says, **"No, it is not."**

~ ~ ~

Then…after electroshock to the left hemisphere, the respondent is presented with the same syllogism and responds with emotional disgust, saying, **"Porcupine? How can it climb trees? It is not a monkey. It is prickly like a hedgehog. It's wrong here!"** [*The emotional-right hemisphere is active*]. Here we see emotions keep thoughts in the context of reality.

~ ~ ~

Next…the emotional right-hemisphere receives electroshock, and the same syllogism is presented. The respondent answers, **"The porcupine climbs trees since it is a monkey."** Notice the initial response is not reality-based. The interviewer then asks, "But is the porcupine a monkey?"

The respondent answers, **"No, the porcupine is prickly, like a hedgehog."** The interviewer asks, "Can it climb trees?" The respondent answers, **"No, it can't. Trees? It can't."** Notice that it took a little prompting (subtle influencing) to get the respondent to answer the question with a reality-based response [*analytical/logical left hemisphere is active here*].

~ ~ ~

When the interviewer *re-presents* the same syllogism while the respondent's emotional right-hemisphere is still suppressed, the respondent answers saying, **"Since the porcupine is a monkey, then it climbs trees."** The interviewer intervenes, saying "But you do know that a porcupine is not a monkey?" And the respondent replies, **"It is written so on the card."**

From this dialogue we see the limits of reason. At the same time, we can see how emotions keep thoughts in the context of reality. Remember when Egyptologist Shafer et al. stressed that in our species' first civilization [Ancient Egypt] "that which stood outside Maat was unreality or falsehood" (128). Is it not rather odd that the white race values falsehood? For example, stop at your local bookstore for a cup of tea or coffee and notice the large selection of fiction, mystery, science-fiction, and romance books; it's certainly a response to consumer demand! And what about Hollywood's big screen dramas, mysteries, romances, space-travel adventures, etc. We can add TV's soap operas, prime-time dramas, etc. Certainly we want to include our elementary and high school, and college miseducation, etc... We are slowly drowning in an ocean of falsehood in real-time daily: and our social institutions have been very busy, creatively, working professionally to ensure this socially-sanctioned falsehood is transmitted from our present generation to future generations, and around the world for political-military reasons. This is the case even with music. In speaking with professional lead-guitarist Clayton T. McLendon, who has played with several well-known musicians and singers during his active years, he mentioned that: "When I was a music education major in college, I had a class entitled, Forms and Analysis. This class broke down the essence of music into its component parts, and sadly generally what passes as music today doesn't even qualify as music in its most theoretical form, because music requires melody and harmonic structure and much of today's music has neither" (McLendon). It appears that since whites have accumulated a long history of avoiding truth they have become masters in the skill of applying falsehood. Traditional people did not and do not rely on fiction in the same sense that industrial people rely on fiction. For traditional societies, fiction could involve storytelling with an emphasis on moral teachings. Industrial societies have taken fiction very very far beyond this point. "Science fiction is literature that explores the impact of real or imaged developments in science or technology. The basic themes of science fiction includes time travel, space travel, marvelous inventions or discoveries, life in other worlds, and invasions of Earth by alien beings" (World Book v17, 205).

In the experiment "Meaning through Fiction: Science Fiction and Innovative Technologies," the authors had this to say: "<u>Our experimental evidence indicates that science fiction provides a clearer understanding of future technologies, which in turn facilitates the perceived connection between the technology and one's own life, resulting in a greater acceptance of this technology</u>" (Appel et al. 478). In a study, "The Future Imagined: Exploring Fiction as a Means of Reflecting on Today's Grand Societal Challenges and Tomorrow's Options," the authors explored:

> **...how speculative and creative fiction offer ways of embodying, telling, imagining, and symbolizing 'futures', that can provide alternative frames and understandings to enrich the grand (European Science Policy) challenges of the 21st century...** The study highlights how fiction sees oppression, inequality and a range of ethical issues linked to human and nature's dignity as central to, and inseparable from, innovation, technology and science. (Bina et al.)

The European Science Policy is a European intergovernmental research organization for the life sciences focusing on "*strengthening life science research in Europe and beyond*" while encouraging the mobility of researchers (EMBL). Cognitive scientist Merciera and Sperbera have mentioned that *reason* often leads to cognitive distortions and poor decisions. So, we must ask the questions, Can anything positive be derived from reasoning inside the context of fiction? Can it produce a balanced ecology? "Researchers are learning that we're prone to believe some lies even when they're unambiguously contradicted by clear evidence. These insights suggest that our proclivity (weakness) for deceiving others, and our vulnerability to being deceived, are especially consequential in the age of social media" (Bhattacharjee 38).

These findings have not gone unnoticed. *Post-truth politics* "is political culture in which debate is framed largely by appeals to emotions disconnected from the details of policy; and by the repeated assertion of talking points to which factual rebuttals (truths) are ignored. ...Oxford Dictionaries declared that its international word of the year in 2016 is "*post-truth*", citing a 2,000% increase in usage compared to 2015. Jennifer Hochschild, H.L. Jayne Professor of Government at Harvard University, has described the rise of *post-truth* as a return to 18th and 19th century political and media practices in the United States, following a period in the 20th century where the media was relatively balanced and rhetoric was toned down" ("Post-Truth"). It is my view that *the scholarly information herein has shown that the 20th century political and media practices have <u>never toned down</u>*!

For example, remember that Sir Francis Bacon was responsible for the celebration of inductive reasoning over deductive reasoning, with the approval of the Catholic Church. *In **inductive reasoning**, the premises are the evidence for the truthfulness of the conclusion, however *the premises may (or) may not be true.* Thus the conclusion "*may*" or "*may not*" be true. Consider the interviewer-respondent dialogue(s) in Chapter 10. Merciera and Sperbera has mentioned that "reason often leads to cognitive distortions and poor decisions." In the paper, "The Relationship between Memory and Inductive Reasoning: Does it Develop?" the authors disclose that there is "<u>considerable developmental continuity in the cognitive processes that underlie memory and inductive reasoning</u>" (Hayes et al). So is our tendency to reason inductively escalating? Feeney and Heit have stated inductive reasoning "corresponds to everyday reasoning." Since industrialized people's inductive reasoning de-emphasizes the subties of spiritual ideas and experiences, and the fact that we tend to lack cultural deductive reasoning experience: our moral reasoning and moral judgment fails to embrace the entire profundity (great depth and meaning) of our global environmental crisis, thanks to Francis Bacon and his Enabler, the Catholic Church. For further clarity we can turn to Australian-American inventor Saul Griffith, Ph.D.'s quote provided by professor emeritus David Owen, Ph.D. in his paper, "The Inventor's Dilemma:" "Al Gore (an American politician and environmentalist)...is the No.1 environmental hypocrite. His house alone uses more energy than an average person uses in all aspects of life, and he flies prodigiously. I don't think we can buy the argument anymore that you get special dispensation just because what you're doing is worthwhile" (qtd. by Owen 50). The Australian-American inventor continues: "Right now, the main thing I'm working on is trying to invent my way out of my own hypocrisy." Today, all of us find ourselves tasked with this same challenge. So my point regarding the European world's 20th century political and media practices not simmering down is quite self-evident by our continuous, unpausing, and intensifying use of inductive reasoning which is based on European logic. In the year 2017, the U.S. population was around 325 million people. Now just imagine, million(s) of industrialized people going about their daily lives giving priority to inductive reasoning! See Diagram 5.

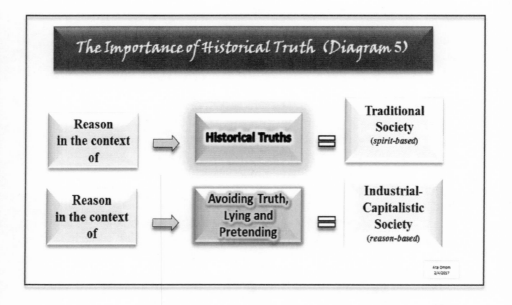

Please note that *in* **deductive reasoning**, the conclusion is based on *premises that are believed to be true or based on experience.* That said, it appear that deductive reasoning was underrated because deductive reasoning would be a roadblock to the advancement of the Enlightenment. Remember the Enlightenment had little or no room for truth or experience. Deductive reasoning helps us to better appreciate the fact that the "ability to generalize behavior-guiding principles and concepts from experience is key to intelligent goal-directed behavior. It allows us to deal efficiently with a complex world and to adapt readily to novel situations" (Miller et al.). Please note that deductive reasoning does not guarantee a conclusion will be true because a "sincere" belief can still be false; and this means we must learn to value truth and our experiences. It can improve our efforts in government and human affairs. Where is western knowledge taking us?? We can see where when we look at the technology: "technology has opened up a frontier for deceit, adding a twentieth (first) century twist to the age-old conflict between our lying and trusting selves" (Bhattacharjee 51). *The Enlightenment is robust and on the move!*

12.4 **Industrialism is an anti-Ecological Defense Mechanism (AEDM)**

We tend to hear that climate change is caused by greenhouse effect, global warming, increased carbon dioxide in the atmosphere, pollution, overconsumption and waste, etc. However, there is a need to put the cause of climate change into more succinct terms in order to improve the world's chances of success.

Climate change is said to be caused by *human activity*. What is the nature of this human activity? The National Academies of Sciences, Engineering, and Medicine state that "climate change is occurring; (it) is caused largely by human activities, and poses significant risks for a broad range of human and natural systems."[xx] The National Aeronautics and Space Administration states, "On Earth, human activities are changing the natural greenhouse. Over the last century, the burning of fossil fuels like coal and oil has increased the concentration of atmospheric carbon dioxide."[xxi] However, it is still possible to be even more succinct about the cause of climate change. It is extremely important to properly identify and define the cause in order to formulate an effective sustainable solution. Below an effort is put forth to clarify what is meant.

During the Age of Discovery, the European world traveled all over the globe exploring and discovering people of color with spiritual-cultures which dominated the globe. The vastness and profoundness of this occurrence was unexpected and mystifying as this new found predicament did not set well with whites' prior assumptions about the world. Haverkort and Reijntjes (12) have indicated that traditional people's knowledge *holistically* embraces the social, natural, and spiritual worlds at all levels. The fact that whites elected to celebrate a society in which reason is the foundation of all knowledge strongly suggests that a society in which spirit is the foundation of all knowledge was inhospitable to whites (despite it being humanity's tradition).

This conclusion that <u>whites viewed spirit-based societies as inhospitable</u> is based on neurologist Calne's opinion that "**reason is simply and solely a tool, <u>without any legitimate claims to moral content</u>. It is a biological product fashioned...to help us survive in an inhospitable and unpredictable physical environment**" (11-12). In creating their *reason-based society* and forcing it upon humanity tells us something about the psychic state of whites in their anti-human deed of being overly preoccupied with isolating and alienating traditional people around the globe from their spiritual bond with the biosphere and ecology, and then wanting to control how traditional people reacted to a spirit-less cultural environment. With such an arrangement racial tension WILL BE perpetual until this bond with the biosphere and ecology are restored!!

But this seems to not bother whites. In their study entitled, "Mad and Misleading: Incidental Anger Promotes Deception," Jeremy Yip, Ph.D., and Maurice Schweitzer, Ph.D., point out that "Anger promotes deception. When individuals feel angry, they are more likely to deceive others. We find that angry individuals are less concerned about the welfare of others, and consequently more likely to exhibit self-interested unethical behavior" (214).

The separation from the spirit-world has contributed to drastic changes in the morality of people of color, bringing us to a moral low. There are obvious barriers to addressing this problem because of the white race's clever preoccupation with avoiding historical truths, lying, and pretending. These three behaviors can be seen as defense mechanisms. In other words, <u>the white race's intellectual movement is a feature of the "anti-ecological defense mechanism (AEDM)" for survival in an animated-spiritual world and universe</u>.

This AEDM is opposite (antagonistic to) the ecological defense mechanism of traditional people. It is *anti* (against). It is a fruitless attempt to achieve security and peace in the world. Traditional people's ecological defense mechanism is consistent with honoring and respecting the spirits in living things, nature (i.e., water, air, earth, sun), and the universe. Here we will look at the anti-ecological defense mechanism from a politico-psychological perspective.

Bhattacharjee (50) points out that "if a fact comes in (to our mind) that doesn't fit into (our frame of reference, we will)…either not notice it, or ignore it, or ridicule it, or be puzzled by it, or attack it if it's threatening." So in response to an imaginary threatening spiritual world, white's devised the AEDM. This is to say, that the comprehensive AEDM consist of (a.) *white supremacy*, (b.) *white race's intellectual movement*, (c.) *Industrial Revolution*, (d.) capitalism and (e.) *imperialism*. These five defenses have minimized whites having to interface regularly with spiritual people, spiritual-natural environment, and the spiritual universe! In other words, white's AEDM minimizes the anxiety of living a daily moral and spiritual life. Steven Pinker, Ph.D., a professor of psychology at Harvard University, who researches cognition, social relationships and language and is the author of *Enlightenment Now: The Case for Reason, Science, Humanism, and Progress*, emphasizes that: "If there's anything the Enlightenment thinkers had in common, it was an insistence that we energetically apply the standard of reason to understanding our world, and NOT FALL BACK on generators of delusions like faith, dogma, revelation, authority, charisma, mysticism, divination, visions, gut feeling, or the (interpretation)…of sacred texts" (Pinker, 8). Pinker's point further adds support to my claim that whites seem to feel uneasy with having to live in spirit-based societies (which are humanity's tradition). I mean, whites have for centuries taken extraordinary steps to avoid spirit-based societies and spiritual people by actively destroying them worldwide with NO JUSTIFICATION, NO REMORSE, and seemingly NO UNDERSTANDING of the relevance of spiritual cultures in balancing Earth's Ecology. These cultures' origin is linked to HUNDREDS OF THOUSANDS OF YEARS of evolutionary experience of striving, surviving and learning how to live cooperatively physically, mentally, and spiritually within the local biosphere and ecology and universe. This long evolutionary journey cultivated our wise ancient ancestors' understanding of how to live in a socially acceptable manner from the standpoint of the personal (ego) and transpersonal (transcendental) self. The personal (ego) is worldly.

The transpersonal self godlike. *Oxford's Dictionary of Psychology* 2006, describes a defense mechanism as "a pattern of FEELINGS, THOUGHTS, or BEHAVIORS arising in response to a 'perception' of psychic danger" (194).

For millennia whites have had the opportunity to study and learn from traditional people's spiritual ways (i.e., Ancient Egyptian, Dogon, Bushman, Native American, Mayan, etc.) and the natural environment too!! Yet we find that the application of traditional people's knowledge in our society is not highly valued. What have whites done with the ancient wisdom acquired and studied over the centuries? After pondering ancient wisdom of traditional people whites *recorded it*, *falsified it* and/or *destroyed it*!

This is done to wipe out traditional people's true "spirital identity." The method used is to destroy traditional people's wisdom acquired from their history, culture, and values; and then replace their source for wisdom with an incompatible alien history, culture and values. In doing so, traditional people eventually loose sight of their true identity and so will everybody else.

Here are two examples that are sufficient for making the point. The Great Sphinx of Giza statue, one of the largest and oldest statues in the world, had its negroid-nose blown off. Some suggest it was done to remove visual evidence that shows Ancient Egypt was a black civilization. According to historian Ivan Van Sertima, Ph.D., the negroid-nose of the Great Sphinx of Giza in Egypt is hidden in the basement of the British Museum away from public's view. An eye-witness who personally saw the recognizable negroid-nose in the British Museum's basement and had pictorial evidence that encouraged Dr. Sertima to put together a team of scholars and they went to the British Museum and requested that the negroid-nose of the Great Sphinx of Giza be return to Egypt so it could be reinstalled on the Great Sphinx of Giza. The British Museum refused to honor their request. Sertima pointed out that Arabs in Egypt today are NOT eager to see the recognizable negroid-nose restored to the Great Sphinx of Giza, because the negroid-nose would prove to traveling tourists and world that modern day Arabs in Egypt are not the true descendants of the Ancient Egyptians. The real Ancient Egyptians and original builders of the Ancient Egyptian Civilization were BLACK AFRICANS (Sertima "Lecture").

German philosopher Georg W.F. Hegel, was known for his influence on Eurocentrism through his political and social philosophical views. Historian Teshale Tibebu, Ph.D. in his book, *Hegel and the Third World: The Making of Eurocentrism in World History*, gives us an example of Eurocentrism as a defense mechanism. Tibebu writes: "In his philosophy of world history, Hegel defines African existence as one confined in the sphere of natural immediacy. Africa is located in the state of nature, and Africans' life is fixated at the level of sense-certainty. This level of consciousness represents the lowest, poorest, and most abstract stage of consciousness" (Tibebu, 171). Hegel had similar views of other nonwhite racial groups, however not as harse. The point being made here is that European social and political philosophies concern themselves with issues that DEEPLY concern the white public. Apparently, a spiritual reality has never fit well into the frame of reference of many whites, so they repeatedly ridicule it. Their social and political philosophies function as an inquiry to understand how to survive in a spiritual world without FALLING BACK to humanity's spiritual indigenous traditions. After all, social and political philosophies are the study of social behavior and why there is a need for a particular political strategy, government, and laws. Political strategies are based on history. From an Eurocentrism perspective this means that whites political strategies are based on their historically insecure and worried relationships with nonwhite people, especially African people—and they govern and create and enforce laws and policies accordingly. African people have not emphasized this point on a widespread basis. Having not done so adequately has hindered many African children and teenagers' capacity to understand the nature and the reality of white supremacy in their local ecological environment.

This occurrence is due to having relinquished our indigenous worldview (African-centrism) and replacing it with an industrial-capitalistic worldview. Behavioral scientists agree that there are differences in worldviews amongst the races. This helps to explain why the African world is having difficulty in clearly seeing, communicating, organizing, and uniting to solve its global white supremacy problem. Let me clarify. From a temperamental standpoint feelings are extremely significant to African people; whereas, for European people feelings are significant to a much lesser degree. For example, Eurocentrism is a manifestation of "diminished power of feelings." The African-centrism is a manifestation of the "power of feelings." So for African people to sub-optimally reason in the context of Eurocentrism is insane.

If we reason with Eurocentrism to solve problems and Eurocentrism is a manifestation of "diminished power of feelings:" then reasoning in the context of Eurocentrism can not help African people to fully embrace their white supremacy problem. Being that we are overly preoccupied with Eurocentrism anyway, as the popular proverb says, "We are our own worst enemy." African-centrism and Eurocentrism both have values that are inherently antagiousness to each other (i.e., truth, communalism, cooperation, peace versus falsehood, individualism, competition, violence). If the Creator, by way of evolution, gave African people the "power of feelings" wouldn't it be sensible to use this God-given power to confront their white adversary. Remember that feelings have specific intra-psychic qualities (i.e., information and consciousness). African-centrism is a byproduct of intra-psychic qualities that have always been valued in government and human affairs by melanated people for millennia. With that said, I don't understand why continental Africa does not establish a mandated Continental Maat Public Policy before it is too late.

For example, the education that cultivates Eurocentrism is unable to embrace the full dimension of the human reality, due to DISREGARD for spirit/truth—which is EVERYWHERE IN THE UNIVERSE. It is this very type of education that created the industrial-capitalistic world and its unnatural and nonspiritual innovations! The perpetuation of this world with its innovations is called "PROGRESS" despite the fact this world is destroying our planet. However, inspite of this reality, many melanated people's so-called leaders encourage their people to find favor with the Eurocentric way of life?!! While on the other hand, the education that cultivates African-centrism is ATTENTIVE to and RESPECTFUL of the guiding consciousness of spirit/truth (Maat). Maat is the universal spiritual principle that regulates the universe, celestial heavenly bodies, nature, human affairs, and guided indigenous people's civilizations and cultures for millennia. African-centrism or the indigenous worldview is the holistic combination of: earthly wisdom of the personal (ego) self AND the spiritual/heavenly wisdom of the transpersonal (transcendental) self. Under the present state of the world it seems that nonwhite people, especially African people, would be eager to learn from and replicate their great historic beginnings before the origin of the Machine.

Generally speaking, it seems to not matter anymore to people of color that their cooperative participation in industrialism and capitalism has caused the extinction of many plants and animals, and the pollution of the air, water and land. Prior to contact with the white race, the air, water and Earth were viewed as a goddess and/or god and respected accordingly. But now we view *materialism* and the *enemy* as a friend; and *Nature* and the *friend* as our enemy. So, who is the enemy? The enemy will appear when we look into the mirror. And who is the friend? The friend will appear from inter-being[xxii] as a result of living a moral-spiritual life.

In this sense, our wise ancestors who adhered to God's prescribed spiritual ways would see us as defectors from the human species. The evidence is we continue to guide each successive generation down the path of industrialism and capitalism despite the fact that both are destroying the planet!! These generations have gone on to acquire prestige and power in the industrial-capitalistic society without understanding the importance of historic truths and moral responsibility to our ancient spiritual ways.

Giving consideration to our historical predicament, Professor of Africana Studies at the University of Maryland (UMBC) Anthony Browder, who has devoted 33 years researching ancient Egyptian history, science, philosophy, and culture raises a rather penetrating question that unveils the deep level of our on going dilemma. Browder's question should inspire all people of ALL RACES to look more cautiously at their leadership, especially African people. Browder, who is also the author of *Nile Valley Contributions to Civilization* asks:

> How do you respond to the faithful followers of a truthful man who presents a falsehood as a sacred fact. Particularly, when these people don't realize that the falsehood was derived from a falsehood which was derived from a falsehood which was derived from a falsehood which was derived from deliberate distortion of sacred truths? Just because a truthful person speaks a falsehood with

truthfulness and conviction doesn't make that falsehood any less false. (Browder)

The AEDM's process is synergistic and lethal in nature. By this it is meant that the process necessitates contact, blending, and injecting European values into a spirit-based society which leads to a multitude of social pathological manifestations in the spirit-based society. This means the factors that are essential for a spiritual culture to emerge: (a.) heredity and environment, (b.) the ability to be attentive to subtle energies in our surrounding environment, (c.) show favor or disfavor to the range of stimuli and events in our environment based on our genotype, and (d.) our degree of openness to sensations and experiences—have been diminishing! **This has made descendants of traditional people vulnerable because it is the vital forces of the entire universe that are the mediums of moral behavior** (Magesa).

There are three degrees of the anti-ecological defense mechanism: *Non-lethal degree* is concerned with the effectiveness of the AEDM to persuade and tame people-of-color to adjust and participate cooperatively in the reason-based society. This is the standard by which whites primarily evaluate race relations, and people of color are treated accordingly. The more tamed one is the more accommodating one is to the white supremacy culture and its values and immorality. One's lifetime labor in contributing to the white supremacy culture is futile in the sense that labor, in short and long-terms; benefits the children of the white oppressors far more than it benefits melanated children of people of color. This is another justification for a socially sanctioned National Maat Public Policy. *Quasi-lethal degree* is concern with imprisonment. *Lethal degree* is kill! There is no order in applying these degrees. The lethal degree can be applied first immediately after contact. A historical pattern of unprovoked mass extinction of traditional people, animals, and plant-life has been eye-witnessed and documented by many generations for centuries! For ecological reasons, it is important for *melanated* people—African people for sure—to act in a manner that is ecologically moral.

To do this there is the need for *melanated* people to be ecologically astute about the temperamental disposition of white people, as it enhances moral reasoning. In accessing past memories involving whites, the emotions associated with the experiences must be retrieved also in order to keep thoughts in the context of reality. This advocacy is not about hate! All living organisms learn from their experiences with their environment. For example, from experience we all know that bees can sting you. There is nothing wrong with knowing that.

Therefore children, teenager, adults, and elders know interacting with bees should be done cautiously. However we also know that bees pollinate beautiful flowers and agricultural crops. To know the pros and cons of our experiences with bees does not make us a lover or hater of bees *per se*, instead it makes us wiser in our interaction with bees. This knowledge of bees is beneficial to all mammals for obvious reasons. This knowledge about bees must be remembered *forever* for ecological reasons. Loss of memory of this ecological reality greatly increases the probability that we will be stung *again* and *again* and *again*. The above logic is applicable to whites as they too are a part of our ecology.

"The thrust toward superiority over people of color, the drive toward material accumulation, the drive toward a technological culture and the drive toward power are all cornerstones of the universal white supremacy culture...a response to the core psychological sense of inadequacy," states Psychiatrist Frances Welsing (10). Welsing is the creator of the Cress-Welsing theory (an analysis of white supremacy) and author of *The Isis Papers: The Keys to the Colors*. In another paper, "Outcasts in a White-Lie Society: Worlds of People with Negative Self-Conception," the scholars report that "behavioral scientists have long wondered why (people with) negative self-concepts and related psychological structures are so stubbornly resistant to change" (Swann et al. 622). They have found "that people with negative self-views may live in social worlds in which they are deprived of corrective feedback that could allow them to improve themselves."

University of South Australia's Professor of Strategic Management Subhabrata Banerjee, Ph.D., at the International Graduate School of Management, offers descriptive insight into this social world of domination in his paper "Corporate Social Responsibility: The Good, the Bad and the Ugly" writing:

The power of science and the scientific method in everyday discourse is an example of how science normalizes social and cultural realms, not because of the superior rationality of science but because of its procedures of normalization arising from its disciplinary power. This disciplinary power is not located at a 'legitimate' site of sovereignty or state but transmits itself through a complex system of institutions, regulations, texts, policies and practices signifying not relations of sovereignty (a government of the people) but relations of domination. (67)

While the above scholar offers a very helpful perspective on how the industrial-technological society works, Nobel Prize recipient and theoretical physicist Albert Einstein explains the ultimate aim of the industrial-technological society with its habitual disregard to how things were established by the act of creation: "The object of all science... is to co-ordinate our experiences and to bring them into a logical system" (qtd. by Welsing x). The logical system will most likely be based on the logic of the Machine rather than the logic of our spiritual temperamental disposition, biosphere, ecology, spirit world, and the universe. Zagorin adds that we should notice that when "imagining the unlimited technological progress to come from a renovated science... he (Bacon) did recognize the destructive effects that might accompany such progress. ...This conclusion...did not cause him to be more cautious...Bacon called the establishment of human dominion over the universe the noblest work of man" (226-227). Of course, for Bacon that really meant: the establishment of white dominion over the universe, wouldn't it??

Earlier Bacevich stated America's "ultimate objective is the creation of an open and integrated international order based on the principles of democratic capitalism, with the United States as the ultimate guarantor of order and enforcer of norms" (3). Such an objective means that all ethical people (white, yellow, red, brown, and black) must be expedient in embracing the whole historic truth of humanity before it is too late!! We need this information to keep us in touch with reality as a species.

Recently, NASA posted a job announcement for a planetary protection officer position (Job No. HQ17S0010). Salary is $124,406 to $187,000 per year. "Planetary protection is concerned with the avoidance of organic-constituent and biological contamination in human and robotic space exploration. NASA maintains policies for planetary protection applicable to all space flight missions that may intentionally or unintentionally carry Earth organisms and organic constituents to the planets or other solar system bodies and any mission-employing spacecraft, which are intended to return to Earth and its biosphere with samples from extraterrestrial targets of exploration. This policy is based on federal requirements and international treaties and agreements."[xxiii] In summary, it is a job to protect Earth from alien contamination. Question: *Now who will protect Earth from White Lies and the Machines*? See Diagram 6.

Whites' practice of resisting corrective feedback that could allow them to improve themselves has unfortunate consequences. Earlier while referring to moral development in military leadership, Professor Thomas pointed out that <u>compliance, moral understanding, moral maturity</u>, and <u>moral ambition,</u> in this order, were the four stages of moral development. He also emphasized that the "most important transitory step from the role of follower to that of leader is the step from <u>compliance</u> to <u>moral understanding</u>" (Thomas). "<u>Moral maturity</u> is not an end-state; rather, *it is the product of continuous evaluation.*" "<u>Moral ambition</u> is the final and ultimate stage of moral development." Moral ambition represents the pinnacle of *self-actualization*, he concludes. Moral reasoning precedes moral understanding; moral reasoning is the Mother of moral understanding!

Research indicates that the application of moral reasoning facilitates higher moral development! Rather than engaging in ego defenses all of time, it is wiser for us to engage in moral reasoning. In the paper, "Moral Reasoning in the Context of Ego Functioning," Kyle Matsuba, Ph.D., and Lawrence Walker, Ph.D., of the University of British Columbia reported that "present findings establish that moral reasoning can be embedded meaningfully in the broader context of personality functioning, that <u>development in moral reasoning</u> can be *predicted* clearly by <u>coping ego processes</u>, and that **moral stagnation** is *predicted* by reliance on **ego defenses**" (464-483). Stated differently, "the role of defense mechanisms in the development of moral judgment has been investigated, with striking results. In two longitudinal studies, it was found that **adolescents with strong (ego) defense use showed lower levels of moral judgment**" (Cramer 640).

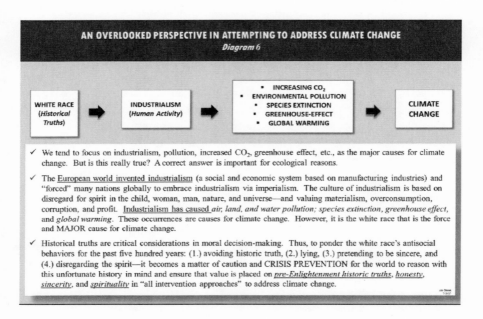

The effect of being: (i) resistant to spiritual guidance, (ii) unable to retrieve historical memory, (iii) resistant to change, and (iv) morally stagnant has caused us to become egoistic, spiritually numb, and BLIND to the fact that continuously without stopping or pausing: we are harming the planet. For example, the Machine culture can be seen in the same light as nuclear weapons. After all nuclear weapons are machines. According to the United Nations, "Nuclear weapons are the most dangerous weapons on earth. One can destroy a whole city...and... the natural environment..." (Nuclear). We also can turn to our usage of "light" in human affairs. The light bulb is a simple machine. "For three billion years, life on Earth existed in a rhythm of light and dark that was created solely by the Sun, Moon and stars. Now, artificial lights overpower the darkness and our cities glow at night... Less than 100 years ago, everyone could look up and see a spectacular starry night sky. Now, millions of children across the globe will never experience the Milky Way where they live. The increased and widespread use of artificial light at night is not only impairing our view of the universe, it is adversely affecting our environment, our safety, our energy consumption and our health" (Light).

"Light pollution poses a serious threat in particular to nocturnal (living things that are active at night) wildlife, having negative impacts on plants and animals physiology. It can confuse animal navigation, alter competitive interactions, change predator-prey relations, and cause physiological harm. The rhythm of life is orchestrated by the natural diurnal patterns of light and dark, so disruption to these patterns impacts the ecological dynamics" (Light "Wikipedia").

We may believe that information digital technology does not contribute to air pollution. Joel Gombiner, Ph.D., of Columbia University in his article, "Carbon Footprinting the Internet" reports that the "Information and Communication Technology (ICT) Industry is responsible for two percent of global $CO2$ emission, the same as aviation" (120). However, it is possible that the percentage "may be twice that of the aviation industry." Writer Anne Quito in her article, "Every Google Search Results in $CO2$ Emission" gives us another way of looking at Gombiner's point and our current lifestyle: "Every Google search comes at a cost to the planet. ...(T)he internet...actually relies on millions of physical servers in data centers around the world, which are connected with miles of undersea cables, switches, and routers all requiring a lot of energy to run. Much of that energy comes from power sources that emit carbon dioxide into the air as they burn fossil fuels."

In closing, this writer takes the stance that the AEDM is not just limited to white people anymore. It is also relevant to black, brown, red, and yellow people since we all are psychologically entangled and mesmerized by the AEDM—as skilled operatives of all degrees of the anti-ecological defense mechanism. It's difficult to argue away the fact that in comparison to how evolution shaped the ORIGINAL HUMAN SPECIES' temperamental disposition, that has been specified by the indefatigability of spiritual cultural behavior(s): 'today's industrialized people are just "little fellas and gals" when compared to our pre-colonial and pre-Enlightenment wise spiritual ancestors.'

U.S. Rep. Alexandria Ocasio-Cortez, D-N.Y., who calls for the establishment of a "Green New Deal" Policy that would transition our whole society from a fossil fuels energy system to renewable sources system (i.e., wind, sun light) "while creating a job guarantee program to facilitate the transition" (Grandoni): gives us a good perspective on the process by which our whole society can transition from a reason-based society to a spirit-based society. Even while the detail of the Green New Deal proposal is being researched and worked out, many voters and Democrat and Republican members of Congress already support the proposal goal. In this legislative process for the Green New Deal, or even, the National Maat Public Policy it is important that corporate values do not become the centerpiece of the legislative process. After all, we are trying to save our planet foremost, not the corporate world. Democrat and Republican legislators must reason ecologically, not corporately! Cornell University professor Hart earlier indicated that the goal is: "getting outside the current corporate straightjacket of central research and development." He continues, this means the "next sustainability challenge...is to become indigenous."

12.5 <u>Morality, Melanin, Biosphere and Universe</u>

Finally, all of this brings us back to Magesa's contention that "agent for moral action...are vital forces of the entire created universe, both visible and invisible worlds" (58). Our *auras, chakras, meridians, nadis* and *melanin* aid our connection to these vital forces. Melanin is found in all organisms (i.e., single-celled life form, plants, fish, birds, and mammals) and the biosphere. Melanin is found throughout the human body (i.e., melanocytes are in hair, eyes, nervous system, organs, and skin). "Melanin is able to transform light energy into chemical energy, and this has been accepted by the countries of the first world patent offices, which leaves no reasonable doubt about our finding," states Mexican Arturo Solis-Herrera, M.D., Pharm.D. (5), who holds doctorates in medicine and pharmacology.

While it is true that skin color is only one attribute of a race, Peter Schalock, MD, a dermatologist and assistant professor at Harvard Medical School, indicates that "Melanin is the brown pigment that produces the various shades and colors of human skin. Coloration (pigmentation) is determined by the amount of melanin in the skin. Without melanin, the skin would be pale white with shades of pink caused by blood flow through the skin. Fair-skinned people produce very little melanin, darker-skinned people produce moderate amounts, and very dark-skinned people produce the most."

According to associate professor of psychology at Clark-Atlanta University T. Owens Moore, Ph.D., "Melanin is black or dark in color" (33). "Melanin…absorbs and converts various forms of electromagnetic energy into energy states that can be used by the nervous system" (32). However, Moore emphasized that it is not "suggested that melanin can make one 'superior' to those who lack melanin" (37). However, he does go on to say "the absence of melanin in the brain (neuromelanin) can be deleterious."

"The melanins are a diverse class of multifunctional bio-macromolecules found throughout nature" (Watt et al. 3754). In their research paper "Supramolecular Structure of Melanin," professors Andrew Watt at University of Oxford, UK; Jacques Bothma at University of California at Berkeley, USA; and Paul Meredith at University of Queensland, Australia, acknowledge that there is "melanin in the biosphere" (3759). According to National Geographic, the "biosphere is made up of the parts of Earth **where life exists**."[xxiv] That would be **land** (the outer layer of the Earth), **water** on the surface of the Earth (oceans/seas/rivers/lakes), water in the ground, water in the air, and the **air itself** (atmosphere) which stretches above the land. "Eumelanin (the most abundant type of human melanin) is the most widely studied form of melanin because of its relevance to human health and wide occurrence in the biosphere" (Watt et al. 3755). This would seem to help explain why most people tend to seek to bond with the biosphere. According to Harvard biologist Edward Wilson, Ph.D., "Our physiology and our minds are adapted for life in the biosphere." (17). People with pigmented skin represent 80 percent of the world's population (Chaplin). Our spiritual anatomy and melanin connect us to the biosphere. "From the depth of the developing zygote (fertilized cell) to the vastness of the dark universe, melanin may be the link between the material and spiritual realms of existence" (Moore 24). When we protect the biosphere and universe, we ARE essentially protecting *ourselves*, the human family and all life!!

Welsing affirms that "...Melanin is a superior absorber of all energy. The fact that whites lack melanin may also help to explain why they have quite a different concept and understanding of God...and why, in the view of many non-white peoples, they lack 'spirituality' and the capacity to tune in to, and thereby establish harmony and justice in the universe. Because they lack the melanin sensory system, they cannot intuit that ALL is ONE" (Jones "Color" 171).

In our world of white supremacy it is important to keep the following into proper perspective: Empathy is the ABILITY to relate to other's feelings (i.e., plants, animals, humans). Feelings are energies which have intra-psychic qualities (VandenBos). Melanin absorbs all energies that can be used by the nervous system (Moore). Being open and empathetic to energies of the spirit world, celestial heavenly bodies, air, water, land, plants, animals [including humans] is the prerequisite for moral action (Magesa). Skin coloration is determined by the amount of melanin in the skin (Schalock). The original human species [Africans] has the most melanin. It is then clear that African people especially, and other people-of-color, have the unavoidable DUTY to be influential moral leaders and outspoken voices in the world's fight to address climate change.

We need to approach climate change from a different perspective, humanity's traditional perspective, if we seriously intend to be successful. In the book *Beyond a Western Bioethics: Voices from the Developing World*, the following is cited: "Conscience is the other self a deep thought that may not have an appeal to the western analytic mind. Interestingly, Filipnos world perceive that *budhi* (conscience)" (Alora et al. 55) as "the innermost core of mankind's being: *kalooban*. Kalooban may be roughly translated as the will. It is the seat of the individual's innermost thoughts and feelings." The authors continues: "thus, for Filipinos, conscience is related to the 'heart' where one can relate with God and one's inner self rather than to the mind."

Buddhist Zen Master Thich Nhat Hanh adds, "To see one in all and all in one is to break through the great barrier which narrows one's perception of reality, a barrier which Buddhism calls the attachment to the false self" (48). Because of this "false self" the "United States with its love of big cars, big houses, and blasting air-conditioners, has contributed more than any other country (in the world) to the atmospheric carbon dioxide that is scorching the planet" (Gillis front page).

With that said, shouldn't it be industrialized people's task to find their compassionate Truer Self. Reflecting on his life experiences, Nobel Prize recipient Dalai Lama (whose religion is Buddhism) had this to say in a meaningful and friendly discussion with Nobel Prize recipient Bishop Desmond Tutu: "After meeting with so many people, thinkers, scientists, educators, healthcare professionals, social workers, and activists... **it is clear that the only way to truly change our world is through teaching compassion**" (Dalai Lama et al., 296). He continues, "Religion is not sufficient. ...So now we have to think seriously. Just to pray or rely on religion faith is not sufficient. ...No matter how excellent, no religion can be universal. So we have to find another way... I think the only way really is....through education. Education is universal. ...**We must teach them that the ultimate source of happiness is within themselves**. Not machine. Not technology. Not money. Not power" (297).

What is compassion? Compassion is understanding, goodwill, generosity, sensitivity, love, care, kindness, sympathy, empathy, pity, benevolence, mercy, warmth, tenderness... The above listed behaviors are best (1.) taught, (2.) cultivated and (3.) sustained in a real-world ethical society. The Machine, technology, money and power are substitutes for the European world's seemingly difficulty to coexist in a compassionate society. In most cases the Machine, technology, money, religion, and greed for power are merely lures (bait), decoys, and/or enticements that are functioning to keep you confused and distracted from your (always) present compassionate nature which is the building block for our spiritual society. Compassion comes from within.

12.6 <u>Beyond the World of Materialism:</u> <u>*Re-Embracing the Spirit World*</u>

In closing, Bacon did not foresee that "he would be called the architect of the modern world's dilemma" or that "'his efforts to establish the Kingdom of Man would come to be regarded as destructive by precisely those generations that inhabit it'" (Zagorin 121). **Today Bacon is viewed as the false prophet who led "mankind to the wilderness of materialism."** This brings to light one of Historian John Henri Clarke's quotes:

> *All too long we have been following people who don't know where they are going. We have to decide where we are going. We have to reject terminology. We have to reject the concept that we are a minority. We have to realize that we are a world people. We must liberate ourselves from depending on other people and reestablish ourselves in the world as a sovereign and self-governing people by any means necessary.* (Freeman 544-545)

If closing the temples of Egyptian mysteries triggered "intellectual darkness (that) descended over Christian Europe and the entire Greco-Roman world in the AD 500's for many centuries" (Sertima 11), one would think that this would be instructive to white people. Not being able to flourish after the closing of the Egyptian's temples of mysteries should inform us that the spiritual way is best for everyone, it is necessity. Then what about the European's resurrection from the depth of the Dark Ages due to the benevolence of the Black Africans who did all they could to civilize and reacquaint whites with humanity's spiritual traditions AGAIN. It is true lies have taken the white race very very far. Nonetheless, now we must be high-minded and learn from our transgressions and reconnect with the practice of learning from history to evaluate the present in order to find moral instructions (Zagorin 206).

Now we should be accepting of the fact that, "Self-concepts vary according to the extent to which a person identifies the self as (1) an autonomous (*self-ruling*) individual, (2) an *integral part of humanity*, and (3) an *integral part of the universe as a whole*" (Cloninger et al., "Psychobiological"). It is the latter two that have been alienated by the European world. Recall it was our concept of an unlimited, orderly, holistic and spiritual differentiated whole universe with values, perfection, harmony, meaning, and moral aim that ruled our concept of the nature of being (Zagorin 127-128). It must be restored as we now know that "Contemporary science reveals a spectrum of reality extending from visible to invisible, from particles to wave functions, from mass to energy…to life-force and psi-force (supernatural). Some societies and cultures, ancient or modern, give more value to one end or the other of the spectrum" (Crosley 4).

"Becoming a virtuous (moral) agent entails the practical refinement of predispositions *in situ* (those unactualized spiritual characteristics) as a member of a ***community of practitioners*** rather than entailing a normative ethical educational project seeking an intellectual resolution of abstract moral questions" (Smith "Virtue" 351). Such an environment ensures the cultivation of a moral ambitious society.

Furthermore, psychiatry now informs us that the ability to (a) direct oneself, (b) cooperate with others, (c) control ones impulses, and (d) self-transcendence are attributes of a healthy personality (Cloninger, "Practical" 99-108). The American Psychological Association defines self-transcendence as "the state in which an individual transcends preoccupation with the self and is able to devote him or herself fully to another person, work, cause, or activity" (VandenBos 833). According to Dr. Filip De Fruyt et al., "*self-transcendence* dimension refers to the experiencing of spiritual ideas" (443).

"Self-transcendence involves the spontaneous feeling of participation in one's surroundings as a unitive whole. It is associated with wise judgement, humble, equanimity (calm), and selfless spirituality, as opposed to egocentric rational materialism. **Individuals who are highly transcendent often report frequent periods of joyful unity and creative inspiration that they do not attribute to self-directed analysis**" (Cloninger, "Temperament" 270). Remember former-President Jomo Kenyatta, Ph.D., in his anthropology study, *Facing Mt. Kenya: The Tribal Life of the Gikuyu* stated that prior to contact with whites, "Their daily lives, both individuals and groups, are influenced at all points by *belief in the supernatural*" (222). He also emphasized that the people were *happy people*!

Social behaviors for living in the spiritual culture include being open-minded, experienced, not easily deceived, moral, trustworthy, loving, cooperative, sincere, and introspective. These behaviors facilitate

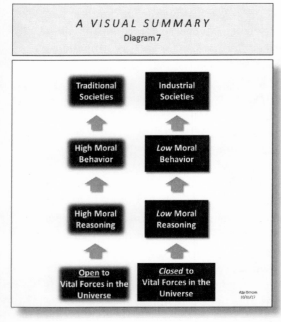

A VISUAL SUMMARY
Diagram 7

Traditional Societies

Industrial Societies

High Moral Behavior

Low Moral Behavior

High Moral Reasoning

Low Moral Reasoning

Open to Vital Forces in the Universe

Closed to Vital Forces in the Universe

bonding and our becoming an integral part of the universe. Specifically, such occurrence makes us more susceptible to subtle spirits that are ever present. In the study "Experimental Dream Telepathy-Clairvoyance and GeomagneticActivity" by Michael Persinger, Ph.D., of Laurentian University (Ontario), and Stanley Krippner, Ph.D., of Saybrook Institute (California), the researchers emphasized the context for studying telepathic-clairvoyant experience in the laboratory setting, stating that "the best index for the study of anomalous (supernatural) behavior of laboratory subjects would be one based on readings from a magnetometer in or adjacent to the laboratory itself. *Optimally, these readings should be considered in relationship to solar and lunar effects, competing electromagnetic field effects, and biological cycles of the subjects being studied.*" Here we have evidence that the biological, electromagnetic, lunar, and solar energies "together" are a larger sphere of reality that is present for us to reason.

For a real-world illustration of reasoning in the context of distant stars, planets, the sun and moon we can turn to the Dogon. "The different Dogon tribes have each specialized in the study of a particular domain of the sky: the Ono study Venus; the Dommo, Orion's shield (brightness); the Aru, the moon; and the Dyon, the sun. Thus the Dogon have the lunar, solar, and sidereal calendars just like the Egyptians" (Diop "Civilization" 318). 'Sidereal' means distant stars. Educational psychologist and Egyptologist Asa Hilliard, Ed.D., a former chairman and dean of the Department of Education at San Francisco State University, reports on a highly significant historical truth that the reader may want to remember forever. Furthermore, maybe all of us will want to take the responsibility to ensure that Hilliard's message is widespread in our present generation and is transmitted to future generations! We can say his research is highly significant because Africa is the birthplace of our species and the place of origin of the first human civilization. However, more so because it gives us some clarity about the temperamental disposition of the First People on earth as established by the act of creation. This knowledge must be digested by this generation because this historic truth will help to keep our thoughts in touch with reality. More importantly, the forthcoming is an indication of being connected with and obedient to God's will and the desire to respond by reciprocating. Surely, Generation X and the Millennials will agree that the practice indicated below means it is wise for America to have an annual "National Awareness Month for the 'First People on Earth'" to commemorate and review the many superlative examples they have left for us to follow and measure our successes, as a society and members of the human species. Hilliard reveals that:

> Abundant oral and written records exist to describe the history of education on the African continent, especially its ancient and indigenous forms. ...(A)n educator who wishes to understand indigenous Africa, must understand how education was conducted in the Nile valley complex. In fact, world education systems, including the Western world, must understand the Nile valley cultures to understand themselves. Africans regarded the education process as a transformative process, one in which a person becomes not only schooled but socialized. A person becomes different, a person becomes more 'godlike,' more human, by virtue of the cultivation rendered through the education and socialization process. It was a process rooted in a world view where there was a belief in human perfectibility, the belief that humans could indeed become more like god. Basic skills were merely the lowest level of education. The development of character, humaneness and spirituality were higher levels of attainment. (Hilliard "Education" 6-9)

Godlike means blessed, angelic, heavenly, celestial, supernatural, etc. Today, there is agreement that self-concept can be individualistic, humanitarian, and/or godlike (Cloninger "Psychobiological'). The above historical truth and psychiatric opinion implies that we have dormant (unseen) potentials that were given to us by an act of creation. These unseen potentials can be cultivated in a real-world ethical environment. Children must start learning AGAIN about how the diverse plants, insects, birds, and wildlife help to shape our local natural ecology; and learn about the songs, sounds, beauty, and the diversity of the architectural constructs (i.e., natural habitats) of insects and wildlife and their harmonious way of life with the local biosphere and ecology. We are urgently tasked with the responsibility, as a species, of re-learning about our natural spiritual relationship with the air, water, land, plants, insects, wildlife, human community, and celestial (heavenly) bodies. Our cultural and moral lives and concept of time must be dominated and regulated by living holistically and harmoniously with the rhythm of our biological clocks, biosphere (i.e., atmosphere, air, water, land), celestial heavenly bodies (i.e., moon, sun, planets, stars), and all living things. Not by the machine called mechanical clock. We are so industrialized that we must re-learn to respect the seasonal migration rhythms of those living things which depend on certain aspects of the biosphere: water (i.e., tunas, whales, sharks, dolphins); land (i.e., bears, wolves, deer, buffalos, humans, imsects); air (i.e., living things, plants); atmosphere (i.e., ducks, owls, red cardinals, eagles, hummingbirds, sea gulls)— because seasonal migration rhythms have a link to the status of all living things' food security, and these living things play diverse specialized roles in our ecosystems through migration. Within their specialty roles these PLANTS (plants can migrate) and animals can do a much better job balancing the ecology than ANY industrialized people! Ok, what is industrialized people's specialty in helping to balance the ecology?? We lost our indigenous specialty when we became industrialized and capitalistic. So now who is ecologically smarter: animals and plants (or) industrialized people? Answer: the animals and plants! We cannot and must not allow corporations to continue to dominate our cultural and moral lives by invading our mental and social space with their many unnecessary artificial replications of nature and environmentally hazardous, disease-causing innovations.

According to Vietnamese sage Hanh, "You carry Mother Earth within you. She is not outside of you. Mother Earth is not just your environment. In that insight of **inter-being**, it is possible to have real communication with the Earth, which is the highest form of prayer."[xxv] "President Carter, in a speech to college students in Atlanta in September 1995, is quoted by Reuters as saying that during his administration, a plane went down in Zaire and a meticulous sweep of the African terrain by <u>American spy satellites failed to locate</u> any sign of the wreckage. It was then 'without my knowledge' that the head of the CIA (Admiral Stansfield Turner) <u>turned to a woman reputed to have psychic powers</u>. As told by Carter, '*She gave some latitude and longitude figures. We focused our satellite cameras on that point <u>and the plane was there</u>*'" (qtd. by Puthoff, 75). It is interesting how the white world seems interested in superhuman powers for selfish reasons, however have not historically allow these normal super human abilities to flourish.

Religious leaders must understand that all people need a spiritual bond with the melanin-saturated local biosphere and the universe— rather than religious sermons. Here the people can have their own heartfelt oration to share with humanity about the awe, splendor, and wisdom derived from ACTUALLY living in harmony with the spirit of the local biosphere (and its diverse life-forms) and universe. This will replace those religious sermons that encourages passiveness and trust that the *Lord is coming soon to deliver the believers* from the white world's social experiment! Educators must see that optimal human potential has a greater grandeur and proficiency than western science, technology, engineering, mathematics (STEM) combined! We already have physicists, mathematicians, chemists, architects, engineers, astronomers, ship navigators, space astronauts, etc. What we desperately need now are human goddesses and gods! Ignoring this point will not make the need go away. Elected-political officials should acknowledge the fact that America is a white supremacy nation. Racism is inherent in our political, economic, legal, religious, educational, and healthcare systems. White and nonwhite politicans must retrieve this valuable historic truth, along with cultural relativism in representing their constituents in: sponsoring and co-sponsoring bills, talking with lobbyists, debating legislation, making laws, spending taxpayers' money, promoting national unity, and in working to solve social problems. The result is enhanced moral reasoning, moral judgment, and moral action. Foremost elected officials at the local, state, and federal levels must now be more responsive to the spiritual needs of their constituents and the natural environment through the sincere vigorous advocacy for a national spiritual way of life and indigenous people. After all, our spiritual disposition has been well-documented by researchers, scholars, experts, and sages around the world: genetically (Hamer), anatomically (Gerber), psychiatrically (Welsing; Cloninger), socio-psychologically (Haverkort and Reijntjes), politically (United Nations), anthropologically (Kenyatta), historically (Hilliard; James; Crosley), spiritually (Hanh; Magesa; Dossey), and medically (Gerber; Greenwood). Thus, for elected-political officials to be NEGLIGENT in this area is a display of moral incompetence.

WE THE PEOPLE, must ensure that our elected-officials at the local, state, and federal levels give the proper attention to the appropriateness of the environments and psycho-social factors (Oreland et al.), because our genes can influence our response to a particular environment since "inherited characteristics (tend to better) fit with some environments than with others" (Reiss et al.).

~ ~ ~

Chapter 13
Conclusion

Whether we use Ta-Seti's date of 17,700 years ago or 5117 years ago (3100 BC) for when civilization began, we know conclusively that the Black Ancient Egyptians were the builders of humanity's first quasi-divine civilization that endured for more than three millennia as an admired and respected civilization. We also know that Ancient Egypt eventually culturally collapsed due to envy, greed, and repetitive invasions from outsiders. By this time, Ancient Egypt had already given the world science, historiography, astronomy, navigation, map-making, shipbuilding, agriculture, craftsmanship, architecture, geometry, calendar-making, art, philosophy, mathematics, writing, administration, medicine, 42 Principles of Maat (code of conduct), law, quasi-divine civilization and much more. Ancient Egypt was a HIGHLY SPIRITUAL CIVILIZATION and Maat proved its effectiveness in government decision-making and human affairs for over three millennia as COMMON LAW. Maat's universal spiritual principles are reflected in the indefatigability of indigenous people's spiritual-cultural ways globally.

The reader may still be questioning the importance of Maat today?? Can we learn from the fact that the European world descended into intellectual darkness from about AD 500's to AD 1500's (an estimated one thousand years). In regard to the beginning of the Dark Ages, John Freely, Ph.D. writes: "The Greco-Roman world was coming to an end, overwhelmed by the onslaught of the 'barbarians,' its ancient gods and learning (from Ancient Egypt) eclipsed by the rise of Christianity" (17). This caused religious wars, military expeditions, disappearance of civilization, and barbarism. WHY did this happen?? This happened because the European world concluded that ANCIENT WISDOM of INDIGENOUS PEOPLE was not necessary for the progress of human knowledge AND confidentially "closed down the temples of Egyptian mysteries" (Sertima). Roman Emperor Theodosius I, a Christian, had earlier ordered the closing of the temples with an imperial decree in AD 391 (Freely 18). It was the Africans who eventually rescued the European world culturally and established and built many of their first major universities. Eventually over a period of time the unforseeable wretched events occurred—Christian Crusades a period of religious wars; European Renaissance an early period of recovery from barbarism toward civility; Age of Discovery a period of European global exploration, discovery, extermination, and exploitation of indigenous people and their natural resources; Age of Enlightenment a beginning period of the European world falsifying knowledge globally; Transatlantic Slave Trade a period when HUNDREDS OF MILLIONS OF AFRICANS (Rodney) died in Atlantic Ocean being transported from Africa to the Americas on slaves ships to work as slaves for nefarious white people; Age of Industrial Revolution a period when the forced-labor of surviving Africans was use to make the industrializing World powerful and rich and when the agricultural economy was replaced by the Machine economy; and finally, Age of Imperialism a period of industrialized countries controlling and exploiting the governments, cultures and natural resources of third world countries. Yes, indeed "lies" have taken the white race very very far—but in the wrong direction!

By successfully forcing humanity to relinquish their focus and guidance away from the ever present invisible subtle spirit-world, with reason as the foundation of all knowledge whites now are better able to manage how people think because they form the logic template for reasoning. The design of the structure of the logic template is POLITICALLY MOTIVATED. It is advantageous to recognize that our rules of cognition (reasoning) are consistent with the ruling class' political goals. Thus, we are reasoning against our divine indigenous voice, thus against future generations. The method used to implement, propagate, and sustain the white supremacy intellectual movement from past generations to our present time "necessarily" involves "daily" avoidance of historic truths, lying, and pretentiousness all while creating philosophies, theories, knowledge, science, and innovations that are necessarily a byproduct of a mixture of intentional lies, truth, guesses and generalizations. In doing so, the white race has created a social world that appears to be more accommodating to psychopaths than to traditional people. In spite of this, we find ourselves still clinging to this comparatively psychopathic way of life and show scorn toward humanity's spiritual way of life—in the midst of a potential global ecological cataclysm that has been generated by the white race's science (the "quiet" anti-ecological storm).

Because our species' historic truths have been turned upside-down, subsequently our moral compass has been mis-directed by an "immoral environment" that we seek to fit into in order to satisfy our basic human needs: we are now unclear about the moral-spiritual dimensions of human behavior; believing materialism, money, competition, and individualism are the paths to happiness and spiritual fulfillment. We mistakenly accept the notion that living in a world of big and tiny Machines is progress, and living in harmony with the natural environment and universe is primitive?! The oddity of this view can be highlighted when we apply economic-historian Arnold Toynbee's recommended test: "Does it fit in with the urgent present requirements of human nature?" Doesn't it look like future generations will unfairly inherit our present dilemma?

After all our social institutions are working to ensure that our behavioral and relationship patterns are interwoven and function no higher than at the personal (ego) level. At this level we are concerned with personal power, self-esteem, and self-perception based on society's expectations and rewards (i.e., money, power, materialism, fame). Gail Berger, Ph.D., states that the desire for tangible or intangible SOCIAL REWARDS when obtained elicits a sense of well-being and feelings of happiness; failure in this regard elicits negative well being and associated feelings. Berger continues: "intangible" social rewards such as receiving · a desired hug, acceptance, validation from another "have been described as 'human needs' and are likely hard-wired and genetic." Our society is exploiting this HARD-WIRED need by rewarding us with money, materialism, power, and fame for staying at the personal (ego) level. We experience well-being and feelings of happiness, however we are still spiritually unfulfilled and enslaved. The white America prefer that people of color, especially African people, are happy and experience well-being staying at personal (ego) level and in religious turmoil rather than being spiritually fulfilled and FREE!! Research informs us that strong ego use lowers our moral judgment. From our transpersonal viewpoint LIVING A LIFE of truth, justice, righteousness, balance, harmony, reciprocity and order is the only social reward that give us that authentic feeling of happiness and well-being. This is because the transpersonal self as our "more highly evolved form of consciousness" is in union with the universe (Winkelman, "Abstract"; Hilliard).

This should tell us that we are one with creation, in the same sense our body parts (i.e., heart, lungs, kidneys) are one with the body. Each body part is a part of the same body. This means humanity must re-cultivate and/or learn the fundamental understanding that humanity must perceive of itself and its activities only by reference to the whole creation. This can help us to find our purpose for being. By not striving to adhere to this understanding has caused us to reason upside-down and this is why humanity cannot solve the "European globally produced problems." We are internally connected to the energetic universe (i.e., Earth, planets, and stars). We must also factor in the fact that melanin is an absorber of all energies. Melanin is present in the biosphere (air, water, land). Melanin is present in all living things. Melanin is significant to our health and moral action.

Our spiritual anatomy and melanin help make possible a relationship with the many cosmological systems which situate possible union amongst humans, natural environment and supernatural. The experience of the experience, if within our conscious awareness, can be meaningful and one may interpret it and describe it in the form of human attributes (i.e. forest, peaceful; deer, friendly; moon, romantic; sunset & flowers, beautiful; a hurricane, ferocious; a breeze, nice; a well-known star cluster, Seven Sisters; spirit, helper; etc.). This behavior is said to be common for humans. This is known as anthropomorphism. If we were to engage in this behavior routinely as a society with emotional sincerity we would improve our relationship with our local ecology. Next, in most traditional societies the belief was/is all natural things and natural phenomena (i.e., air, water, plants, rocks, animals, thunder, earthquakes, forest fires, celestial bodies, universe) has a spirit (soul). In this context with the cosmological systems these collectively play an ongoing role in organizing the biosphere, ecology, and universe. This belief is known as animism. In summary, this is an open-ended brief perspective on our "old ontology." Next, in humanity's long-lasting quasi-divine civilization the two most important aspects of kingship was "divinity" and "unification!" Divinity is receiving insight and judgment through supernatural means.

Patristic specialist Donald Fairbairn, Ph.D., indicates that: "From a Western point of view, the first issue which one must consider in formulating theology is that of Authority. ...As soon as we ask about authority...we discover that this question is inappropriate.... Because of the difference....(in views) of reality...." (Fairbairn 11). For example, "...Protestantism located authority with Bible alone and Roman Catholicism with the Church hierarchy (principally the pope himself)..." (12). Here we can see that authority is an object. However, quoting theologian Vladimir Lossy, Fairbairn continues with the following that is complementary to our species' tradition, he writes: "God no longer present himself as object, for it is no more a question of knowledge but of union" (qtd. by Fairbairn 52). We have discussed OUR spiritual anatomy. According to medical doctor and acupuncturist Michael Greenwood, M.D.: "Many people live from the first 3 (lower) chakras, NEVER accessing the transcendent resources of the Heart and upper centers" (27). Couldn't we say this occurrence has an exceptionally high probability of being related to our daily ongoing De-Enlightenment and further emphasizes the need for the intervention of a National Maat Public Policy for its mind, body, spirit therapeutic benefits, for example: "The HEART, as the sovereign (ruler) of the body-mind-spirit...functions to integrate the personal (ego) and the transpersonal (truer self) into a unified whole." Earlier in Chapter 7, it was pointed out that the first step to initiate this transformative process involves unconditional love. This is INSTRUCTIVE in terms of the need to reevaluate our legal, political, educational, health, economic, cultural, familial, and religious social institutions and their missions. This is to say, all social institutions must highly value this transformative process as it is the gateway to our lost "old" ontology that we need so dearly to re-establish a paradise on Earth.

This transformative process make possible a clearer perception of the true nature of our reality as it gives access to our transcendental point-of-view through our upper chakra centers. The following provides a perspective on the transformative process. Full body sculptures of pharaohs and royalty in Ancient Egypt are commonly portrayed with the left foot symbolically moving forward. Our heart is located more on the left side. The left foot moving forward symbolizes MAKE WAY FOR THE HEART the ruler of our body-mind-spirit functions!! Since unconditional love opens the heart to our upper centers, then the strategy for making the way for the heart is strample down bigotry and wickedness.

Remember in the latter part of Chapter 4, a perspective on the African personality was presented which reflects union. It is from one of the oldest spiritual text in the world, Pyramid Text of King Unas: "Thou are pure, thy bones are the gods and goddesses of heaven, thou existest at the side of God, thou art unfastened, thou comest forth toward thy soul." And what about the Tibetan mystic's statement: "To the enlighten man...whose consciousness embraces the universe, to him the universe becomes his body, while his physical body becomes a manifestation of the universal mind, his inner vision an expression of HIGHER REALITY, and his speech an expression of ETERNAL TRUTHS and mantric powers."

What are the upper centers? The upper centers are the throat chakra which is the voice of the body which emerges without reason, forehead (third-eye) chakra is associated with psychic abilities "inner vision that sees the truth directly" (31). Here, there is no reason! And crown chakra blossoms open to the Ultimate Void/Divine. It is through your union that "knowing is experienced as being," states Greenwood. There is no reason! Remember neurologist Calne stated, "reason is simply and solely a tool, without any legitimate claim to moral content. It is a biological product fashioned...to help us survive in an inhospitable and unpredictable physical environment." Thus, reason's appropriateness in an industrialized society is clearer. However, reason is less needed in a spirit-based society because the society would be preoccupied with striving to live life in harmony with the cosmological systems rather than with corporations' values; thus experiencing less social difficulties, complications, and uncertainties. Since it is clear that REASON CANNOT DEVELOP HUMANITY'S HIGHER FACULTIES, humanity must now turn to that which will develop humanity's higher faculties. Our Heart opens the way to a higher form of self-expression and listening, psychic powers (ESP), and Universal Mind. This is The Way. Physician Gerber has indicated that the "true nature of reality is beyond the scope of our ordinary sensory channels" (i.e., smell, touch, taste, hearing, vision). The Way, as a "transformational experience in which the ego **temporarily** is transcended" (Greenwood 30), can revive humanity's understanding, appreciation, and interactions amongst all living things in their ecological environments, thus improving our adjustment to life and the True Nature of Being. Hence, the present urgent requirement of human nature is the restoration of spiritual traditions and cultures in order to re-establish our natural bond!!

Ethnic and racial groups in America have been searching for spiritual fulfillment for centuries. It has been demonstrated that this can only be "obtained" and "sustained" in a spirit-based society. This writer has proven that Americans live in a reason-based society and has provided sound justifications as to why *all* American people must live in a spirit-based society as spiritual beings!! Now that we know what the problem is, and know what the solution is: What are we going to do?? For a good start we can familiarize ourselves with the 42 Principles of Maat (E.A. Wallis Budge's translation) and advocate for a National Maat Public Policy!! **Regardless of how one chooses to reason, one's education level, or one's income status—running away from a spiritual way of life in a spiritual world and universe IS NOT a solution.** Instead it is irrevocably anti-life and the definitive problem!

A public policy is a strategy that benefits the whole society; its principles are reflected in the U.S. Constitution; and its principles effect the process of making law, and the execution and interpretation of law. If needed, the American people can have the Constitution amended to make it more complete and supportive of a National Maat Public Policy. This should not be a problem assuming that the majority of the democrat and republican Members of Congress have a self-concept that is an integral part of humanity [humanitarian] and/or an integral part of the universe as a whole [godlike]—and NOT individualistic and self-ruling (Cloninger). A public policy regulates the whole society's behavior. Because the federal government policies and decisioning strategies have been ineffective in complementing the spiritual temperament of the American people—a mandated National Maat Public Policy is the most effective, dignified, and honorable way to improve our social interactions—as a nation—in the 21st Century.

❖ A <u>National Maat Public Policy</u> is a government administrative and management decision-making strategy, which gives forthright consideration to the spirits of children, women, men, nature, and universe in addressing government and human affairs.

As such, it is expedient for the supreme legislative body of this nation—the U.S. Congress—to lay aside this nation's historical legacy of unrestrained willingness to engage in lawmaking with favoritism to transnational corporation (TNC) and the wealthy, while overlooking the spirit in children, women, men, natural environment and universe, FOREVER!

In conclusion, it is especially important that every local, state, and federal politician (even the U.S. President) know that they too are a "victim" or "perpetrator" of the European De-Enlightenment. Therefore it has been recommended that all politicians give attention to the National Maat Public Policy decision-making strategy!! A **National Maat Public Policy** will <u>drastically reduce</u> the workload of legislative, judicial, and executive branches of the *federal, state* and *local* governments while also reducing government expenditures. This policy can generate a NEW ETHICAL STANDARD IN INTERNATIONAL DIPLOMACY that will improve the world's chances of achieving sustainable peace. Because world governments will also discover the rich and enduring benefits of this proven efficient and effective government decision-making strategy in addressing human rights, corporate crimes, and climate change. These three concerns are global and therefore there should be intense global competition amongst nations concerning who will lead the way in establishing the first National Maat Public Policy (based on the 42 Declarations of Innocence) in the world, in the twenty-first century? Will it be America (possibly), Brazil, Canada, China, Egypt, France, Ghana, India, Japan, Kenya, Mexico, Nigeria, Russia, South Africa, Vietnam, etc. The **National Maat Public Policy** will empower the federal, state, and local governments to legally and ethically confront and stop the wealthy and transnational corporations' crimes against the biosphere, ecology and universe. Foremost, the policy will finally prevent our government from becoming an "oligarchy" and <u>terminate the wealthy and corporations' control of human consciousness and human cultures</u> and, thereby, restore this right to the people so we can once again have possession and control of our moral, spiritual and cultural lives as truly free spiritual beings once again—and **SAVE OUR PLANET**! Does it help to know that the WORLD CITIES REPORT 2016, states: "It is clear that continuing along the current model of urbanization is no longer an option?"

. . .

References

Abrams, Herbert. "A Short History of Occupational Health." *Journal of Public Health Policy*, vol. 22, no.1, Jan. 2001.

African-Native American Genealogy Homepage, "Cow Tom." http://www.african-nativeamerican.com/cow-tom. Accessed 23 March 2018.

African-Native American Genealogy Homepage, "Harry Island." http://www.african-nativeamerican.com/harry_island.htm. Accessed 23 March 2018.

Alexander, Amir. "Infinitesimal," *Scientific American*, 2014.

Alora, Tan and Lumitao, Josephine. *Beyond A Western Bioethics: Voices from the Developing World*, Georgetown University Press, 2001.

Ambady, Nalini. "Group-Based Discrimination in Judgments of Moral Purity-Related Behavior: Experimental and Archival Evidence." *Journal of Experimental Psychology 2014*, vol. 143, no. 6, American Psychological Association, 2014, pp. 2135-2152.

"American Enlightenment." *Wikipedia: the free Encyclopedia*, Wikimedia Foundation, 2015, en.wikipedia.org/wiki/American_Enlightenment. Accessed 3 Nov. 2015.

"American Psychological Association Survey Shows Money Stress Weighing on Americans' Health Nationwide." *American Psychological Association*, 4 Feb. 2015, www.apa.org/news/press/releases/2015/02/money-stress.aspx. Accessed 2 Nov. 2015.

"Announcement of U.S. Support for the United Nations Declaration on the Rights of Indigenous Peoples," U.S. Department of State. January 12, 2011.
https://2009-2017.state.gov/s/srgia/154553.htm.
Accessed 10 Feb 2018.

Appel, Markus et al. "Meaning Through Fiction: Science Fiction and Innovative Technologies." *Psychology of Aesthetics, Creativity, and the Arts*, vol. 10, no. 4, 2016, pp. 472-480.

Appleby, Joyce. *The Relentless Revolution: A History of Capitalism*. W.W. Norton, 2010.

Arcand, Kimberly, and Megan Watzke. *Light: The Visible Spectrum and Beyond*. Black Dog & Leventhal Publishers, 2015.

Armaline, William et al. *Human Rights in Our Own Backyard: Injustice and Resistance in the United States*. University of Pennsylvania Press, 2011.

Asante, Molefi. "The Idea of the Soul in Ancient Egypt." *Gaudium Sciendi*, Numero 6, Junho 2014, p. 48.
http://www2.ucp.pt/resources/Documentos/SCUCP/GaudiumSciendi/Revista_Gaudium_Sciendi_N6/14%20ASANTE.pdf.
Accessed 3 Mar. 2017.

"Autonomous Flying Microrobots (RoboBees)," Wyss Institute, Harvard University,
wyss.harvard.edu/technology/autonomous-flying-microrobots-robobees.
Accessed 16 Feb. 2017.

Babiak, Paul, Craig Neumann, and Robert Hare. "Corporate Psychopathy: Talking the Walk." *Behavioral Science & the Law*, vol. 28, no. 2, 2010, pp. 174-193.

Babiak, Paul, and Robert Hare. *Snakes in Suits: When Psychopaths Go To Work*. Harper Publisher, 2006.

Babiak, Paul, and Robert Hare. "Psychopathy: An Important Forensic Concept for the 21st Century," *FBI Law Enforcement Bulletin*, Federal Bureau of Investigation, July 2012. Accessed 19 May 2016.

Bacevich, Andrew. *American Empire: The Realities and Consequences of U.S. Diplomacy*. Harvard University Press, 2002.

Ball, Philip. *The Devil's Doctor: Paracelsus and the World of Renaissance Magic and Science*. Farrar, Straus & Giroux, 2006.

Bandura, Albert. "Self-Efficacy." *Encyclopedia of Human Behavior*, edited by V.S Ramachandran, vol. 4, Academic Press, 1994, pp. 71-81, www.uky.edu/~eushe2/Bandura/BanEncy.html. Accessed 5 April 2017.

Banerjee, Subhabrata. "Corporate Social Responsibility: The Good, the Bad and the Ugly." *Critical Sociology*, vol. 34, no.1, 2008, pp. 51-79.

Banerjee, Subhabrata. "Whose Land Is It Anyway? National Interest, Indigenous Stakeholders and Colonial Discourses." *Organization & Environment*, vol. 13, no.1, March 2000, pp. 3-38. Accessed 9 March 2017.

Baptist, Edward. *The Half Has Never Been Told: Slavery and the Making of American Capitalism*. Basic Books, 2014.

Barker, Eric. "Which Professions Have the Most Psychopaths? The Fewest?" *Time Magazine*: Career and Workplace, 20 March 2014. http://time.com/32647/which-professions-have-the-most-psychopaths-the-fewest/. Accessed 2 October 2017.

Barnes, John. *A Pack of Lies: Towards A Sociology of Lying.* Cambridge University Press, 2014.

Barzun, Jacques. *From Dawn to Decadence.* Harper Perennial, 2000.

Bassoff, Evelyn. "Neglecting the Negative: Shortcomings in Reasoning." *Journal of Counseling & Development*, vol. 63, no. 6, Feb. 1985, pp, 368-71.

Bauman, Zygmunt. *Does Ethics Have a Chance In a World of Consumers?* Harvard University Press, 2008.

Beinfield, Harriet, and Efrem Korngold. *Between Heaven and Earth.* Ballantine Books, 1991.

Ben-Jochannan, Yosef et al. *The African Origins of the Major World Religions.* Karnak House, 1991.

Berger, Gail. "Motivation for Social Reward," Psychotherapy and Neuroscience (Social Reward), protected by Creative Commons Deeds, 2018.
https://www.nature-nurture.org.
Accessed 10 Nov 2017.

Bernstein, Irving. "The Growth of American Unions." *American Economic Review*, vol. 44, no.3, 1954, pp. 301-318.

Berry, Thomas. *The Great Works: Our Way into the Future.* Bell Tower. 1999.

Bhattacharjee, Yudhijit. "Why We Lie." *National Geographic Magazine*, National Geographic Society, June 2017.

Bhawuk, Dharm. *Spirituality and Indian Psychology.* Springer, 2011.

Bina, Olivia, Sandra Mateus, Lavinia Pereira, and Annalisa Caffa. "The Future Imagined: Exploring Fiction As A Means Of Reflecting On Today's Grand Societal Challenges And Tomorrow's Options." *Futures*, vol. 86, Feb. 2017, pp. 166-184.

"Biological Aspects of Race." *American Association of Physical Anthropologists*, 2015, www.physanth.org/about/position-statements/biological-aspects-race. Accessed 5 Aug. 2015.

Birbaumer, Niels, et al. "Deficient Fear Conditioning in Psychopathy: A Functional Magnetic Resonance Imaging Study." *Archives of General Psychiatry*, vol. 62, no 7, 2005, pp: 799-805. *JAMA Psychiatry*, American Medical Association, abstract.

Black, Jeremy. *The Power of Knowledge: How Information & Technology Made the Modern World*. Yale University Press, 2014.

Bomey, Nathan. "For Millennials, is the American Dream dead?" *USA Today News: College*, 9 Dec. 2016, college.usatoday.com/2016/12/09/millennials-american-dream-stats/. Accessed 10 Dec. 2016.

Bouchard, Thomas, Jr. "Genes, Environment and Personality." *Science*, vol. 264, no. 17, June 1994, p. 1701.

Box, George. "Science and Statistics." *Journal of the American Statistical Association*, vol. 71, no. 356, Dec.1976, pp. 791-799.

Box, George, and Norman Draper. *Empirical Model-Building and Response Surfaces*. Wiley & Son Publisher, 1987.

Boxill, Bernard, and Thomas E. Hill, Jr. "Chapter 18: Kant and Race." *Race and Racism*, Oxford University Press, 2001.

Brennan, Barbara. *Hands of Light: A Guide to Healing Through the Human Energy Field*. Bantam Books, 1988.

Brinkley, Joel. "American Indians Say Documents Show Government Has Cheated Them Out of Billions," (U.S.) The New York Times, January 7, 2003.

Brooke, John. *Science and Religion: Some Historical Perspectives*. Cambridge University Press, 1991.

Browder, Anthony. "Anthony Browder Nile Valley Civilization," [time 1:36:26] Trans Atlantic Production, Published May 21, 2018. (Youtube). https://www.youtube.com/results?search_query=anthony+browder+nile+valley+ Accessed 29 May 2018.

Brown, Chip. "Kayapo Courage." *National Geographic*, vol. 225, no. 1, Jan. 2014.

Brown, Lester. *World on the Edge*. W.W. Norton & Co., 2011.

Budge, E.A. Wallis, translator. *Book of the Dead*. Gramercy Books, 1960.

- - -. 1995.

Buchanan, Jas. S. "Alfred Barnett Interview," May 24, 1937. Works Progress Administration, Indian-Pioneer History Project for Oklahoma. Received electronically on Apr 23, 2018 from Jeffrey D. Kennedy.

Bunson, Margaret. *Encyclopedia of Ancient Egypt*. Revised ed., Facts on Files, Inc., 2002.

Calne, Donald. *Within Reason: Rationality and Human Behavior*. Vintage Books, 1999.

Cameron, Daryl et al. "A Constructionist Review of Morality & Emotions: No Evidence for Specific Links Between Moral Content and Discrete Emotions." *Personality & Social Psychology Review*, vol.19, no. 4, Nov. 2015, pp.371-394, abstract.

Campbell, Robert. *Campbell's Psychiatric Dictionary*. 7th Ed., Oxford University Press, 1996.

- - -. 2009.

Capra, Fritjof. *The Tao of Physics*. Shambhala, 2010.

Carey, Bjorn. "The Industrial Revolution Of The Oceans Will Imperil Wildlife, Says Stanford Scientist." *Stanford News*, 16 Jan. 2015, news.stanford.edu/2015/01/16/oceans-extinction-cycle-011615/. Accessed 30 Sept. 2016.

Carter, Jimmy. "A Cruel and Unusual Record." *The New York Times, The Opinion Pages*, www.nytimes.com/2012/06/25/opinion/americas-shameful-human-rights-record.html?_r=0. Accessed 1 May 2016.

Caruso, Anthony. "Statistics of U.S. Businesses Employment and Payroll Summary: 2012 (Economy-Wide Statistics Briefs)." *U.S. Census Bureau*, Feb. 2015, p. 7, www.census.gov/content/dam/Census/library/publications/2015/econ/g12-susb.pdf. Accessed 20 Sept. 2016.

Castanha, Tony. "Address on the Revocation of the Papal Bull 'Inter Caetera.'" *National Conference on Peacemaking and Conflict*

Resolution 2001, 10th Biennial Conference, George Mason University, 2001,
www.uctp.comoj.com/papalbull1.htm.
Accessed 30 Aug. 2011

"Catholic Church."
Wikipedia: The Free Encyclopedia, Wikimedia Foundation,
en.wikipedia.org/wiki/Catholic_Church.
Accessed 22 Sept. 2011.

Chang, David. "An Equal Interest in the Soil," *The American Indian Quarterly* Vol. 33, No. 1, Winter 2009.

Chaplin, G. "Geographic Distribution of Environmental Factors Influencing Human Skin Coloration," *American Journal of Physical Anthropology*, Nov 2004; 125 (3): 292-302.

Chengu, Garikai. "How African Muslims Civilized Spain."
The Islamic Post, vol.1, 2017.

Chengu, Garikai. "Libya: From Africa's Richest State Under Gaddafi, to Failed State After NATO Intervention." Global Research/Centre for Research on Globalization, first published 19 October 2014.
https://www.globalresearch.ca/libya-from-africas-richest-state-under-gaddafi-to-failed-state-after-nato-intervention/5408740.
Accessed 26 Oct. 2017.

Chetty, Raj, and Nathaniel Hendren, principal investigators.
The Equality of Opportunity Project.
www.equality-of-opportunity.org/.
Accessed 9 Dec. 2016.

"Child Poverty." *National Center for Children in Poverty, 2014*,
www.nccp.org/topics/childpoverty.html.
Accessed 16 Sept. 2015.

"Children of the Sun: Native: Native Culture Following the Old Ways" (website). Home: Muscogee Creek Language and Pronounication Guide.
childrenofthesunnativeculture.com.
Accessed 21 Apr 2018.

Cirino, Erica. "Industrialization of the Oceans: Is it time to Dive into the 'Blue Economy.'" Ocean Views, *National Geographic Society*, 27 May 2016,
voices.nationalgeographic.com/2016/05/27/industrialization-of-the-oceans-is-it-time-to-dive-into-the-blue-economy/.
Accessed 28 Nov. 2016.

Clark, Desmond (Editor). *The Cambridge History of Africa*.
Cambridge University Press, 1982.

"Climate Change Collection," The National Academies of Sciences, Engineering, Medicine, 500 Fifth St. N.W., Washington, D.C. 20001
https://www.nap.edu/collection/34/climate-change?gclid=EAIaIQobC
hMIjJ7yk5CR1Qy0sNCh2uFgDjEAAYAiAAEgJtEfD_BwE.
Accessed 16 Jul 2017.

Cloninger, Robert. "Temperament and personality. *Current Opinion in Neurobiology*, vol. 4, no. 2, 1994, pp. 266-273, abstract,
www.sciencedirect.com/science/science/article/
pii/0959438894900833.
Accessed 20 March 2012.

Cloninger, Robert. "A Practical Way to Diagnosis Personality Disorders: A Proposal," *Personality and Individual Differences*, vol. 29, no. 3, 2000, pp. 441-452.

Cloninger, Robert. "A Psychobiological Model of Temperament and Character," *Archive of General Psychiatry*, vol. 50, no. 12, 1993, pp. 975-90, abstract.

Cobban, Alfred. *The Eighteenth Century: Europe in the Age of Enlightenment*. McGraw-Hill Books, 1969.

Cohen, Lisa. *The Handy Psychology Answer Book*. Visible Ink, 2016.

Collas, Ion. *Madame Bovary: A Psychoanalytic Reading*. Librairie Droz, 1985.

Cooke, Jacob. *Encyclopedia of the North American Colonies*. vol. 3 Charles Scribner's Sons, 1993.

Cow Tom-The Oklahoma Cow Keeper-History of the Cow Keep Dynasty thur Jake Simmons 1968-1974, Author Unknown. (courtesy of Tsai-Chin Harrison). Received electronically on April 23, 2018 from Jeffery D. Kennedy.

Cox, Daniel, Rachel Lienesch, and Robert Jones. "Beyond Economics: Fears of Cultural Displacement Pushed the White Working Class to Trump." PRRI, 9 May 2017, https://www.prri.org/research/white-working-class-attitudes-economy-trade-immigration-election-donald-trump/. Accessed 19 Sep. 2017.

Cramer, Phebe. "Defense Mechanisms in Psychology Today," *American Psychologist*, June 2000, pp. 637-643.

Crane, Andrew. "Modern Slavery as a Management Practice: Exploring the Conditions and Capabilities for Human Exploitation." *Academy of Management Review*, vol. 38, no. 1, pp. 49-69.

Crocker, Lester (Editor). *The Age of Enlightenment*, Harper & Row, 1969.

Crosley, Reginald. *Alternative Medicine and Miracles: A Grand Unified Theory*. University Press of America, 2004.

Cummings, Elijah. "To be Black in America is also to Be Green in America." *The Afro-American*, vol. 125, no. 39, 27 April 2017, p. A-3.

Dalai Lama & Tutu, Desmond. *The Book of Joy*. Avery, 2016.

Daniels, Patricia, and Stephen Hyslop. *Almanac of World History*. National Geographic, National Geographic Society, 2015.

Davies, Brenda. *The 7 Healing Chakras*. Ulysses Press, 2000.

Derber, Charles. *Sociopathic Society: A People's Sociology of the United States*. Routledge Publishing, 2013.

De Fruyt, Filip et al., "Cloninger's Psychobiological Model of Temperament and Character and the Five-Factor Model of Personality," *Personality and Individual Differences*, 29 (3), September 2000, 441-452.

Deglin, Vadim, and Marcel Kinsbourne. "Divergent Thinking Styles of the Hemispheres: How Syllogisms Are Solved during Transitory Hemisphere Suppression." *Brain and Cognition*, vol. 31, no.3, Aug. 1996, pp. 285-307.

D'Espagnat, Bernard. *On Physics and Philosophy*, Princeton University Press, 2006.

Diop, Cheikh Anta. *Precolonial Black Africa: A Comparative Study of the Political and Social Systems of Europe and Black Africa, from Antiquity to the Formation of Modern States*. Lawrence Hill & Co., 1987.
http://jroan.com/Cheikh%20Anta%20Diop%20-%20Precolonial%20Black%20Africa.pdf.
Accessed 9 October 2017

Diop, Cheikh Anta. *Civilization or Barbarism: An Authentic Anthropology*. Lawrence Hill Books, 1991.

- - -. *The African Origin of Civilization: Myth or Reality*. Lawrence Hill & Co., 1974.

Dobbin, Frank, and Alexandra Kalev. "Why Diversity Programs Fail: And What Works Better," *Harvard Business Review*, July-August 2016.

Dossey, Larry. *Healing Beyond the Body*. Shambhala, 2001.

Editors of Encyclopedia Britannica. "Aurignacian Culture." *Encyclopædia Britannica*, www.britannica.com/topic/Aurignacian-culture. Accessed 25 July 2015.

EMBL: European Molecular Biology Laboratory/About Us, "European Science Policy/International Relations," https://www.embl.de/aboutus/international-relations/european-science-policy/. Accessed 20 Sep 2017

Encyclopedia Americana. Encyclopedia Center, Inc., 2000-2002, vols. 7 & 10.

Encyclopedia Britannica. Encyclopedia Britannica, Inc., 2002-2007, vols. 4 & 4.

"Encyclopédie." *Wikipedia: The Free Encyclopedia*, Wikimedia Foundation, en.wikipedia.org/wiki/Encyclop%C3%A9die. Accessed 20 March 2016.

Fairnbairn, Donald. Eastern Orthodoxy through Western Eyes, Westminster John Knox Press, 2002.

Fanon, Frantz. *The Wretched of the Earth*. Grove Press, 2004.

Faragher, John. *American Heritage Encyclopedia of American History*. Henry Holt & Co., 1998.

Feeney, Aidan, and Evan Heit. *Inductive Reasoning: Experimental, Developmental and Computational Approaches*. Cambridge University Press, 2007.

Ferguson, Niall. *The Ascent of Money: A Financial History of the World*. Penguin Books, 2008.

"Finance and Insurance: NAICS 52." Bureau of Labor Statistics, U.S. Department of Labor, www.bls.gov/iag/tgs/iag52.htm#workforce. Accessed 30 April 2017.

Flynn, John. *As We Go Marching*. Doubleday & Co., 1944.

Forster, Greg. "Sacred Enterprise." *Claremont Review of Books*, vol. 9, no. 3, Summer 2009, p. 40.

Freedman, Monroe, and Abbe Smith. *Understanding Lawyers Ethics*. 4th ed., Matthew & Bender, 2010.

Freely, John. *Before Galileo: The Birth of Modern Science in Medieval Europe*, Overlook Duckworth Publishers, 2012.

Freeman, Iam. *Seeds of Revolution: A Collection of Axioms, Passages and Proverbs* (Volume 1), iUniverse LLC, 2014.

Gadalla, Moustafa. *Egyptian Cosmology: The Animated Universe*. Tehuti Research Foundation, 2001.

Gentile, Mary C. "Turning Values into Action." *Stanford Social Innovation Review*, vol. 8, no. 4, Fall 2010, pp. 42-47.

Gerber, Richard. *Vibrational Medicine*. 3rd ed., Bear & Co., 2001.

Gillis, Justin. "World's Unity on Warming Pivots on U.S." *New York Times*, 1 June 2017, p. A1.

Goldschmidt, Arthur. *A Brief History of Egypt*. Checkmark Books, 2008.

Goleman, Daniel. *Emotional Intelligence: Why It Can Matter More than IQ*. Bantam Books, 1995.

Gombiner, Joel. 2011. "Carbon Footprinting the Intermet," *Consilience: The Journal of Sustainable Development*, Vol. 5, Issue 1, 2011, p.119-124.
https://journals.cdrs.columbia.edu/wp-content/uploads/
sites/25/2016/10/141-370-2-P8.pdf.
Accessed 10 May 2018.

Gordon, Wendy. "A Property Right in Self-Expression: Equality and Individualism in the Natural Law of Intellectual Property." *The Yale Law Journal*, vol. 102, no.7, May 1993, p. 1540.

Gottlieb, Anthony. *The Dream of Enlightenment: The Rise of Modern Philosophy*. Liveright Publishing Co., 2016.

Grandoni, Dino. "The Energy 202: Lots of People Support the 'Green New Deal': So What is it?" Washington Post, 12/19/2018 (online).

Greenberg, Jonathan. *Staking a Claim: Jake Simmons, Jr. and the Making of an African-American Oil Dynasty.* Informing to Empower Publishing, 1990.

Greenwood, Michael. "Acupuncture and the Chakras," Medical Acupuncture, Vol 17, No. 3, 2006.

Gugliotta, Guy. "The Great Human Migration." *Smithsonian*, vol. 39, no. 4, July 2008, pp. 56-64.

Gwaambuka, Tatenda. "New Evidence: The Real Reason Gaddafi Was Killed." *The African Exponent*, 6 April 2016.

Hall, Alfred R. *A History of Technology*. Oxford University Press, 1957.

Hamer, Dean. *The God Gene.* Doubleday, 2004.

Hanh, Thich Nhat. *The Miracle of Mindfulness*. Beacon Press, 2016.

Hannam, James. *The Genesis of Science*. Regnery Publishing, 2011.

Harari, Yuval. *Sapiens: A Brief History of Mankind*. Harper Collins Publishers, 2015.

Hare, Robert. "Focus on Psychopathy." *FBI Law Enforcement Bulletin*, Federal Bureau of Investigation, July 2012, leb.fbi.gov/2012/july/leb-july-2012.
Accessed 23 May 2016.

Harris, Grant, and Marnie Rice. "Treatment of Psychopathy: A Review of Empirical Findings." *Handbook of Psychology*, ch. 28. Guilford Press, 2005.
www.gwern.net/docs/algernon/2006-harris.pdf.
Accessed 10 Sept. 2016.

Hart, Stuart. *Capitalism at the Crossroads*. 3rd ed., Pearson Education, 2010.

Harvey, Paul, and Edward Blum. *The Columbia Guide to Religion in American History*. Columbia Press, 2012.

Haveman, Christopher. "The Removal of the Creek Indians from the Southeast, 1825-1838." (Dissertation) Auburn University, Alabama, August 10, 2009.
https://etd.auburn.edu/bitstream/handle/10415/2184/Haveman.pdf?sequence=2.
Accessed 22 March 2018.

Haverkort, Bertus, and Coen Reijntjes. "Diversities of Knowledge Communities, Their Worldviews and Sciences: On the Challenges of their Co-Evolution." *Traditional Knowledge in Policy and Practice: Approaches to Development and Human Well-being*, United Nations University Press, 2010,
collections.unu.edu/eserv/UNU:2546/ebrary9789280811919.pdf.
Accessed 11 Oct. 2015.

Hayes, Brett et al. "The Relationship between Memory and Inductive Reasoning: Does it Develop?" *Developmental Psychology*, 2013 May; 49 (5): 848-60
https://www.ncbi.nlm.nih.gov/pubmed/22686173

Hercz, Robert. "Psychopaths Among Us." *Without Conscience*, 2001, www.hare.org/links/saturday.html.
Accessed 1 March 2016. (* You can hear Robert Hare, Ph.D., a criminal psychologist, explain his same experience on YouTube video: "Are Corporate Leaders Psychopaths?" Open Mind, published June 30, 2016, time 1:18:17). Accessed 10 Sep 2018.

Herper, Matthew. "Solving Pharma's Shkreli Problem." *Forbes*, 8 Feb. 2016.

Herrera, Arturo. "The Unsuspected Capacity of Melanin to Transform Light Energy into Chemical Energy and the Surprising Anoxia Tolerance of Chrysemys Picta." *MOJ Cell Science & Report*, vol. 2, no. 3, 2015.

Hignett, Katherine. "Scott Kelly: NASA Twins Study Confirms Astronauts DNA Activity Changed in Space," *Newsweek*, 3/9/18. www.newsweek.com.
Accessed 10 March 2018.

Hiller, Fernando. "The Deductions of Freedom/Morality-as-Autonomy and the Categorical Imperative in Groundwork III and Their Problems." *Tópicos, Revista de Filosofía*, 1 Jan. 2016, eds.a.ebscohost.com/eds/pdfviewer/pdfviewer?vid=1&sid=04d6757b-beb7-4ebe-92db-2e1c25d2bb99%40sessionmgr4007&hid=4111.
Accessed 11 Dec. 2016.

Hilliard, Asa. April 2000, "The State of African Education" (Paper). American Educational Research Association Plenary Presentation Commission on Research in Black Education/April 2000 in New Orleans, LA. (Dr. Asa Hilliard III is a Fuller E. Calloway Professor of Education, Georgia State University, Atlanta, Georgia). http://www.coribe.org/pdf/hilliard.pdf.
Accessed 16 April 2018.

Hilliard, Asa. "Kemet Chronology: A Summary." *Scribd*, 1988, www.scribd.com/doc/162114321/Asa-Hilliard-Kemet-Timeline.
Accessed 8 March 2017.

Hilliard, Asa. "Teacher Education from an African American Perspective." PUB DATE Nov 95 NOTE 39 p.; Paper presented at an Invitational Conference on "Defining the Knowledge Base for Urban Teacher Education" (Atlanta, GA, November 11, 1995). PUB TYPE Viewpoints (Opinion/Position Papers, Essays, etc.)(120) Speeches/ Conference Papers (150). https://files.eric.ed.gov/fulltext/ED393798.pdf.
Accessed 2 Feb. 2018.

Hoff, Brad. "Hillary Emails Reveal True Motive for Libya Intervention." *Foreign Policy Journal*, 6 Jan. 2016,

www.foreignpolicyjournal.com/2016/01/06/new-hillary-emails-reveal-true-motive-for-libya-intervention/.
Accessed 3 April 2017.

Holony, Elena. "Isaac Newton was a Genius, But Even He Lost Millions in the Stock Market." *Business Insider: Wealth Advisor*, 20 Jan. 2016,
www.businessinsider.com/isaac-newton-lost-a-fortune-on-englands-hottest-stock-2016-1.
Accessed 8 Feb. 2017.

Imhotep, David. *The First Americans were Africans: Documented Evidence*. Author House, 2011.

Ingraham, Joseph. *Negro Plot: An Account of the Late Intended Insurrection Among A Portion of the Blacks of the City of Charleston*. Printed and published by Joseph W. Ingraham, 1822. Published by the Authority of the Corporation of Charleston. Call Number F279. C4 C31 1822 (Rare Book Collection, University of North Carolina at Chapel Hill).
http://docsouth.unc.edu/church/hamilton/hamilton.html
Accessed 2 Nov. 2017.

"Inter Caetera." *Wikipedia: The Free Encyclopedia*,
Wikimedia Foundation,
en.wikipedia.org/wiki/Inter_caetera.
Accessed 24 July 2011.

International Council of Thirteen Indigenous Grandmothers. "Letter to Cardinal Kasper, Secretary of the Pontifical Council for Promoting Christian Unity-Vatican." *Taowhywee, Agnes Baker Pilgrim*, 2005,
http://www.agnesbakerpilgrim.org/Page.asp?PID=96.
Accessed 20 July 2011.

Irwin, Harvey. *An Introduction to Parapsychology.* McFarland & Co. Publisher, 1999.

Ishay, Micheline. *The Human Rights Reader.* 2nd ed., Routledge, 2007.

Iyengar, B.K.S. . *Light of Yoga.* Schocken Books, 1976.

Jackson, Vanessa. "An Early History-African American Mental Health." *Race, Health Care and the Law: Speaking Truth to Power!,* academic.udayton.edu/health/01status/mental01.htm. Accessed 9 July 2016. Originally published as "In Our Own Voices: African American Stories of Oppression, Survival and Recovery." *Off Our Backs*, vol.33, no. 7/8, July-Aug 2003, pp 19-21.

James, George. *Stolen Legacy: Greek Philosophy is Stolen Egyptian Philosophy.* The Journal of Pan African Studies, 2009, www.jpanafrican.org/ebooks/eBook%20Stolen%20Legacy.pdf. Accessed 5 April 2017.

Jaumotte, Florence, Subir Lall, and Chris Papageorgiou. "Rising Income Inequality: Technology, or Trade and Financial Globalization?" International Monetary Fund, 2008, www.imf.org/external/pubs/ft/wp/2008/wp08185.pdf. Accessed 30 April 2017.

Jones, Charles and Woodson, Carter. The Religious Instruction of African Americans & The History of Their Church in the United States, CreateSpace Independent Publishing Platform, 2011. (** This book is an original combination compliation consisting of the following two complete titles: The Religious Instruction of the Negroes in the United States by Charles C. Jones, publisher Thomas Purse, copyrighted 1842; and The History of the Negro Church by Carter G. Woodson, publisher The Associated, copyrighted,1921.)

Jones, Major. *The Color of God: The Concept of God in Afro-American Thought.* Mercer University Press, 2000.

Jones, Owens. "Law, Evolution, and the Brain: Applications and Open Questions." *Philosophical Transactions of the Royal Society: Biological Science*, vol. 359, 26 Nov. 2004, pp. 1697-1707.

Joseph, Sarah. "Transnational Corporations and Indigenous People Rights." *Balayi: Culture, Law, and Colonialism*, vol. 8, no. 1, 2006, pp.70-82.

"Kant's Moral Philosophy." Stanford Encyclopedia of Philosophy, July 2016 revised edition, Stanford Center for the Study of Language and Information, 23 Feb. 2004, (see first paragraph), plato.stanford.edu/entries/kant-moral/.
Accessed 12 Dec. 2016.

Karenga, Maulana. *Maat, the Moral Ideal in Ancient Egypt: A Study in Classical African Ethics. Routledge, 2004.*

Kelly, Scott. "Space Odyssey." *National Geographic Magazine*, National Geographic Partners, LLC, Aug. 2017.

Kenny, Sir Anthony. "Aristotle: Greek Philosopher."
Encyclopedia Britannica,
www.britannica.com/biography/Aristotle.
Accessed 10 Oct. 2015.

Kenyatta, Jomo. *Facing Mt. Kenya: The Tribal Life of the Gikuyu.* Vintage Books, 1965.

Kouchaki, Maryam, et al. "Seeing Green: Mere Exposure To Money Triggers A Business Decision Frame And Unethical Outcomes." *Organizational Behavior and Human Decision Processes*, vol. 121, no. 1, May 2013, pp. 53-61.

Kreitner, Roy. "Legal History of Money." *Annual Review of Law and Social Science*, vol., no. 8, 2012, pp. 415-431.

Kuppens, Peter, Anu Realo, and Ed Diener. "The Role of Positive and Negative Emotions in Life Satisfaction Judgment Across Nations." *Journal of Personality and Social Psychology*, vol. 95, no. 1, 2008, pp. 66–75.

Lease, Mary. "In Defense of Home and Hearth: Mary Lease Raises Hell Among the Farmers." *History Matters: the U.S. Survey Course on the Web*,
historymatters.gmu.edu/d/5304/.
Accessed 27 July 2016.

Lerman, Lisa, and Philip Schrag. *Ethical Problems in the Practice of Law*. 2nd ed., Aspen Publisher, 2008.

Levine, Timothy. "Active Deception Detection." *Policy Insight from the Behavioral and Brain Sciences*. vol. 1, no. 1, 2014, p. 122-128.

Levine, Timothy, Rachel Kim, and Lauren Hamel. "People Lie for a Reason: Three Experiments Documenting the Principle of Veracity." *Communication Research Reports*, vol. 27, no. 4, Oct.-Dec. 2010, pp.271-285.

"Light Pollution." (Consequences), Wikipedia.
https://en.m.wikipedia.org/wiki/Light_pollution.
Accessed 27 Dec 2017.

"Light Pollution," International Dark-Sky Association.
http://www.darksky.org/light-pollution/.
Accessed 28 Dec 2017.

Lopez-Perez, Raul, and Eli Spiegelman. "Why do People Tell the Truth? Experimental Evidence for Pure Lie Aversion." *Experimental*

Economics, Journal of Economic Science Association, vol. 16, no. 3, Springer International Publishing, 2013, pp 233-247. doi: 10.1007/s10683-012-8324-x.

Macionis, John, and Linda Gerber. *Sociology*. 7th ed., Pearson Education, 2010.

Madrick, Jeff. *Seven Bad Ideas: How Mainstream Economist Have Damaged America and the World*. Vintage Books, 2014.

Magesa, Laurenti. *African Religion: The Moral Traditions of Abundant Life*. Orbis Books, 1997.

Malinowski, Sharon, and Anna Sheets, editors. *The Gale Encyclopedia of Native American Tribes*. Gale Publishing, 1998.

Manuel, Frank. "The Luddite Movement in France." *The Journal of Modern History*, vol. 10, no. 2, June 1938, pp. 180-211.

Martin, Denise. "Maat and Order in African Cosmology: A Conceptual Tool for Understanding Indigenous Knowledge." *Journal of Black Studies*, vol. 38, no. 6, July 2008, pp. 951-967.

Martin, Tony. "Tactics of Organized Jewry in Suppressing Free Speech." *Institute for Historical Review*. 2002, www.ihr.org/other/tonymartin2002.html. Accessed 1 Oct. 2016.

Matsuba, Kyle & Walker, Lawrence. (1998). "Moral Reasoning in the Context of Ego Functioning." *Merrill-Palmer Quarterly*, 1998, 44, 464-483. (*see discussion section*).

McElhaney, Kellie. *Just Good Business: The Strategic Guide to Aligning Corporate Responsibility and Brand*. Berrett-Koehler, 2008.

McLendon, Clayton T. This information was derived by the author from a conversation with Clayton on July 9, 2018.

Mellars, Paul. "The Impossible Coincidence. A Single-Species Model for the Origins of Modern Human Behavior in Europe." *Evolutionary Anthropology*, 2005, vol. 14, pp. 12-27.

Merciera, Hugo, and Dan Sperbera. "Why do Humans Reason? Arguments for an Argumentative Theory." *Behavioral and Brain Sciences, vol. 34, no. 2*, Cambridge University Press, April 2011, pp 57- 74, abstract.

Merriam Webster's Collegiate Dictionary: Tenth Edition, Springfield, Massachusetts, Merriam-Webster, 1993.

Miller, Earl, et al. "The Prefrontal Cortex: Categories, Concepts and Cognition." *Philosophical Transactions of the Royal Society: Biological Science*, 2002 Aug 29; vol. 357, no. 1424, The Royal Society Publishing, pp. 1123–36, www.pubmedcentral.nih.gov/articlerender fcgi?tool=pmcentrez&artid=1693009. Accessed 9 April 2012.

Montagu, Ashley. "Genetical Theory of Race, and Anthropological Method," *American Anthropology*, New Series, Vol. 44, No.3, Jul-Sep 1942, pp. 369-275.

Moore, T. Owens. *The Science of Melanin: Dispelling the Myths*. Venture Books, 1995.

Morris, Ian. *Why the West Rules—For Now*. Farrar, Straus, Giroux Press, 2010.

Muscogee Creek Indian Freedmen Band: The Official Website of the Muscogee Creek Indian Freedmen. (see Little Known History: Cow Tom).

http://www.1866creekfreedmen.com/media.
Accessed 23 March 2018.

Muscogee Creek Nation Official Website, (Home page).
https://www.mcn-nsn.gov/.
Accessed 25 Apr 2018.

Muscogee (Creek) Nation (Official Website), "Muscogee (Creek) Nation History."
http://www.mcn-nsn.gov/culturehistory/.
Accessed 23 March 2018.

Muzinic, Lana et al. "Psychiatric Aspects of Normal and Pathological Lying," *International Journal of Law and Psychiatry,* Volume 46, May-June 2016, pages 88-93.

Nantambu, Kwame. "Real Origin of the Ten Commandments." *Trinicenter*, 2009,
www.trinicenter.com/kwame/2009/1812.htm.
Accessed 27 Aug. 2016.

NAACP Resolution, National Association for the Advancement of Colored People, 102nd Annual Convention in Los Angeles, California. (See the official Website of the Muscogee Creek Indian Freedmen Band).
http://www.1866creekfreedmen.com/
Accessed 29 Apr 2018.

NASA: Global Climate Change. Earth Science Communications Division of the National Aeronautics and Space Administration, 16 Sept. 2015,
climate.nasa.gov/news/2340/.
Accessed 16 Sept. 2015.

"National Defense Budget Summary." *National Defense Budget Estimates for FY 2015*, p. 6, U. S. Department of Defense, comptroller.defense.gov/Portals/45/Documents/defbudget/fy2015/FY15_Green_Book.pdf.
Accessed 16 Sept. 2015.

"Native American Religion & Spirituality."
JR's Free Thought Pages: No Gods-No Master,
www.skeptic.ca/Native_Religion.htm.
Accessed 9 March 2017.

Neisser, Ulric, et al. "Intelligence: Knowns and Unknowns."
American Psychologist, vol. 51, no.2, American Psychological Association, Feb. 1996, pp. 77-101,
www.mensa.ch/sites/default/files/Intelligence_Neisser1996.pdf.
Accessed 3 Feb. 2017.

Neumann, C. S., R. D. Hare, and D. A. Pardini. "Antisociality and the Construct of Psychopathy: Data From Across the Globe." *Journal of Personality*, vol. 83, 18 Oct. 2014, pp. 678–692, doi: 10.1111/jopy.12127.

"Nuclear Weapons." United Nations Office for Disarmament Affairs,
https://www.un.org/disarmament/wmd/nuclear/.
Accessed 28 Dec 2017.

O'Connor, Anahad. "New York Attorney General Targets Supplements at Major Retailers." *New York Times*, 3 Feb. 2015,
well.blogs.nytimes.com/2015/02/03/new-york-attorney-general-targets-supplements-at-major-retailers/.
Accessed 12 June 2016.

O'Dell, Larry. "Simmons, Jake, Jr. (1901-1981),"
Oklahoma Historical Society, 2009.
www.okhistory.org.
Accessed 22 March 2018.

Oreland, Lar, et al. "Gene-Environment Interaction and Personality/ Behaviour." *International Society on Brain and Behaviour: 2nd International Congress on Brain and Behaviour, Annuals of General Psychiatry*, vol. 5, no. 1, 2 Jan. 2006.

Ortiz, Roxanne. An Indigenous Peoples' History of the United States. Beacon Press, 2014.

Owen, David. "The Inventor's Dilemma: A Eco-minded Engineer Discusses the Limits of Innovation," The New Yorker, May 17, 2010, p.42-50.

Oxford Companion to the Mind. Oxford University Press, 2004.

Palmarini, Massimo. *Inevitable Illusions: How Mistakes of Reason Rule Our Minds*. John Wiley & Son, 1994.

"Paterson, NJ: A History." *Paterson History*, www.patersonhistory.com/. Accessed 13 Sept. 2015.

Pearce, Fred. "Global Extinction Rates: Why Do Estimates Vary So Wildly?" *Yale Environment360*, Yale School of Forestry & Environmental Studies, 17 Aug. 2015, e360.yale.edu/features/global_extinction_rates_why_do_estimates_vary_so_wildly. Accessed 3 May 2017.

Peck, M. Scott. *People of the Lie*. Touchstone, 1983.

Peek, Philip, and Kwesi Yankah. *African Folklore: An Encyclopedia.* Routledge, 2004.

Pentland, John. "Religion and Money." *Quest Magazine*, vol.102, no 3, Summer 2014, pp. 96-99.

Persinger, Michael, and Stanley Krippner. "Experimental Dream Telepathy-Clairvoyance and Geomagnetic Activity." *Central Intelligence Agency: Library*, www.cia.gov/library/readingroom/document/cia-rdp96-00792r000400030001-0. Accessed 2 July 2017.

Piff, Paul. "Wealth and the Inflated Self: Class, Entitlement, and Narcissism." *Personality and Social Psychology Bulletin*, vol. 40, no.1, 2014, pp. 34-43.

Piff, Paul, et al. "Higher Social Class Predicts Increased Unethical Behavior." *Proceedings of the National Academy of Science*, vol. 109, no.11, 13 March 2012, pp. 4086-4091.

Pinker, Steven. *Enlightenment Now: The Case for Reason, Science, Humanism, and Progress.* Viking Publisher, 2018.

Pizarro, David. "Nothing More than Feelings? The Role of Emotions in Moral Judgment." *Journal for the Theory of Social Behavior*, vol. 30, no. 4, 2000, pp. 355-375.

Platz, Jeppe. "Singularity Without Equivalence: The Complex Unity of Kant's Categorical Imperative," *Journal of Value Inquiry*, vol. 50, 2016, pp. 369-384, http://eds.b.ebscohost.com/edspdfviewer/pdfviewer?vid=1&sid=8b594ab0-0d3d-4db2 Accessed 27 Sept 2017.

"Pope Francis Apologizes to Indigenous Peoples for 'Grave Sins' of Colonialism," Indian Country Today, July 10, 2015 https://indiancountrymedianetwork.com/news/indigenous-peoples/pope-francis-apologizes-to-indigenous-peoples-for-grave-sins-of-colonialism/. Accessed 9/5/2017

"Positivism." *Wikipedia: The Free Encyclopedia*, Wikimedia Foundation,
en.wikipedia.org/wiki/Positivism.
Accessed 30 Sept. 2015.

Posner, Eric. "Law and the Emotions." *Chicago Unbound*,
University of Chicago Law School, 2001,
chicagounbound.uchicago.edu/cgi/viewcontent.
cgi?article=1013&context=occasional_papers.
Accessed 3 April 2017.

"Post-Truth Politics," Wikipedia,
https://en.wikipedia.org/wiki/Post-truth_politics.
Assessed 27 Aug. 2017.

Prakasha, Padma. *The Nine Eyes of Light: Ascension Keys from Egypt*,
North Atlantic Books, 2010.

Puthoff, Harold. "CIA-Initiated Remote Viewing Program at Stanford
Research Institute." *Journal of Scientific Exploration*, vol. 10, no.1,
1996, pp. 63-76.

"Quick Facts about Nonprofits."
National Center for Charitable Statistics,
http://nccs.urban.org/data-statistics/quick-facts-about-nonprofits
Accessed 15 Oct. 2015.

Quirin, Markus, Martin Beckenkamp, and Julius Kuhl. "Giving or
Taking: The Role of Dispositional Power Motivation and Positive
Affect in Profit Maximization." *Mind and Society*, vol. 8, no. 1,
June 2009, pp. 109-126.

Quito, Anne. "Every Google Search Results in CO2 Emissions,"
Quartz, May 7, 2018.

https://qz.com/1267709/every-google-search-results-in-co2-emissions-this-real-time-dataviz-shows-how-much/.
Accessed 12 May 2018.

Raphael, Marc. *Jews and Judaism in the United States: A Documentary History*. Behrman House, 1983.

Rascovar, Barry. "Rascovar: Judge Williams Applied The Law, Not Emotion." *Maryland Reporter*, 26 June 2016, marylandreporter.com/2016/06/26/rascovar-judge-williams-applied-the-law-not-emotion/.
Accessed 3 March 2017.

Reiss, David, Leslie Leve, and Jenae Neiderhiser. "How Genes And The Social Environment Moderate Each Other." *American Journal of Public Health*, vol. 103, no. 1, Oct, 2013, pp.S111-S121.

"Revival of Pan-Africanism Forum," Asante, Molefi. March 24, 2012, Hilton Hotel, 1750 Rockville Pike, Rockville, MD 20852 (Obama Presidency and its Impact on Africa and the Global African Diaspora) http://www.youtube.com/watch?v=BH1tkF4DvzU

Rice, Doyle. "175 Nations Sign Historic Paris Climate Deal on Earth Day." *USA Today News*, 22 April 2016, www.usatoday.com/story/news/world/2016/04/22/paris-climate-agreement-signing-united-nations-new-york/83381218/.
Accessed 24 April 2016.

Roberts, J.M., and Odd Arne Westad. *The History of the World*. Oxford University Press, 2013.

"Robobee," *Wikipedia: The Free Encyclopedia*, Wikimedia Foundation, en.wikipedia.org/wiki/RoboBee,
Accessed 28 March 2017.

Rodney, Walter. *How Europe Underdeveloped Africa*, Bogle-L'Ouverture, 1972.

Rodriquez, Junius. *The Historical Encyclopedia of World Slavery*. Vol.1, ABC-CLIO, Inc., 1997.

"Romanus Pontifex." *Wikipedia: The Free Encyclopedia*, Wikimedia Foundation, en.wikipedia.org/wiki/Romanus_Pontifex. Accessed 20 May 2016.

Rotman, David. "How Technology is Destroying Jobs." *MIT Technology Review: Business Impact*, 12 June 2013, www.technologyreview.com/s/515926/how-technology-is-destroying-jobs/. Accessed 6 March 2017.

"Royal African Company." *Wikipedia: The Free Encyclopedia*, Wikimedia Foundation, en.wikipedia.org/wiki/Royal_African_Company. Accessed 20 May 2016.

Safi, Michael. "India Launches Record-breaking 104 Satellites from Single Rocket." *The Guardian*, Science section: Space, 15 Feb 2017, www.theguardian.com/science/2017/feb/15/india-launches-record-breaking-104-satellites-from-single-rocket. Accessed 15 Feb. 2017.

Sale, Kirkpatrick. *Rebel against the Future: The Luddites and their War on the Industrial Revolution*. Addison-Wesley Publishing, 1995.

Schalock, Peter. "Overview of Skin Pigment." *Merck Manual*, consumer version,

www.merckmanuals.com/home/skin-disorders/pigment-disorders/
overview-of-skin-pigment.
Accessed 21 Nov. 2016.

Schouten, Ronald. "Psychopaths on Wall Street." *Harvard Business Review*, 14 March 2012.

Schrijver, Karel and Schrijver, Iris. *Living With the Stars: How the Human Body Is Connected to the Life Cycles of Earth, the Planets, and the Stars*. Oxford University Press, 2015.

Seara-Cardoso, Ana, and Essi Viding. "Functional Neuroscience of Psychopathic Personality in Adults." *Journal of Personality*, vol. 8, no. 6, Dec. 2015, pp. 723-737. Doi: 10.1111/jopy.12113. First published 2014.

Sertima, I.V., "Dr. Ivan Van Sertima-They Came Before Columbus," YouTube (published March 4, 2014), Category: Education, Black History/365, [time 1:02:36.]; Accessed 24 August 2018. A valuable lecture.

Sertima, Ivan. *Golden Age of the Moor*. Journal of African Civilizations Ltd., Inc., 1992.

Seventh Annual Report of the Commission to the Five Civilized Tribes to the Secretary of the Interior, June 30, 1900, (v. 7-8), U.S. Government Printing Office, 1900. Washington. Hathi Trust Digital Library [original from Harvard University].

Shafer, Byron, et al. *Temples of Ancient Egypt*. I. B. Tauris Publisher, 1997.

Shapiro, Fred (editor). *Yale Book of Quotations*, Yale University Press, 2006.

Sheppard, Stephen, editor. *Wolters Kluwer Bouvier Law Dictionary*. Wolters Kluwer Law & Business, 2011.

Shields, Christopher. "Aristotle: Living Beings." Rev. 2015, *Stanford Encyclopedia of Philosophy*, 2008, https://plato.stanford.edu/search/searcher. py?query=Aristotle%3A+Living+Beings Accessed 30 Sept. 2015.

Shuren, Jeffrey, and Jordan Grafman. "Neurology of Reasoning." *Arch Neurology*, vol. 59, June 2002. https://jamanetwork.com/journals/jamaneurology. Accessed 8 Oct. 2015.

Simon, Herbert. *Reason in Human Affairs*. Stanford University Press, 1983.

Singh, Simon. *Big Bang*. Harper Perennial, 2004.

Slater, Timothy, and Lydia Pozzato. "Psychopathy." *FBI Law Enforcement Bulletin*, Federal Bureau of Investigation, July 2012, https://www.hsdl.org/?view&did=718311. Accessed 1 Nov 2017.

Smith, Cara L., et al. "Personality Contributions to Belief in Paranormal Phenomena." *Individual Differences Research*, vol. 7, no.2, pp. 85-96.

Smith, Eugene. "Before Virtue: Biology, Brain, Behavior, and the Moral Sense." *Business Ethics Quarterly*, vol. 22, no. 2 Cambridge University Press, April 2012, doi 10.5840/beq201222223.

"Social Justice in an Open World: The Role of the United Nations." *Development of Economic and Social Affairs*, Division of Social Policy and Development, United Nations, 2006.

"Space Debris: Orbiting Debris Threatens Sustainable Use of Outer Space." *United Nations*, www.un.org/en/events/tenstories/08/spacedebris.shtml. Accessed 4 Jan. 2016.

Starcher, Dale, and Sarah Allen. "A Global Human Potential Movement and a Rebirth of Humanistic Psychology." *The Humanistic Psychologist*, vol. 44, no. 3, American Psychological Association, 2016, pp. 227-241.

Stavrova, Olga and Siegers, Pascal. "Religious Prosociality and Morality Across Cultures: How Social Enforcement of Religion Shapes the Effects of Personal Religiousity on Prosocial and Moral Attitudes and Behavior", *Personality and Social Psychology Bulletin*, March 2014 40 (3): 315-333; first published November 11, 2013.

State of the World's Indigenous People. United Nations, 2009, pg. 59-62, www.un.org/esa/socdev/unpfii/documents/SOWIP/en/SOWIP_web.pdf. Accessed 15 Aug. 2015.

Stout, Martha. "The Ice People." *Psychology Today*, vol. 38, no. 1, Jan./Feb. 2005, pp. 72-78.

- - -. *The Sociopath Next Door.* Harmony Books, 2005.

Strach, Eric. "Astronomy and Medicine." *Journal of the British Astronomical Association*, vol.92, no.4, 1982, p.164-169.

Subrahmanyam, Sanjay. *Europe's India: Words, People, Empire, 1500-1800*. Harvard University Press, 2017.

Sussman, Dalia. "Negative View of U.S. Race Relations Grows, Poll Finds." *New York Times*, 4 May 2015,

www.nytimes.com/2015/05/05/us/negative-view-of-us-race-relations-grows-poll-finds.html?_r=0.
Accessed 16 Sept. 2015.

Swann, William B. Jr., Alan Stein-Seroussi, and Shawn McNulty. "Outcasts in a White-Lie Society: The Enigmatic Worlds of People with Negative Self-Conceptions." *Journal of Personality and Social Psychology, 1992 Apr. vol. 62, no. 4, pp. 618-624.*

Teeter, Emily. "The Presentation of Maat: Ritual & Legitimacy in Ancient Egypt." *Studies in Ancient Oriental Civilization*, no. 57, The Oriental Institute of the University of Chicago, 1997.
oi.uchicago.edu/sites/oi.uchicago.edu/files/uploads/shared/docs/saoc57.pdf.
Accessed 5 April 2017.

Thornton, Richard. "Meso American and South American Words Found in the Native Languages of Southeastern United States." History, Language, Mexico, Native American Community, Savannah River, South America.
https://peopleofonefire.com.
Accessed 21 Apr 2018.

Thomas, Joseph. "The Four Stages of Moral Development in Military Leaders." *The ADM James B. Stockdale Center for Ethical Leadership*, United States Naval Academy,
www.usna.edu/Ethics/_files/documents/Four%20Stages%20of%20Moral%20Development%20Thomas.pdf.
Accessed 9 Sept. 2013.

Tibebu, Teshale. *Hegel and the Third World: The Making of Eurocentrism in World History*, Syracuse University Press, 2011.

Toynbee, Arnold. *The Industrial Revolution*, Beacon Press, 1956.

"United Nations Declaration of Indigenous People's Rights." *United Nations*, March 2008.
www.un.org/esa/socdev/unpfii/documents/DRIPS_en.pdf.
Accessed 14 Aug. 2015.

"U.S. Patent Activity Calendar Years 1790 to the Present; Table of Annual U.S. Patent Activity Since 1790." *United States Patent and Trade Office*,
www.uspto.gov/web/offices/ac/ido/oeip/taf/h_counts.htm.
Accessed 27 Oct. 2015.

VandenBos, Gary, editor. *APA Dictionary of Psychology*. American Psychology Association, 2007.

Vanderslice, Lane. "Vested Interests and the Common People in Developing Countries: Understanding Oppressive Societies and Their Effects." *Journal of Economic Issues*, vol. LI, no. 2, June 2017, doi 10. 1080/00213624.2017.1320509.

Van Slyke, James. "Understanding the Moral Dimension of Spirituality: Insights from Virtue Ethics and Moral Exemplars." *Journal of Psychology & Christianity*, vol. 34, no. 3, Fall 2015, p.205-215.

Watt, Andrew, Jacques Bothma, and Paul Meredith. "The Supramolecular Structure of Melanin." *Soft Matter*, no. 19, Royal Society of Chemistry, pp. 3754-3760.

Welner, Michael.. "Response to Simon: Legal Relevance Demands That Evil Be Define and Standardized." *Journal of the American Academy of Psychiatry and the Law*, vol. 31, no. 4, 2003, pp 417-421.

Welsing, Frances. *The Isis Papers: The Keys to the Colors*. Third World Press, 1995.

Westfall, Richard. *Science and Religion in Seventeenth Century England*. Yale University Press, 1958.

"What is a Gene Mutation and How do Mutations occur?" *Genetics Home Reference: Your Guide to Understanding Genetic Conditions*, U.S. National Library of Medicine, ghr.nlm.nih.gov/handbook/mutationsanddisorders/genemutation. Accessed 28 July 2015.

"Who Are Indigenous People?" *Indigenous Peoples, Indigenous Voices*, U.N. Permanent Forum on Indigenous Issues, www.un.org/esa/socdev/unpfii/documents/5session_factsheet1.pdf. Accessed 15 Aug. 2015.

Wiener, Martin. *English Culture and the Decline of the Industrial Spirit: 1850-1980*. Cambridge University Press, 1981.

Wilder, Craig Steven. *Ebony and Ivy*. Bloomsbury Press, 2013.

Wilkinson, Richard. *The Complete Gods and Goddesses of Ancient Egypt*. Thames and Hudson, 2003.

Williams, Chancellor. *The Destruction of a Black Civilization: Great Issues of a Race from 4500 B.C. to 2000 A.D.* Third World Press, 1974.

Wilson, Edward. *Half-Earth: Our Planet's Fight for Life*, Liveright Publishing, 2016.

Winkelman, Michael. "The Evolution of Consciousness? Transpersonal Theories in Light Cultural Relativism," *Anthropology of Consciousness*, Vol 4, Issue 3, American Anthropology Association (AnthroSource) Sep 1993. https://anthrosource.onlinelibrary.wiley.com Accessed 7 Nov 2018.

Winters, Clyde. "Ancient African Kings of India" Rasta Livewire, October 09, 2006. http://www.africaspeaks.com/reasoning/indexphp?topic=11100.0;wap2.

World Book Encyclopedia. World Book Publications, 1998-2015, vol. 1-6.

World Book Encyclopedia. World Book Publications, 2016, vol. 17.

World Cities Report 2016, "The Need for a New Urban Agenda (1.10, p. 25), United Nations.

World Population Prospects: The 2017 Revision, 21 June 2017. United Nations, https://www.un.org/development/desa/publications/world-population-prospects-the-2017-revision.html Accessed 24 October 2017

Wright, Robert, and Vincenzo Quadrini. "Chapter 3, Section 3.1: Of Love, Money, and Transactional Efficiency." *Money and Banking*, Flat World Knowledge, 2009.

Yip, Jeremy and Schweitzer, Maurice. "Mad and Misleading: Incidental Anger Promotes Deception," *Organizational Behavior and Human Decision Processes*, 137 (2016) 207-217.

Zagorin, Perez. *Francis Bacon*. Princeton University Press, 1998.

• • •

Endnotes

[i] "The Aurignacian culture is an archaeological culture of the Upper Paleolithic located in Europe and southwest Asia. It lasted broadly within the period from ca. 45,000 to 35,000 years ago." "Aurignacian," Wikipedia: The Free Encyclopedia, en.wikipedia.org/wiki/Aurignacian," Accessed 10 Oct. 2016.

[ii] Professor George G. M. James died a violent death shortly after he published his book, Stolen Legacy: Greek Philosophy Is Stolen Egyptian Philosophy. According to the *Encyclopedia of Black Studies* (2005) edited by Molefi Kete Asante and Ama Mazazma: "Shortly after the publication of *Stolen Legacy*, which he completed while at the University of Arkansas, James died under mysterious circumstances. Popular rumors suggested he might have been killed because he exposed intimate knowledge related to the Masonic tradition (p. 440)." Author of article is Gwinyai Muzorewa.

[iii] "Definition of Marketing," American Marketing Association, www.ama.org/AboutAMA/Pages/About.aspx. Accessed 30 May 2017.

[iv] Sir Richard Arkwright (1732-1792) of England is the innovator of the factory system.

[v] U.S. Fish and Wildlife Service: Environmental Conservation Online System. Endangered Species. https://www.fws.gov/Endangered/. Accessed 22 Oct. 2017.

[vi] "Blue Whales and Communication," National Geographic Magazine, 26 March 2011, www.nationalgeographic.com.au/science/blue-whales-and-communication.aspx, accessed 25 Aug. 2016. Also see: Mark McDonald, John Hildebrand,

and Sarah Mesnick, "Worldwide Decline In Tonal Frequencies Of Blue Whale Songs" Inter-Research Endangered Species Research, vol. 9, no. 1, pp. 13-21, www.int-res.com/abstracts/esr/v9/n1/p13-21. Accessed 13 April 2017.

vii Thomas Paine, The Age of Reason,1796, Reprinted 2016. Also note the Dedication., www.deism.com/images/theageofreason1794.pdf. Accessed 9 March 2017.

viii Stockholm syndrome is when a captured person, over a period of time, develops indefensible feelings for his or her captor. "Psychologists who have studied the syndrome believe that the bond is initially created when a captor threatens a captive's life, deliberates, and then chooses not to kill the captive. The captive's relief at the removal of the death threat is transposed into feelings of gratitude toward the captor for giving him or her life." www.britannica.com/topic/Stockholm-syndrome. Accessed 13 April 2017.

ix Vishwaguru Mahamandaleshwar Paramhans Sri Swami Maheshwaranandaji., "Chakras and Nadis," Celje, 5 Oct 2008. YouTube, youtube.com/watch?v=o8UEo2QkQwA. Accessed 12 April 2017. Maheshwarananda is the founder of Yoga in Daily Life System.

x Jacqui Frank and Kara Chin, "Jim Rogers: The Worst Crash in Our Lifetime is Coming," Business Insider, 9 June 2017. www.businessinsider.com/jim-rogers-worst-crash-lifetime-coming-2017-6. Accessed 21 June 2017

^{xi} Quote taken from: Richard Clarida, Jordi Gali, and Mark Gertler. "The Science of Monetary Policy: A New Keynesian Perspective," National Bureau of Economic Research, NBER Working Paper Series, May 1999,
www.nber.org/papers/w7147.
Accessed 16 Jan. 2017.

^{xii} Henry Ford's quote was taken from the video entitled "Who Controls the Money Controls the World." Youtube. Nov. 13, 2011 published. https://www.youtube.com/watch?v=YDYfyAQ8lUI
Accessed 1 Nov. 2017.
Also see T. Gordon Larsen, *Apocalypse Survival: Preparing for the Unthinkable*, Dog Ear Publishing, 2015. (p. 41).

^{xiii} "Net Worth of United States Senators and Representatives," Ballotpedia: The Encyclopedia of American Politics, U.S. Congress Ballotpedia, 6 June 2017,
ballotpedia.org/Net_worth_of_United_States_Senators_and_Representatives.
Accessed 31 October 2017

^{xiv} James Delaney, "Jean-Jacques Rousseau (1712-1778)." Internet Encyclopedia of Philosophy (IEP): A Peer-Reviewed Academic Resource, Niagara University, par. 1,
www.iep.utm.edu/rousseau/.
Accessed 17 April 2017.

^{xv} Syllogisms are a form of reasoning in which a conclusion is drawn from two given propositions (premises).

^{xvi} Electroconvulsive therapy (ECT)-"a form of somatic treatment for certain psychiatric conditions in which electrical current is applied to the brain through two electrodes placed on the skull" (Campbell's Psychiatric Dictionary, 9th ed., 2009).

---

xvii Equador [*sic*]: this is the researchers' spelling in this research article. Equador is also spelled "Ecuador."

xviii "Limits" is the actual word used in the research article.

xix The title of this chapter is actually a Yiddish proverb. It was taken from inside the paper cover of Karine Tuil's hardback novel, The Age of Reinvention, Atria Books, 2013.

xx "Climate Change Collection,"
The National Academies of Sciences, Engineering, Medicine, www.nap.edu/collection/34/climate-change?gclid=EAIaIQobChMIjJ 7yk5CR1Qy0sNCh2uFgDjEAAYAiAAEgJtEfD_BwE. Accessed 16 July 2017.

xxi "A Blanket Around the Earth," Global Climate Change: Vital Signs of the Planet/Causes, NASA climate.nasa.gov/causes/.
Accessed 16 July 2017.

xxii The term "*inter-being*" means inter-dependency, all is One.

xxiii Planetary Protection Officer,
National Aeronautics and Space Administration, USAJOBS, www.usajobs.gov/GetJob/ViewDetails/474414000.
Accessed 7 Aug. 2017.

xxiv "Biosphere," National GeographicEducation www.nationalgeographic.org/encyclopedia/biosphere/.
Accessed 18 March 2017. Also see: NASA Earth Observatory, earthobservatory.nasa.gov/Features/WorldOfChange/biosphere.php.
Accessed 13 April 2017.

---

xxv BrainyQuote, (Communication, Mother, Earth), www.brainyquote.com/search_results.html?q=thich+nhat+thanh. Accessed 16 July 2017.

• • •

About the Author
Ata Uchenna Omom

Ata Omom (birth name Alvin Lee Rentie) was born in the U.S. Army Hospital at Ft. Leavenworth, Kansas (military family); and raised in the City of Leavenworth, KS. The City of Leavenworth is known as the "supply base" and "spring board" of American westward expansion; hot bed of anti-slavery and pro-slavery activism before the Civil War; and destination for runaway African (slaves) refugees. Bethel AME Church of Leavenworth, the church that Ata and his family attended, was part of the Underground Railroad during the Civil War. The first African American mayor of the City of Leavenworth was the Honorable Mayor Benjamin Day, 1972. Day was the author's 6th grade teacher.

Ata is a graduate of Malcolm X City College (AAS)/Chicago; Howard University (BS)/Washington, D.C.; Morgan State University (MS)/Baltimore; and Baltimore School of Massage (Therapeutic Massage/Professional Certification). Ata studied tai chi chuan under Grandmaster Chien Liang Huang. He is also a military veteran. Hobbies are walking and meditation.